Counseling the
Culturally Different

Wiley Series in Counseling and Human Development
Leo Goldman, Editor

Community Counseling: A Human Services Approach
Judith A. Lewis and Michael D. Lewis

Research Methods for Counselors:
Practical Approaches in Field Settings
Leo Goldman, Editor

Dimensions of Intervention for Student Development
Weston H. Morrill, James C. Hurst, and E. R. Oetting, Editors

Counseling the Culturally Different: Theory and Practice
Derald Wing Sue, Edwin I. Richardson, Rene A. Ruiz, and
Elsie J. Smith

Counseling the
Culturally Different

Theory and Practice

DERALD WING SUE
CALIFORNIA STATE UNIVERSITY—HAYWARD

with chapter contributions by

Edwin H. Richardson
PRESIDENT'S COMMISSION ON MENTAL RETARDATION,
WASHINGTON, D.C.

Rene A. Ruiz
NEW MEXICO STATE UNIVERSITY
LAS CRUCES

Elsie J. Smith
STATE UNIVERSITY OF NEW YORK AT BUFFALO

A WILEY-INTERSCIENCE PUBLICATION

JOHN WILEY & SONS
New York • Chichester • Brisbane • Toronto • Singapore

7/62 Taylor .24.95

This publication is designed to provide accurate and
authoritative information in regard to the subject
matter covered. It is sold with the understanding that
the publisher is not engaged in rendering legal, accounting,
or other professional service. If legal advice or other
expert assistance is required, the services of a competent
professional person should be sought. *From a Declaration
of Principles jointly adopted by a Committee of the
American Bar Association and a Committee of Publishers.*

Library of Congress Cataloging in Publication Data:

Sue, Derald Wing.
   Counseling the culturally different.

   (Wiley series in counseling and human development)
   "A Wiley-Interscience publication."
   Includes index.
   1. Cross-cultural counseling. I. Title.

BF637.C6S85   158'.3   80–24516
ISBN 0–471–04218–8

Printed in the United States of America

10 9 8 7 6 5 4 3

This book is dedicated to
Paulina Wee Sue and Derald Paul Sue.

Foreword

Recognizing that human and cultural diversity are important factors deserving our increased sensitivity and awareness, this task group submits the following recommendation:

That the provision of professional services to persons of culturally diverse backgrounds not competent in understanding and providing professional services to such groups shall be considered unethical. It shall be equally unethical to deny such persons professional services because the present staff is inadequately prepared. It shall therefore be the obligation of all service agencies to employ competent persons or to provide continuing education for the present staff to meet the service needs of the culturally diverse population it serves.*

This key recommendation of the Vail Conference undergirds this book and the future growth of psychology in this country. Historically, counseling and therapy have been white middle-class professions implicitly and sometimes explicitly serving to acculturate and inculcate peoples of diverse backgrounds into a relatively narrow picture of mental health. Even the most hallowed concept of counseling—facilitating *individual* development—may be considered culturally biased when related to other cultural systems such as those of Asians or American Indians that may be more family or group centered.

Counseling the Culturally Different: Theory and Practice is an important and vital instructional aid for beginning and experienced practitioners. Rather than say "something must be done," this book does something. It clearly describes some of the central cultural characteristics of varying groups in this country. Without this information, it is difficult, and—as the Vail Conference recommendation indicates—unethical to counsel with a person of a different culture. This book,

*Korman, M. *Levels and Patterns of Professional Training in Psychology*. Washington, D.C.: American Psychological Association, 1973, p. 105.

however, moves beyond information to some useful "how's" suggesting to the professional *what* can be done as well as *why* it should be done. This combination of information, theory, and practice results in a work that can make a difference in the lives of many clients and still be culturally appropriate.

During my presidency of the Division of Counseling Psychology of the American Psychological Association, I made one of my primary efforts the increased involvement of psychologists in issues of cross-cultural counseling. My presidential address focused on the present state of counseling and therapy theory and how it has failed to cope with issues of cross-cultural differences. In my own work, I have put forth the notion of *cultural expertise* as a target goal for both counselors and their clients. Simply put, it means that the counselor or client is able to commit himself or herself to culturally appropriate actions, while being aware of their potential impact and reaction among several cultural groups. Derald Sue's outstanding work is a key step toward a more relevant psychology of counseling and therapy.

This book builds cultural expertise. The book demonstrates the political and social base of counseling and therapy. Crisp discussion of barriers and credibility in counseling should help us get started and understand the task before us if we are to become culturally expert. Derald Sue's chapter on dimensions of world views shows us how we must develop our own cultural identity so that we can better understand cultures different from our own. Perhaps a special weakness of the white Anglo is her or his fear and lack of understanding of others, which may come from a lack of our own cultural identity.

To me, the book becomes rich in specifics in Part II. Here we have the opportunity to learn specifics of counseling and therapy with peoples different from ourselves. Whether one is white, black, red, or yellow, one will learn from and enjoy this section. For example, while I cannot fully agree with Richardson's chart (Chapter 9) describing differences in Indian and Anglo values, it is one instance of how my own understanding (and I assume that of other counselors and therapists) has been limited within a narrow perspective. Unless we are able, regardless of our racial and ethnic background, to consider and understand these challenging alternative perspectives, we are not ready to cope with the even more challenging critical incidents in counseling described in Part III. Moreover, unless we are willing to take our cultural biases and put them on the shelf, we are almost totally unable to work in the actual counseling and therapy relationship with those who are different from ourselves.

I commend this book to you. Scholarship, challenge, information, new questions combine in an exciting mix. Derald Sue and his colleagues have given us something to think about and, more important, something to act upon.

ALLEN E. IVEY

University of Massachusetts, Amherst
February 1981

Preface

Counseling the Culturally Different: Theory and Practice was written for several reasons. The first and most basic reason is the serious lack of texts devoted to this important topic. Ever since the 1960s, the counseling and mental health fields have been challenged about the appropriateness of the services they offer to minority clients. A barrage of criticisms has been leveled against traditional counseling practices as being demeaning, irrelevant, and oppressive toward the culturally different. Admonitions to develop new methods, concepts, and services more appropriate to the life experiences of minority clients have been plentiful. Yet, to this date, the number of texts addressing these issues or devoted solely to cross-cultural counseling and used in mental health training programs cannot even be counted on the fingers of one hand.

Second, of the texts available, few present an integrated conceptual framework by which to view how cross-cultural counseling relates to the wider social forces, the counselor-client relationship, and the culturally different in the United States. Most published materials on working with minority clients are notoriously fragmented and/or myopic. For example, in looking at the mental health literature on minority issues, one can find isolated topics discussed (racism, stereotypes, value conflicts, normative data, etc.) and/or reference to the unique needs/concerns/problems of specific racial and ethnic minorities (American Indians, Asian Americans, Blacks, Hispanics, etc.) without regard for one another. There have been few attempts (*a*) to present a theory or conceptual framework by which to add meaning to the mental health literature and counseling issues of *all* minority groups, (*b*) to identify similarities and differences among the various ethnic groups as they relate to mental health notions and practices, and (*c*) to provide a wider focus on how the sociopolitical system affects minorities and counseling.

One of the primary strengths of this book is that it attempts to rectify these issues. It is intended to fill the large void in current counselor education programs by providing a basic text appropriate for courses in counseling the culturally different and serving as an adjunct to courses in school counseling, social change, counseling theories, foundations of counseling, and so on. While training in cross-cultural counseling is more than cognitive understanding and insight, it provides a much-needed starting point by which to take the first step.

Furthermore, *Counseling the Culturally Different* is unique in that it presents a discussion of issues relevant to the culturally different in the United States that cuts across all ethnic/racial minorities. It provides a conceptual framework by which to understand the minority experience in the United States, the role counseling has played with respect to larger societal forces, and the practice of cross-cultural counseling in the public schools, mental health agencies, industries, correctional settings, and the like. In addition, specific minority groups are given individual treatment to contrast similarities with differences.

ORGANIZATION

The text is organized into three main parts: (*a*) Part I: "Issues and Concepts in Cross-Cultural Counseling," (*b*) Part II: "Counseling Specific Populations," and (*c*) Part III: "Critical Incidents in Cross-Cultural Counseling." Each part was written in such a manner so that it could be used independently or in conjunction with the other parts. It is my belief, however, that maximal learning and benefit will take place when all three parts are integrated with one another. Part I, "Issues and Concepts in Cross-Cultural Counseling," deals with the broad conceptual and theoretical foundations of cross-cultural counseling. The main purpose of this part is to discuss issues, to critically analyze data, and to propose concepts of cross-cultural counseling common to most culturally different groups in the United States. Chapter 1, "The Politics of Counseling," traces and discusses the historical and contemporary role of counseling as it relates to the culturally different. Counseling and its relationship to the culturally different are seen within the political framework of the larger society. The racist and damaging effects of the mental health fields on minorities are revealed to the reader. These effects permeate the mental health literature, standards used to judge normality and abnormality, and our graduate training programs. Chapter 2, "Barriers to Effective Cross-Cultural Counseling," extends this thesis to the actual process of counseling. The values and life experiences of minorities are compared and contrasted to certain generic characteristics of counseling. Culture-bound values, class-bound values, and verbal-nonverbal factors are systematically presented. The fact that most counselors and mental health practitioners adhere to these values and unwittingly impose them on the culturally different is a source of serious concern. These values, oftentimes, act as barriers to effective cross-cultural counseling.

Chapter 3, "Credibility and Racial/Cultural Similarity in Cross-Cultural Counseling," uses social influence theory to (a) identify the important factors that make a counselor influential, (b) discuss how these may be differentially operative for culturally different clients, and (c) address the question of whether a counselor who is culturally different can work effectively with a client.

The very act of counseling may become a form of cultural oppression. This is especially true when the counselor and client do not hold the same world view. Chapter 4, "Dimensions of World Views: Cultural Identity," proposes a general working theory of how race- and culture-specific factors interact to produce people with differing world views. It is suggested that one of these world views, internal locus of control and responsibility, is characteristic of Western counseling approaches and assumptions. The counseling implications of each world view are discussed.

Chapter 5, "The Culturally Skilled Counselor," attempts to discuss and present characteristics that contribute to the culturally effective counselor, thereby minimizing the dangers of oppression. In addition, a cross-cultural counseling model is presented.

While Part I deals primarily with concepts common to most racial/ethnic minorities, Part II, "Counseling Specific Populations," recognizes the uniqueness of culturally diverse populations. Thus a separate chapter discussing the cultural and historical perspective of each individual group (Chapter 6, "Asian Americans," Chapter 7, "Blacks," Chapter 8, "Hispanics," and Chapter 9, "American Indians") and the group's implications for counseling is critically presented. The strength of these chapters is twofold: first, each is written by individuals who are counselors/mental health professionals thoroughly familiar with the particular ethnic group. Counseling implications for each group are integrated and evolve from the historical and cultural discussion. Second, each chapter provides specific, concrete suggestions for counseling the various groups and thus are highly valuable to practitioners.

Part III, "Critical Incidents in Cross-Cultural Counseling" (Chapter 10), presents a series of case vignettes portraying cross-cultural counseling issues/dilemmas. These cases may be used for teaching/training and are all related to the first two sections. They are intended to help students and professionals (*a*) identify cultural points of view and responses, (*b*) show how two cultural dictates may lead to misunderstandings, (*c*) increase awareness of sociopolitical ramifications in cross-cultural counseling, (*d*) reveal how traditional counseling approaches may clash with cultural values, and (*e*) suggest alternative ways of dealing with the critical incident. The chapter is divided into three parts. The first part describes the critical incidents, the second suggests how the critical incidents may be used to enhance learning, and the third describes themes and issues most likely to be raised for each case. I hope that this text will prove valuable to students and professionals alike in increasing their sensitivities, knowledge, understanding, and skills important to effective cross-cultural counseling. Cross-cultural counseling is an exciting and challenging field, and we must all take the initiative in reaching out to learn, advance, and grow.

Part of this text was developed from National Institutes of Mental Health Grant No. 1-T24MH15552-01 on Developing Interculturally Skilled Counselors.

In closing, I would like to mention a few special individuals who have had a significant impact on my personal and professional life. In many respects, these are the people who have not only influenced my thoughts, but also have given me much personal support. First and foremost is my wife, Paulina, and son, Derald Paul. The years I spent conceptualizing and writing this book would not have been possible without their love and understanding. Second, thanks to my parents, who taught me to be proud of who and what I am—Chinese American. Third, many thanks to colleagues and tutors Leo Goldman, Barbara Kirk, Paul Pedersen, Allen Ivey, Ed Richardson, Art Ruiz, Elsie Smith, and Stephen Weinrach. Finally, thanks to all my Third World students who helped me understand their many world views.

DERALD WING SUE

Hayward, California
February 1981

Contents

I
Issues and Concepts in Cross-Cultural Counseling

What is cross-cultural counseling? Is it any different from other forms of counseling? Do we really need to view minority clients as being different from anyone else? How can couseling be accused of being a form of cultural oppression? Why do minority clients distrust counseling so much? Can a person of another race/culture counsel a client effectively? What are some barriers to effective cross-cultural counseling? How may they be overcome? What are some characteristics of the culturally skilled and effective counselor?

These are just a few of the important questions Part I attempts to address. More than anything else, Chapters 1 to 5 make it clear that cross-cultural counseling cannot be separated from the broader socio-political environment. How counseling is rooted in and reflects the dominant values, beliefs, and biases of the larger society, how the minority experience in the United States have influenced the culturally different's world views, how traditional counseling may represent cultural oppression for the minority client, and how counselors must take steps to view the minority client in a different way are the themes presented throughout.

1
The Politics of Counseling

Almost all definitions of counseling encompass certain philosophical assumptions: (*a*) a concern and respect for the uniqueness of clients; (*b*) an emphasis on the inherent worth or dignity of all people regardless of race, creed, color, or sex; (*c*) a high priority placed on helping others to attain their own self-determined goals; (*d*) valuing freedom and the opportunity to explore one's own characteristics and potentials; and (*e*) a future-oriented promise of a better life (Tolbert, 1969; Belkins, 1975; Hansen, Stevic, & Warner, 1977; Aubrey, 1977; Brammer, 1977). Many of these goals had their roots in the educational guidance movement of the early 1900s and reflected democratic ideals such as "equal access to opportunity," "pursuit of happiness," "liberty and justice for all," and "fulfillment of personal destiny." While these lofty ideals may seem highly commendable and appropriate for the counseling profession, they have oftentimes been translated in such a manner as to justify support for the status quo (Adams, 1973).

That counseling has failed to fulfill its promises to the culturally different has been a frequent theme voiced by minority group authors since the mid-1960s. In reviewing the minority group literature on counseling, Pine (1972) found the following views to be representative of those held by many minority individuals:

. . . that it is a waste of time; that counselors are deliberately shunting minority students into dead end nonacademic programs regardless of student potential, preferences, or ambitions; that counselors discourage students from applying to college; that counselors are insensitive to the needs of students and

Permission granted to reproduce all or any parts of the following articles: D.W. Sue & D. Sue, Ethnic minorities: Failures and responsibilities of the social sciences. *Journal of Non-White Concerns in Personnel and Guidance,* 1977, **5**, 99–106. And Sue, D.W., & Sue, S. Ethnic minorities: Resistance to being researched. *Professional Psychology,* 1972, **2**, 11–17.

the community; that counselors do not give the same amount of energy and time in working with minority as they do with white-middle-class students; that counselors do not accept, respect, and understand cultural differences; that counselors are arrogant and contemptuous; and that counselors don't know how to deal with their own hangups. (p. 35)

Pine's cogent summary of minority group perceptions of the counseling profession indicates a gap existing between the ideals of counseling and its actual operation with respect to the culturally different. While counseling enshrines the concepts of freedom, rational thought, tolerance of new ideas, and equality and justice for all, it can be used as an oppressive instrument by those in power to maintain the status quo. In this respect, counseling becomes a form of oppression in which there is an unjust and cruel exercise of power to subjugate or mistreat large groups of people. When used to restrict rather than enhance the well-being and development of the culturally different, it may entail overt and covert forms of prejudice and discrimination.

In this first chapter, an attempt is made to explore the many ways in which counseling and psychotherapy have failed with respect to the culturally different. This failure can be seen in three primary areas: (*a*) counselor education and training programs, (*b*) counseling and mental health literature, and (*c*) the counseling process and practice. We deal with only the first two areas in this chapter. The counseling process and practice is discussed in Chapter 2.

COUNSELOR EDUCATION AND TRAINING PROGRAMS

There is a growing awareness that the human service professions, especially counseling and clinical psychology, have failed to meet the particular mental health needs of ethnic minorities. Most graduate programs give inadequate treatment to mental health issues of ethnic minorities. Cultural influences affecting personality formation, career choice, educational development, and the manifestation of behavior disorders are infrequently part of mental health training programs. McFadden & Wilson (1977) report that less than 1% of the respondents in a survey of counselor education programs reported instructional requirements for the study of nonwhite cultures. When minority group experiences are discussed, they are generally seen and analyzed from the "white-middle-class perspective." As a result, professionals who deal with mental health problems of ethnic minorities lack understanding and knowledge about ethnic values and their consequent interaction with a racist society (D.W. Sue & D. Sue, 1977a).

Furthermore, the traditional training of mental health practitioners has often resulted in counselors inheriting the racial and cultural bias of their forebears. Several investigators (Bell, 1971; Franklin, 1971) point out that it is the training of practitioners that is at the heart of the problem. In many graduate education programs, the topic of counseling minorities is either ignored or given token treatment. In programs where minority experiences have been discussed, the focus tends to be on their pathological life styles and/or a maintenance of false stereotypes. Thus counseling practitioners are graduated from our programs believing that minorities are inherently pathological and that counseling involves a simple modification of white intrapsychic models.

Definitions of Mental Health

Counselor education programs have often been accused of fostering "cultural encapsulation," a term first coined by Wrenn (1962). The term refers specifically to (a) the substitution of model stereotypes for the real world, (b) the disregarding of cultural variations in a dogmatic adherence to some universal notion of truth, and (c) the use of a technique-oriented definition of the counseling process. The results are that counselor roles are rigidly defined, implanting an implicit belief in a universal concept of "health" and "normal."

If we look at criteria used by the mental health profession to judge normality and abnormality, this deficiency becomes glaring. Buss (1966) has identified three fundamental approaches: (a) normality as a statistical concept, (b) normality as ideal mental health, and (c) abnormality as the presence of certain behaviors (research criteria).

First, "statistical concepts" define *normality* as whatever tendencies occur most frequently in the population. "Abnormality" is equated with those traits or attributes that occur with the least frequency. The normal probability curve used so often in intelligence quotient (IQ) tests, achievement tests, and personality inventories is an example of such a measurement. Although this criterion is widely used, it actively places the culturally different at a disadvantage. First, the standard of comparison tends to be a white middle-class norm group. If deviations from the majority are considered abnormal, then many ethnic minorities would have to be so classified. For example, if a group of Blacks were to be administered a personality test and it were found that they were more suspicious than their white counterparts, what would this mean? Some psychologists and educators have used such findings to label Blacks as paranoid. Statements by Blacks that "The Man" is out to get them may be perceived as supporting a paranoid delusion.

Grier & Cobbs (1968) state that minorities who are reared under different norms and who have been consistently victims of oppression in a racist society may have a legitimate right to be suspicious and distrustful of white society. In their book, *Black Rage,* they point out how Blacks, in order to survive in a white racist society, have had to be suspicious and distrustful of whites. The so-called "paranoid" orientation is a functional rather than a dysfunctional mechanism used by Blacks to protect themselves from possible physical and psychological harm. Grier and Cobbs perceive this "cultural paranoia" as adaptive and healthy. Indeed, some believe that the lack of a paranorm among minorities may be more indicative of pathology than its presence! The absence of a paranorm in minorities may indicate poor reality testing (denial of oppression-racism in society).

Second, using "ideal mental health" as a criterion of normality or abnormality has many deficiencies. Such an approach stresses the importance of attaining some ideal goal such as a consciousness-balance of psychic forces (Freud, 1960; Jung, 1960), self actualization-creativity (Rogers, 1961; Maslow, 1968), or competence, autonomy, and resistance to stress (Allport, 1961; White 1963). The discriminatory nature of such approaches is grounded in the belief of a universal application (all populations and all situations) and a failure to recognize the value base from which the criteria derive. The particular goal or ideal used is intimately linked to a theoretical frame of reference and values held by the practitioner. For example, the psychoanalytic emphasis on "insight" as a determinant of mental health is a value in itself (London, 1964; Lowe, 1969). Many writers (Calia, 1968; Bryson & Bardo, 1975; D.W. Sue & D. Sue, 1977b), have pointed out that certain socioeconomic groups and ethnic minorities do not particularly value "insight."

Furthermore, definitions of mental health such as competence, autonomy, and resistance to stress are related to white middle-class notions of "individual" maturity. Shertzer and Stone (1974) and Banks (1977) discuss how the counseling profession originated from the ideological milieu of individualism. Individuals make their lot in life. Those who succeed in society do so on the basis of their *own* efforts and abilities. Successful people are seen as mature, independent, and possessing great ego strength. Apart from the potential bias in defining what constitutes competence, autonomy, and resistance to stress, the use of such a person-focused definition of maturity places the blame on the individual. When a person fails in life, it is because of his/her own lack of ability, interest, maturity, or some inherent weakness of the ego. If we see minorities as being subjected to higher stress factors in society (Deloria, 1969; Smith 1973; Ruiz & A.M. Padilla, 1977; D.W. Sue,

1975) and placed in a one-down position by virtue of racism, then it becomes quite clear that the definition will tend to portray the life-style of minorities as inferior, underdeveloped, and deficient. Ryan (1971) and others (Ivey & Authier, 1978; Banks & Marsten, 1973; Caplan & Nelson, 1973; Avis & Stewart, 1976) have referred to this process as "blaming the victim." Yet a broader system analysis would show that the economic, social, and psychological conditions of minorities are related to their oppressed status in America.

Third, an alternative to the previous two definitions of defining abnormality is a research one. For example, in determining rates of mental illness in different ethnic groups, "psychiatric diagnosis," "presence in mental hospitals," and scores on "objective psychological inventories" are frequently used. Diagnosis and hospitalization present a circular problem. The definition of normality-abnormality depends on what mental health practitioners say it is! In this case, the race or ethnicity of mental health professionals is likely to be different from that of minority clients. Bias on the part of the practitioner with respect to diagnosis and treatment is likely to occur. Yamamoto, James, & Palley (1968) found that minority clients tended to be diagnosed differently and to receive less preferred modes of treatment.

Furthermore, the political and societal implications of psychiatric diagnosis and hospitalizations have been forcefully pointed out by Laing (1967, 1969) and Szasz (1961, 1970). Laing believes that individual madness is but a reflection of the madness of society. He describes schizophrenic breakdowns as desperate strategies by people to liberate themselves from a "false self" used to maintain behavioral normality in our society. Attempts to adjust the person back to the original normality (sick society) is unethical.

Szasz states this opinion even more strongly:

In my opinion, mental illness is a myth. People we label "mentally ill" are not sick, and involuntary mental hospitalization is not treatment. It is punishment . . . The fact that mental illness designates a deviation from an ethical rule of conduct, and that such rules vary widely, explains why upper-middle-class psychiatrists can so easily find evidence of "mental illness" in lower-class individuals; and why so many prominent persons in the past fifty years or so have been diagnosed by their enemies as suffering from some types of insanity. Barry Goldwater was called a paranoid schizophrenic . . . Woodrow Wilson, a neurotic . . . Jesus Christ, according to two psychiatrists . . . was a born degenerate with a fixed delusion system. (Szasz 1970, pp. 167–168).

Szasz sees the mental health professional as an inquisitor, an agent of society exerting social control on those individuals who deviate in thought and behavior from the accepted norms of society. Psychiatric hospitalization is believed to be a form of social control for persons who annoy or disturb us. The label "mental illness" may be seen as a political ploy used to control those who are different, and counseling is used to control, brainwash, or reorient the identified victims to fit into society. It is exactly this concept that many minorities find frightening. For example, many Asian Americans, Blacks, Chicanos, Puerto Ricans, and American Indians are increasingly challenging the concepts of normality and abnormality. They feel that their values and life-styles are often seen by society as pathological and thus are unfairly discriminated against by the mental health professions.

In addition, the use of "objective" psychological inventories as indicators of maladjustment may also place minorities at a disadvantage. One example concerning the paranorm has already been given. Most minorities are aware that the test instruments used on them have been constructed and standardized according to white middle-class norms. The lack of culturally unbiased instruments makes many feel that the results obtained are invalid. The improper use of such instruments can lead to an exclusion of minorities in jobs and promotion (American Psychological Association, Task Force on Employment Testing of Minority Groups, 1969), to discriminatory educational decisions (Russell, 1970), and to biased determination of what constitutes pathology and cure in counseling/therapy (Halleck, 1971; London, 1964). These factors lend support to the belief that counseling is an egocentric part of the Establishment that interprets behavior exclusively from its reference point and attempts to fit minorities into the "white experience."

These universal definitions of "health" and "normal" that are accepted unquestioningly in most graduate programs also guide the delivery of mental health service. Thus the culturally encapsulated counselor may become a tool of his/her own dominant political, social, or economic value. Ethnocentric notions of adjustment tend to ignore inherent cultural-class values, allowing the encapsulated person to be blind to his/her own cultural baggage. The net result has been that mental health services have demanded a type of racial and cultural conformity in client behavior that has been demeaning and that has denied different ethnic minorities the right of their cultural heritage.

Curriculum Deficiencies

While universal definitions of mental health pervade all aspects of the counseling profession, such has been able to happen primarily because of the graduate curriculum. D.W. Sue & Pedersen (1977) in examining mental health training programs have concluded that the collection and dissemination of information on cross-cultural counseling and the training of culturally skilled counselors have been hindered by several problems.

First, while there has been much talk about what is wrong with things and what needs to be done, little action has taken place. Much of the problem resides in a lack of direction and the tedious process of developing new programs and practices. Our failure to advance quickly can be traced to the haphazard manner in which we have approached the task and the low priority given to this area.

Second, cross-cultural training programs are noticeably deficient in relating race- and culture-specific incidents in counseling to skills the culturally competent counselor must possess. Effective interracial or cross-cultural counseling has suffered because a systematic approach to teaching counseling skills relevant to the culturally different has not occurred. While consciousness raising, cognitive understanding, and affective dimensions are important, there is a strong need to relate these components to specific skills in working with the culturally different. The gap between awareness, understanding, and behavior has led to failure in training programs.

Third, many successful programs and practices in interracial communication and cross-cultural counseling are scattered in the literature or in local publications. Program designers and researchers are generally unaware of the programs that have been developed elsewhere. The result is a lack of any sophisticated critical analyses of existing programs and unnecessary duplication of programs or studies investigating similar problems. Consequently, there is an inability to improve on other studies and to build on past research. This problem has severely limited the development of sophisticated theory on cross-cultural training. A viable conceptual framework is sorely needed in this area.

Last, and related to the previous point, the use of media-based training packages is beginning to play a broad and important role in the training of school counselors and mental health practitioners. Especially noteworthy are those by Carkhuff (1975) Hosford (American Personnel and Guidance Association, APGA, 1975; Hosford & deVisser, 1974), Ivey (Ivey & Gluckstern, Microtraining Associates, 1976; Ivey & Authier, 1978), and Kagan (1976). These four media-based packages present systems for teaching basic helping skills. They have pulled the veil of mystery from professional helpers to reveal the principle components of the therapeutic act. These helping skills and attitudes can be taught to the uninitiated, as well as prospective professionals.

While such systems are available for the general teaching of counseling skills to school counselors and mental health practitioners, they (excluding Ivey's) are not designed for training in cross-cultural counseling or therapy. They are heavily based on a Western framework and lack validation regarding their appropriateness for cross-cultural counseling/therapy modes. Furthermore, while the specific skills they identify seem to constitute the basic helping ones for any mental health professional, the differential use of these skills and the particular combinations most appropriate to the culturally different have not been researched. The result is the lack of any comparable cross-cultural training system of the caliber and specificity to the ones mentioned previously.

It is this very issue of cultural encapsulation and its detrimental effects on minorities that have generated training recommendations from the Vail Conference (Korman, 1974), Austin Conference (1975), and Dulles Conference (1978). All conferences noted the serious lack and inadequacy of psychology training programs in dealing with religions, racial, ethnic, sexual, and economic groups. Selected recommendations included advocating (a) that professional psychology training programs at all levels provide information on the potential political nature of the practice of psychology; (b) that professionals need to "own" their value positions; (c) that client populations ought to be involved in helping determine what is "done to them"; (d; that evaluation of training programs include not only the content, but also an evaluation of the graduates; and (e) that continuing professional development occur beyond the receipt of any advanced degree.

Perhaps the most important recommendation to arise from these conferences and echoed by others (Society for the Psychological Study of Social Issues, SPSSI, 1973, McFadden, Quinn, & Sweeney, 1978) President's Commission on Mental Health, 1978) was the importance of identifying and assessing competencies of psychologists as they relate to the culturally different.

In a recent action, the APA Council of Representatives voted the following resolution at its January 1979 meeting:

It is the sense of APA Council that APA accreditation reflect our concern that all psychology departments and schools should assure that their students receive preparation to function in a multi-cultural, multi-racial society. This implies having systematic exposure to and contact with a diversity of students, teachers and patients or clients, such as, for example, by special arrangement for interchange or contact with other institutions on a regular and organized basis. (p. 5)

The importance of providing educational experiences that generate sensitivity to the appreciation of the history, current needs, strengths, and resources of minority communities was stressed. Students and faculty members should be helped to understand the development and behavior of the group being studied, thus enabling them to (a) use their knowledge to develop skills in working with minority groups; and (b) develop strategies to modify the effects of political, social, and economic forces on minority groups. The curriculum must focus on immediate social problems and needs. It must stimulate an awareness of minority problems caused by economic, social, and educational deprivation. The curriculum must also be designed to stimulate this awareness not solely at a cognitive level. It must enable students to understand feelings of helplessness and powerlessness, low self-esteem, poor self-concept, and how they contribute to low motivation, frustration, hate, ambivalence, and apathy. Each course should contain (a) a *consciousness raising* component, (b) an *affective component,* (c) a *knowledge* component, and (d) a *skills* component.

COUNSELING AND MENTAL HEALTH LITERATURE

Many writers have noted how the social science literature and specifically research have failed to create a realistic understanding of various ethnic groups in America (Bryde, 1971; D.W. Sue & S. Sue, 1972; Thomas & Sillen, 1972; Williams, 1970; Smith, 1973; A.M. Padilla & Ruiz, 1974; Sumada, 1975). In fact, certain practices are felt to have done great harm to minorities by ignoring them, maintaining false sterotypes, and/or distorting their life-styles. As mentioned previously, mental health definitions may be viewed as encompassing the use of social power (Tedeschi & O'Donovan, 1971; and functioning as a "handmaiden of the status quo" (Halleck, 1971, p. 30). Sanford (1969) points out that organized social science is part of the Establishment from which its researchers are usually drawn; moreover, organized social science often is dependent on the Establishment for financial support. Ethnic minorities frequently see counseling in this fashion too, as a discipline concerned with maintaining the status and power of the Establishment. As a result, the person collecting and reporting data is often perceived as possessing the social bias of his/her society.

D.W. Sue (1975) notes that social sciences have generally ignored the study of Asians in America. This deficit has contributed to the perpetuation of false stereotypes that has angered many of the younger Asians concerned with raising consciousness and group esteem. When studies have been conducted on minorities, research has been appallingly unbalanced. In a hard-hitting article, Billingsley (1970) points out how "white social science" has tended to reinforce a negative view of

Blacks among the public by concentrating on unstable Black families instead of the many stable ones. Such unfair treatment has also been the case of studies on Chicanos that have focused on the psychopathological problems encountered by Mexican Americans (E.R. Padilla, 1971). Other ethnic groups such as the Native Americans (Deloria, 1969) and Puerto Ricans (A.M. Padilla & Ruiz, 1974) have fared no better. Even more disturbing is the assumption that the problems encountered by minorities are due to intrinsic factors (racial inferiority, incompatible value systems, etc.) rather than to the failure of society (D.W. Sue & S. Sue, 1972).

S. Sue & Kitano (1973) in their analysis of the literature portrayal of the Chinese and Japanese in the United States conclude that there is a strong correlation between stereotypes and the conditions of society. When economic conditions were poor, Asians were portrayed as unassimilable, sexually aggressive, and treacherous. However, when economic conditions dictated a cheap labor supply, stereotypes became more favorable.

While there are many aspects of how minorities are portrayed in the social science literature, two of them seem crucial for us to explore: (a) minorities and pathology and (b) the relevance of research.

Minorities and Pathology

When we seriously study the "scientific" literature of the past relating to the culturally different, we are immediately impressed with how an implicit equation of minorities and pathology is a common theme. The historical use of science in the investigation of racial differences seems to be linked with white supremacist notions. A. Thomas and Sillen (1972) refer to this as "scientific racism" and cite several historical examples to support their contention: (a) 1840 census figures (fabricated) were used to support the notion that Blacks living under unnatural conditions of freedom were prone to anxiety; (b) mental health for Blacks was contentment with subservience; (c) psychologically normal Blacks were faithful and happy-go-lucky; (d) influential medical journals presented fantasies as facts supporting the belief that the anatomical, neurological, or endocrinological aspects of Blacks were always inferior to whites; (e) the Black person's brain is smaller and less developed; (f) Blacks were less prone to mental illness because their minds were so simple; and (g) the dreams of Blacks are juvenile in character and not as complex as whites.

Furthermore, the belief that various human groups exist at different stages of biological evolution was accepted by G. Stanley Hall (1904). He stated explicitly that Africans, Indians, and Chinese were members of adolescent races and in a stage of incomplete development. In most cases, the evidence used to support these conclusions were fabricated, extremely flimsy, or distorted to fit the belief in nonwhite inferiority (A. Thomas & Sillen, 1972). For example, Gossett (1963) reports how when one particular study in 1895 revealed that sensory perception of Native Americans were superior to Blacks and that of Blacks to whites, the results were used to support a belief in the mental superiority of whites. "Their reactions were slower because they belonged to a more deliberate and reflective race than did the members of the other two groups" (p. 364). The belief that Blacks are "born athletes" as opposed to scientists or statesmen derive from this tradition. The fact that Hall was a well-respected psychologist often referred to as "the father of child study" and first president of the APA did not prevent him from inheriting the racial biases of his times.

The Genetic Deficient Model   The portrayal of the culturally different in literature has generally taken the form of stereotyping them as "deficient" in certain "desirable" attributes. For example, de Gobineau's (1915) *Essay on the Inequality of the Human Races* and Darwin's (1859) *The Origin of Species by Means of Natural Selection* were used to support the genetic intellectual superiority of whites and the genetic inferiority of the "lower races." Galton (1869) wrote explicitly that African "Negros" were "half-witted men" who made "childish, stupid and simpleton like mistakes," while Jews were inferior physically and mentally and only designed for a parasitical existence on other nations of people. Terman (1916) using the Binet scales in testing Spanish Indian, Mexican American, and Black families concluded that they were uneducable.

That the genetic deficient model still exists can be seen in the writing of Shuey (1966), Jensen (1969), Herstein (1971), and Shockley (1972). These writers have adopted the position that genes play a predominant role in the determination of intelligence. Shockley (1972) has expressed fears that the accumulation of weak or low intelligence genes in the Black population will seriously affect overall intelligence. Thus he advocates that low IQ people should not be allowed to bear children; they should be sterilized.

Even more disturbing has been recent allegations that the late Cyril Burt, eminent British psychologist, fabricated data to support his contention that intelligence is inherited and that Blacks have inherited inferior brains. Such an accusation is immensely important when one considers that Burt is a major influence in American and British psychology, is considered by many to be the father of educational psychology, was the first psychologist to be knighted, was awarded the

APA's Thorndike Prize and that his research findings form the foundations for the belief that intelligence is inherited. The charges, leveled by several people (Dorfman, 1978; Kamin, 1974; Gillie, 1977) can be categorized into four assertions: (a) that Burt guessed at the intelligence of parents he interviewed and later treated his guesses as scientific facts, (b) that two of Burt's collaborators never existed and Burt wrote the articles himself while using their names, (c) that Burt produced identical figures to three decimal points from different sets of data (a statistical impossibility), and (d) that Burt fabricated data to fit his theories. In a thorough review of one of Burt's most influential publications, Dorfman (1978) concludes:

Cyril Burt presented data in his classic paper "Intelligence and Social Class" that were in perfect agreement with a genetic theory of IQ and social class. A detailed analysis of these data reveals, beyond reasonable doubt, that they were fabricated from a theoretical normal curve, from a genetic regressions equation, and from figures published more than 30 years before Burt completed his surveys. (p. 1177)

The Cyril Burt fiasco may represent another instance of scientific racism.

The questions about whether there are differences between races in intelligence is both a complex and emotional one. The difficulty in clarifying this question is compounded by many factors. Besides the difficulty in defining "race," there exists questionable assumptions regarding whether research on the intelligence of whites can be generalized to other groups, whether middle-class and lower-class ethnic minorities grow up in similar environments to middle- and lower-class whites, and whether test instruments are valid for both minority and white subjects. More important, we should recognize that the "average values" of different populations tell us nothing about any one individual. Hereditability is a function of the population *not* of a trait. Ethnic groups all have individuals in the full range of intelligence; and to think of any racial group in terms of a single stereotype goes against all we know about the mechanics of heredity. Yet much of the social science literature continues to portray ethnic minorities as being genetically deficient in one sense or another.

The Culturally Deficient Model   Well-meaning social scientists who challenged the genetic deficit model by placing heavy reliance on environmental factors, nevertheless, tended to perpetuate a view that saw minorities as culturally "disadvantaged," "deficient," or "deprived." Instead of a biological condition that caused differences, the blame now shifted to the life-styles or values of various ethnic groups (Baratz & Baratz, 1970; Sumada, 1975; Smith, 1977). The term "cultural deprivation" was first popularized by Riessman's widely read book, *The Culturally Deprived Child* (1962). It was used to indicate that many groups perform poorly on tests or exhibit deviant characteristics because they lack many of the advantages of middle-class culture (education, books, toys, formal language, etc.). In essence, these groups were culturally impoverished! Sumada (1955) summarizes studies which take the position that a host of factors place many minority persons in such a position as to hinder their success in school and society at large: (*a*) nutritional factors–malnutrition contributes to physical and mental impairment; (*b*) environmental factors—crowded and broken homes, dilapidated and unaesthetic areas (lack of books, toys, pictures, etc); (*c*) psychological factors—lower self-concepts, poor motivation, absence of successful male models, lack of parental encouragement and interest in education, and fear of competing with whites; (*d*) sociocultural factors—exposure to a culture with slum and ghetto values; and (*e*) linguistic factors—an adulterated form of their own language and English.

While Riessman meant such a concept to add balance to working with minorities and ultimately improve their condition in America, some educators (Clark, 1963; Mackler & Giddings, 1965; Clark & Plotkin, 1972) strenuously objected to the term. First, the term "culturally deprived" means to lack a cultural background (slaves arrived in America culturally naked), which is contradictory because everyone inherits a culture. Second, such terms cause conceptual and theoretical confusions that may adversely affect social planning, educational policy, and research. For example, the Moynihan Report (1965) asserts that "at the heart of the deterioration of the Negro society is the deterioration of the Black family. It is the fundamental source of the weakness of the Negro community" (p. 5). Action thus was directed toward infusing "white" concepts of the family into the Black ones. Third, Baratz & Baratz (1970) point out that cultural deprivation is used synonymously with the deviation from and superiority of white middle-class values. Fourth, these deviations in values become equated with pathology in which a group's cultural values, families, or life-styles transmit the pathology. Thus it provides a convenient rationalization and alibi for the perpetuation of racism and the inequities of the socioeconomic system (Smith, 1977).

The Culturally Different Model   There are many who now maintain that the culturally deficient model only serves to perpetuate the myth of minority inferiority. The focus tends to be a person-blame one, an emphasis on minority pathology, and a use of white middle-class definitions of desirable and undesirable behavior. D. W. Sue (1975) states that our use of a common standard assumption implies that to be different is to be deviant, pathological, or sick. Mercer (1951) claims that intelligence and personality scores for minority group children really measure how "Anglicized" a person has become. Baratz & Baratz (1970) suggest that minorities should no longer be viewed as deficient but rather "culturally different." The goal of society should be to recognize the legitimacy of alternative life-styles, the advantages of being bicultural (capable of functioning in two different cultural environments), and the value of differences.

Relevance of Research

So far, our discussion of minority portrayal in the professional literature has been a general one. We have made minimal reference to research as it relates to minorities in particular. Research findings are supposed to form the basis of any profession that purports to be a science. The data generated from research should be objective and free of bias. Yet what a researcher proposes to study and how he/she interprets such findings are intimately linked to a personal, professional, and societal value system. We have already seen how personal and societal values may affect the interpretation of data as it relates to minorities. A very similar analogy can be drawn with respect to the counseling profession. For example, the profession's preoccupation with pathology tends to encourage the study of personality deficits and weaknesses rather than strengths or assets. Racist attitudes may intensify this narrow view as minorities may be portrayed in professional journals as a neurotic, psychotic, psychopath, parolee, and so on, instead of a well-rounded person.

It is not surprising that minority groups are often suspicious of the motives of the researcher. The researcher of ethnic matters may find his/her attitudes and values toward minority groups being challenged. No longer can the researcher claim that research is solely in the interest of science and morally neutral. Carl Rogers, a well-known humanistic psychologist, has stated, "If behavioral scientists are concerned solely with advancing their science it seems most probable that they will serve the purpose of whatever group has the power" (Brecher & Brecher, 1961). C. W. Thomas (1970) has even voiced this thought in stronger form.

White psychologists have raped Black communities all over the country. Yes raped. They have used Black people as the human equivalent of rats run through Ph.D. experiments and as helpless clients for programs that serve middle-class white administrators better than they do the poor. They have used research on Black people as green stamps to trade for research grants. They have been vultures. (p. 52)

Williams (1974) discusses two scientific research projects that illustrate this statement: the Tuskegee experiment and the Colville Indian Reservation Study.

The Tuskegee experiment was a 40-year federal experiment in which 600 Alabama Black men were used as guinea pigs in the study of what damage would occur to the body if syphilis were left untreated. Approximately 200 were allowed to go untreated even when medication was available for it. Records indicated that 7 died as a result of syphilis, and an additional 154 died of heart disease that may have been caused by the untreated syphilis! Experiments of this type are ghastly and give rise to suspicions that minorities are being used as guinea pigs in other experiments of this sort.

That exploitation occurs in other ethnic communities is exemplified in the Colville Indian reservation disposition (Williams, 1974). An anthropologist, after gaining the trust and confidence of the Colville Indians in Washington conducted a study of factionalism among the tribe. A subsequent study by another group of white researchers recommended that the best course of action for the Colville reservation was to liquidate its assets, including land, rather than consider economic development. Part of the justification for liquidation was based on the factionalism results obtained from the first study, and termination of the reservation was recommended. There were several primary issues about the actions that merit attention. First, the reservation was composed of 1.4 million acres of land that was rich in timber and minerals. There was strong pressure on the part of whites to obtain the land. Second, the problems of factionalism were actually created by a society that attempted to "civilize" the Indians via Christianity and by white businesses which offered promises of riches. Third, many of the Indians confided in the white researcher and were led to believe that the information obtained would not be released.

It is studies such as these and the continual portrayal of ethnic communities and groups as deviant that make minorities extremely distrustful about the motives of the white researcher (Rainwater & Pittman, 1967). Whereas social scientists in the past have been able to enter ethnic communities and conduct their studies with only minimal justification to those studied, researchers are now being received with suspicion and overt hostility. Minorities are actively raising questions and issues regarding the value system of researchers and the outcome of their research. The publication of the *Ethical Principles in the Conduct of Research with Human Participants* (the Ad Hoc committee of the APA, 1973) is an acknowledgment of these issues.

Under what conditions is it ethically acceptable to study residents of the ghetto, the intellectually handicapped, the poor, prisoners or even college students? The researcher who undertakes to study these groups is sometimes charged with being opportunistic, exploitative, and potentially damaging to the target populations. (p. 16)

Furthermore, many members of ethnic minorities find it difficult to see the relevance of applicability of much research conducted on them. This is especially true when they view the researcher as a laboratory specialist dealing with abstract, theoretical ideas rather than with the real human conditions. Much hostility is directed toward the researcher who is perceived in this way. There is a growing feeling among ethnic minorities that research should go beyond the mere explaining of human behavior. Research should contribute to the concerns and betterment of the groups being studied. This concern is not only voiced by minorities, but also by many students, scholars, and the public. Ethnic minorities often view the researcher as a laboratory specialist interested in abstract theoretical ideas rather than a person interested in the applicability of his/her findings. Baron (1971) points out that psychological researchers are often guilty of perpetuating this belief by failing to make clear and explicit the goals behind their pursuits. Indeed, many find this task distasteful. Much hostility, therefore, is directed to the researcher of ethnic matters whom many minorities feel conduct narrow irrelevant studies that will not improve the human condition. There seems to be much justification for these charges.

First, graduate programs in the social sciences have traditionally been much more concerned with the training of academicians rather than practitioners. Several psychologists (Patterson, 1972; Thoresen, et al., 1972; Proshansky, 1972, 1976) in their analyses of graduate education point out that most programs use as the "root model" the experimental research-scientist as the psychological paradigm. Patterson (1972) points out that this model has frequently hindered research dealing with social and psychological problems facing humankind. Since much exploratory work is needed in investigating complex social problems, the strong emphasis on rigorous methodology discourages much meaningful research dealing with problems of complex social issues. This discouragement is often seen in the status hierarchy of graduate programs. Experimental research is at the top of the ladder, with exploratory work at the bottom. Furthermore, manuscripts that may have meaningful implications in social contexts but which may not lend themselves to rigorous experimentation are difficult to publish in the professional journals. Ethnic minorities who may desire to seek solutions to pressing social problems become alienated from such programs that they feel are irrelevant and encapsulated from real social settings. Proshansky (1972) voices concern about the need for psychology to attract and train individuals to play roles other than the experimental research scientist. He states that "the real tragedy, however, lies in my conviction that students come into psychology with a variety of interests, abilities, and talents and what we do is to impose on them a ready-made professional self-identity" (p. 208).

Second, many social researchers feel that their responsibility is discharged with the publication of their results. Research data reported in the professional journals may be understandable to fellow professionals but certainly not to many students and laypeople. All too often the publication of articles is written to impress colleagues and insure promotion and tenure (Goldman, 1977). The individuals and communities in such studies are often forgotten. Feedback in intelligible and usable form to the particular communities is seriously lacking and contributes to feelings of exploitation. Researchers are increasingly being asked, "How will this study help us? Tell us in concrete terms without your professional rationalizations and jargon and we will decide whether you can have access to us or not."

A CALL TO THE PROFESSION

If counseling, as a profession, is to receive acceptance from the culturally different, it must demonstrate, in no uncertain terms, its good faith and ability to contribute to the betterment of a group's quality of life. This demonstration can take several directions.

First, the counseling profession must take initiative in confronting the potential political nature of counseling. For too long we have deceived ourselves into believing that the practice of counseling and the data base which underlie the profession are morally, ethically, and politically neutral. The results have been (*a*) subjugation of the culturally different, (*b*) perpetuation of the view that minorities are inherently pathological, (*c*) perpetuation of racist practices in counseling, and (*d*) provision of an excuse to the profession for not taking social action to rectify inequities in the system.

Second, the counseling profession must move quickly to challenge certain assumptions that permeate our training programs. We must critically reexamine our concepts of what constitutes normality and abnormality, begin mandatory training programs that deal with these issues, critically examine and reinterpret past and continuing literature dealing with the culturally different, and use research in such a manner as to improve the life conditions of the researched population.

Educational programs can no longer present a predominately white Anglo-Saxon Protestant (WASP) orientation. Minority groups must receive equal treatment and fair portrayal on all levels of education. Courses dealing with minority group experiences must become a required part of the educational curriculum. If teachers feel that textbooks have not adequately portrayed ethnic minorities, they should feel some obligation to supplement their reading lists or refuse to use such texts. Pressure can then be brought to bear on the authors and publishers. Also, the professional reward structure in counseling needs to be radically altered. The practitioner should receive equal status as the academician. Action or applied research should be encouraged even though it may not be the epitome of rigorous experimental controls.

Third, research can be a powerful means of combating stereotypes and of correcting "biased" studies. The fact that previous studies have been used to perpetuate stereotypes (Billingsley, 1970) does not preclude the usefulness of research. If social scientists believe that research has been poorly conducted or misinterpreted to the detriment of minority groups, they should feel some moral commitment to investigate their beliefs. Unfortunately, this self-correcting process of ethnic research has been underdeveloped, since there is a shortage of minority social scientists contributing a minority group point of view. The researcher cannot escape the moral and ethical implications of his/her research and must take responsibility for the outcome of his/her study. He/she should guard against misinterpretations and take into account cultural factors and the limitations of his/her instruments.

Fourth, there is a strong need for counseling to attract more ethnic minorities to the profession, complex as this issue is. Although many white professionals have great understanding and empathy for minorities, they can never fully appreciate the dilemmas faced by a minority member. Ethnic minorities can offer a dimension and viewpoint that act as a counterbalance to the forces of misinterpretation. Furthermore, Proctor (1970) feels that the cry for more minority professionals demonstrates the presence of a "credibility gap" between counseling and minority members. With this addition of more minority counseling psychologists, trust among ethnic minorities may be enhanced.

Fifth, counselors must realize that many so-called pathological socioemotional characteristics of ethnic minorities can be directly attributed to unfair practices in society. Herzog (1971) and Blau (1970) advocate a shift in research from the poor and culturally different to that of groups and institutions that have perpetuated racism and obstructed needed changes.

Another shift in focus can be the study of positive attributes and characteristics of ethnic minorities. Social scientists have had a tendency to look for pathology and problems among minorities. Beckman et al., (1970) have stated that too much research has concentrated on mental health problems and culture-conflict of minorities, while little has been done to determine the advantages of being bicultural. Hopefully, such an orientation will do much to present a more balanced picture of different minority groups.

It must be noted, however, that the researcher cannot selectively publish findings that perpetuate "good" characteristics of minority groups and that censure "bad" ones. This selectivity is not only unethical, but also serves to maintain misunderstandings in the long run.

Last, making research with minorities a community endeavor can do much to lower hostility and develop trust between researcher and subject. For example, a social scientist investigating minority groups in the community is often more effective if he/she discusses his/her ideas with community leaders and obtains their cooperation (Goering & Cummins, 1970; Klein, 1968). The inclusion of community members in different phases of research (interviewers, coordinators, etc.) can facilitate trust. This would require that social scientists clearly articulate their goals and methods to the community. Sanford (1970), in his discussion of student activism, notes that many students seldom know the implications or outcomes of the research conducted on them. He points out that research with student involvement can benefit its subjects by (a) helping them answer their questions and concerns, (b) helping them acquire understanding of themselves, and (c) helping them learn research skills. In this way, research will be educational for those being studied as well.

REFERENCES

Ad Hoc Committee on Ethical Standards in Psychological Research. *Ethical principles in the conduct of research with human participants.* Washington, D.C.: APA, 1973.

Adams, H. J. Progressive heritage of guidance: A view from the left. *Personnel and Guidance Journal*, 1973, **51**, 531–538.

Allport, G. W. *Pattern and Growth in Personality*. New York: Holt, Rinehart & Winston, 1961.

American Personnel and Guidance Association. *Behavioral Counseling Film Series* (Hosford). Washington, D.C.: APGA, 1975.

American Psychological Association, Council of Representatives' minutes from the meeting of January 19–20, 1979, p. 5.

American Psychological Association Task Force on Employment Testing of Minority Groups. Job testing and the disadvantaged. *American Psychologist*, 1969, **24**, 637–649.

Aubrey, R. F. Historical development of guidance and counseling and implications for the future. *Personnel and Guidance Journal*, 1977, **55**, 288–295.

Avis, J. P., & Stewart, L. H. College counseling: Intentions and change. *The Counseling Psychologist*, 1976, **6**, 74–77.

Banks, W. Group consciousness and the helping professions. *Personnel and Guidance Journal*, 1977, **55**, 319–330.

Banks, W., & Marsten, K. Counseling: The reactionary profession. *Personnel and Guidance Journal*, 1973, **41**, 457–462.

Baratz, S., & Baratz, J. Early childhood intervention: The social sciences base of institutional racism. *Harvard Educational Review*, 1970, **40**, 29–50.

Baron, J. Is experimental psychology relevant? *American Psychologist*, 1971, **26**, 713–716.

Beckman, G. M., Henthorn, W. E., Niyakawa-Howard, A., & Passin, H. *Culture Learning Program Proposal*. Honolulu: East-West Center, 1970.

Belkin, G. S. *Practical Counseling in the Schools*. Dubuque, Iowa: W. C. Brown, 1975.

Bell, R. L. The culturally deprived psychologist. *Counseling Psychologist*, 1971, **2**, 104–106.

Billingsley, A. Black families and white social science. *Journal of Social Issues*, 1970, **26**, 127–142.

Blau, T. APA Commission on accelerating Black participation in psychology. *American Psychologist*, 1970, **25**, 1103–1104.

Brammer, L. M. Who can be a helper? *Personnel and Guidance Journal*, 1977, **55**, 303–308.

Brecher, R., & Brecher, E. The happiest creatures on earth? *Harpers*, 1961, **222**, 85–90.

Bryde, J. F. *Indian Students and Guidance*, Boston: Houghton Mifflin, 1971.

Bryson, S., & Bardo, H. Race and the counseling process: An overview. *Journal of Non-White Concerns in Personnel and Guidance*, 1975, **4** (1), 5–15.

Buss, A. H. *Psychopathology*, New York: Wiley, 1966.

Calia, V. F. The culturally deprived client: A reformulation of the counselor's role. In J. C. Bently (Ed.), *The Counselor's Role: Commentary and Readings*. Boston: Houghton Mifflin, 1968, 41–49.

Caplan, N., & Nelson, S. D. On being useful—The nature and consequences of psychological research on social problems. *American Psychologist*, 1973, **28**, 199–211.

Carkhuff, R. R. *Human Resource Development Videotape Series—Life Skills*. Amherst, Mass.: Human Resource Development Press, 1975.

Carkhuff, R. R., & Pierce, R. Differential effects of therapist race and social class upon patient depth of self-exploration in the initial clinical interview. *Journal of Consulting Psychology*, 1967, **31**, 632–634.

Clark, K. B. Educational stimulation of racially disadvantaged children. In A. H. Passow (Ed.), *Education in Depressed Areas*. New York: Teachers College Press, 1963, 142–162.

Clark, K. B., & Plotkin, L. A review of the issues and literature of cultural deprivation theory. In K. B. Clark (Ed.), *The Educationally Deprived*. New York: Metropolitan Applied Research Center, 1972, 47–73.

Darwin, C. *On the Origin of Species by Natural Selection*, 1859.

Deloria, V. *Custer Died for Your Sins*. New York: Macmillan, 1969.

de Gobineau, A. *The Inequality of Human Races*. New York: Putnam, 1915.

Dorfman, D. D. The Cyril Burt question: New findings. *Science*, 1978, **201**, 1177–1186.

Franklin, A. J. To be young, gifted and black with inappropriate professional training: A critique of counseling programs. *Counseling Psychologist*, 1971, **2**, 107–112.

Freud, S. Psychopathology of everyday life. In *Standard Edition*, vol. 6. London: Hogarth Press, 1960.

Galton, F. *Hereditary genius: An Inquiry into Its Laws and Consequences*. London: Macmillan, 1869.

Gillie, D. *Phi Delta Kappan*, **58**, 1977, 469.

Goering, J. M., & Cummins, M. Intervention research and the survey process. *Journal of Social Issues*, 1970, **26**, 49–55.

Goldman, L. Toward more meaningful research. *Personnel and Guidance Journal*, 1977, **55**, 363–368.

Gossett, T. F. *Race: The History of an Idea in America*. Dallas: Southern Methodist University Press, 1963.

Grier, W., & Cobbs, P. *Black Rage*. New York: Basic Books, 1968. Hall, G. S. *Adolescence*. New York: Appleton, 1904.

Halleck, S. L. Therapy is the handmaiden of the status quo. *Psychology Today*, 1971, **4**, 30–34, 98–100.

Hansen, J. C., Stevic, R. R., & Warner, R. W. *Counseling: Theory and Process*. Boston: Allyn & Bacon, 1977.

Hernstein, R. IQ. *Atlantic Monthly*, 1971, 43–64.

Herzog, E. Who should be studied? *American Journal of Orthopsychiatry*, 1971, **41**, 4–11.

Hosford, R. E., & deVisser, L. A. J. M. *Behavioral Approaches to Counseling: An Introduction*. Washington, D.C.: APGA, 1974.

Ivey, A., & Authier, J. *Microcounseling: Innovations in Interviewing Training*. Springfield, Ill.: Charles C. Thomas, 1978.

Ivey, A. E., & Gluckstern, N. B. *Systematic Videotraining for Beginning Helpers*. Amherst, Mass.: Microtraining Associates, 1976.

Jensen, A. How much can we boost IQ and school achievement? *Harvard Educational Review*, 1969, **39**, 1–123.

Jung, C. G. The structure and dynamics of the psyche. In *Collected Works*, vol. 8. Princeton: Princeton University Press, 1960.

Kagan, N. *Interpersonal Process Recall: A Method of Influencing Human Interaction.* Washington, D.C.: APGA, 1976.

Kamin, L. *The Science and Politics of I.Q.* Potomac, Md.: Eribaum, 1974.

Klein, D. C. *Community Dynamics and Mental Health.* New York: Wiley, 1968.

Korman, M. National conference on levels and patterns of professional training in psychology. *American Psychologist*, 1974, **29**, 441–449.

Laing, R. D. *The Divided Self.* New York: Pantheon, 1967.

Laing, R. D. *The Politics of Experience.* New York: Pantheon, 1969.

London, P. *Modes and Morals of Psychotherapy.* New York: Holt, Rinehart & Winston, 1964.

Lowe, C. M. *Value Orientations in Counseling and Psychotherapy.* San Francisco: Chandler, 1969.

McFadden, J., Quinn, J. R., & Sweeney, T. J. Position paper: Commission on non-white concerns. Association of Counselor Educators and Supervisors. APGA Washington, D.C., 1978.

McFadden, J., & Wilson, T. Non-white academic training within counselor education, rehabilitation counseling and student personnel programs. Unpublished research, 1977.

Mackler, B., & Giddings, M. G. Cultural deprivation: A study in mythology. *Teachers College Record*, 1965, **66**, 608–613.

Maslow, A. H. *Toward a Psychology of Being.* Princeton: Van Nostrand, 1968.

Mercer, J. R. Institutionalized anglocentrism. In P. Orleans & W. Russel (Eds.), *Race, Change and Urban Society.* Los Angeles: Sage Publications, 1971.

Moynihan, D. P. Employment, income and the ordeal of the Negro family. *Daedalus*, 1965, 745–770.

Padilla, A. M., & Ruiz, R. A. *Latino Mental Health.* Washington, D.C.: U. S. Department of Health, Education and Welfare, 1974.

Padilla, E. R. The relationship between psychology and Chicanos: Failures and possibilities. In N. N. Wagner & M. R. Haug (Eds.), *Chicanos: Social and Psychological Perspectives.* St. Louis, Mo.: Mosby, 1971, 286–294.

Patterson, C. H. Psychology and social responsibility. *Professional Psychology,* 1972, **3**, 3–10.

Pine, G. J. Counseling minority groups: A review of the literature. *Counseling and Values*, 1972, **17**, 35–44.

President's Commission on Mental Health. Report to the President. Washington, D.C.: U. S. Government Printing Office, 1978.

Proctor, S. A. Reversing the spiral toward futility. *The Personnel and Guidance Journal*, 1970, **48**, 721–728.

Proshansky, H. M. Environmental psychology and the real world. *American Psychologist*, 1976, **31**, 303–310.

Proshansky, H. M. For what are we training our graduate students. *American Psychologist*, 1972, **27**, 205–212.

Rainwater, L., & Pittman, D. J. Ethical problems in studying a politically sensitive community. *Social Problems*, 1967, **14**, 357–366.

Riessman, F. *The Culturally Deprived Child.* New York: Harper & Row, 1962.

Rogers, C. R. *On Becoming a Person.* Boston: Houghton Mifflin, 1961.

Ruiz, R.A., & Padilla, A.M. Counseling Latinos. *Personnel Journal*, 1977, **55**, 401–408.

Russel, R. D. Black perceptions of guidance. *Personnel and Guidance Journal*, 1970, **48**, 521–728.

Ryan, W. *Blaming the Victim.* New York: Pantheon, 1971.

Sanford, N. Research with students as action and education. *American Psychologist*, 1969, **24**, 544–546.

Sanford, N. Whatever happened to action research? *Journal of Social Issues*, 1970, **26**, 3–23.

Shertzer, B., & Stone, S. *Fundamentals of Counseling.* Boston: Houghton Mifflin, 1974.

Shockley, W. *Journal of Criminal Law and Criminology*, 1972, **7,** 530–543.

Shuey, A. *The Testing of Negro Intelligence.* New York: Social Science Press, 1966.

Smith, E. J. Counseling Black individuals: Some stereotypes. *Personnel and Guidance Journal, 1977,* **55**, 390–396.

Smith, E. J. *Counseling the Culturally Different Black Youth.* Columbus, O.: Charles E. Merrill, 1973.

Society for the Psychological Study of Social Issues. Document entitled "Graduate Programs in Psychology, in the Sciences, in Education, Social Work, Public Health, Suitable to the Needs of Minority Students," Los Angeles, 1973.

Sue, D. W. Asian Americans: Social-psychological forces affecting their life styles. In S. Picou & R. Campbell (Eds.), *Career Behavior of Special Groups.* Columbus, O.: Charles E. Merrill, 1975.

Sue, S., & Kitano, H. H. L. Stereotypes as a measure of success. *Journal of Social Issues*, 1973, **29**, 83–98.

Sue, D. W., & Pedersen, P. Cross-cultural training modules for mental health practitioners: Development and evaluation. Research grant proposal submitted to NIMH, 1975.

Sue, D. W., & Sue, D. Barriers to effective cross-cultural counseling. *Journal of Counseling Psychology*, September 1977b.

Sue, D. W., & Sue, D. Ethnic minorities: Failures and responsibilities of the social sciences. *Journal of Non-White Concerns in Personnel and Guidance*, 1977a, **5**, 99–106.

Sue, D. W., & Sue, S. Ethnic minorities: Resistance to being researched. *Professional Psychology, 1972,* **2**, 11–17.

Sumada, R. J. From ethnocentrism to a multicultural perspective in educational testing. *Journal of Afro-American Issues*, 1975, **3**, 4–18.

Szasz, T. S. The crime of commitment. *Readings in Clinical Psychology Today*. Del Mar, Calif.: CRM Books, 1970, 167–169.

Szasz, T. S. *The Myth of Mental Illness.* New York: Hoeber, 1961.

Tedeschi, J. T., & O'Donovan, D. Social power and the psychologist. *Professional Psychology*, 1971, **2**, 59–64.

Terman, L. M. *The Measurement of Intelligence.* Boston: Houghton Mifflin, 1916.

Thomas, A., & Sillen, S. *Racism and Psychiatry.* New York: Brunner/Mazel, 1972.

Thomas C.W. Different strokes for different folks. *Psychology Today*, 1970, **4**, 49–53, 80

Thoresen, R. W., Krauskopf, C. J., McAleer, C. A., & Wenger, D. H. The future of applied psychology: Are we building a buggy whip factory? *American Psychologist*, 1972, **27**, 134–139.

Tolbert, E. L. *Introduction to Counseling*. New York: McGraw-Hill, 1969.

White, R. W. Ego and reality in psychoanalytic theory: A proposal regarding independent ego energies. *Psychological Issues*, 1963, **3**, 1–210.

Williams, R. L. Black pride, academic relevance and individual achievement. *Counseling Psychologist*, 1970, **2**, 18–22.

Williams, R. L. The death of white research in the Black community. *Journal of Non-White Concerns in Personnel and Guidance*, 1974, **2**, 116–132.

Wrenn, G. The culturally encapsulated counselor. *Harvard Educational Review*, 1962, **32** (4), 444–449.

Yamamoto, J., James, Q. C., & Palley, N. Cultural problems in psychiatric therapy. *Archives of General Psychiatry*, 1968, **19**, 45–49.

2
Barriers to Effective Cross-Cultural Counseling

In the last chapter, we mentioned how the counseling profession had failed to contribute to the betterment of Third World groups in America. Counselor training programs and the portrayal of minorities in both the popular and scientific literature have oftentimes instilled within counselor trainees (*a*) monocultural assumptions of mental health, (*b*) negative stereotypes of pathology for minority life-styles, and (*c*) ineffective, inappropriate, and antagonistic counseling approaches to the values held by minorities. Nowhere is this damage seen more clearly than in the actual practice of counseling and therapy.

Counseling and psychotherapy may be viewed legitimately as a process of interpersonal interaction and communication. For effective counseling to occur, the counselor and client must be able to *appropriately* and *accurately send* and *receive* both *verbal* and *nonverbal* messages. While breakdowns in communication often happen between members who share the same culture, the problem becomes exacerbated between people of different racial or ethnic backgrounds. Many mental health professionals have noted that racial or ethnic factors may act as impediments to counseling (Carkhuff & Pierce, 1967; Vontress, 1971; Attneave, 1972; Sue, D.W., 1975; Ruiz & Padilla, 1977). Misunderstandings that arise from cultural variations in communication may lead to alienation and/or an inability to develop trust and rapport. As suggested by Yamamoto, James, & Palley (1968), this may result in early termination of therapy.

In one of the most comprehensive studies ever conducted on Third World clients, S. Sue and associates (S. Sue et al. 1974; S. Sue &

Permission granted to reproduce any or all of the following article: D.W. Sue, & D. Sue, Barriers to effective cross-cultural counseling. *Journal of Counseling Psychology*, 1977, **24**, 420–429

McKinney, 1975; S. Sue, Allen, & Conaway, 1975) found that Asian Americans, Blacks, Chicanos, and Native Americans terminated counseling after only one contact at a rate of approximately 50%. This was in sharp contrast to a 30% rate for Anglo clients. These investigators believe that it is the inappropriateness of interpersonal interactions, what happens between counselor and client, which accounts for the premature termination. Padilla, Ruiz, & Alvarez (1975), while referring to a Latino population, identify three major factors that hinder the formation of a good counseling relationship: (a) a language barrier which often exists between the counselor and client, (b) class-bound values which indicate that counselors conduct treatment within the value system of the middle class, and (c) culture-bound values which are used to judge normality and abnormality in clients. All three of these variables seem to interact in such a way as to seriously hinder and distort communications.

First, this chapter focuses on how the values of counseling and psychotherapy may be antagonistic to the values of Third World clients. Second, how these values may distort communication and/or affect the counseling relationship between members of different backgrounds is explored. Third, implications for counseling are discussed. A conceptual scheme is presented that can be used to compare and contrast how language, culture, and class variables can be used to determine appropriate interventions. Such a comparative analysis is not only helpful in providing a means for examining the appropriateness of counseling approaches for Third World clients, but also for other special populations (women, the physically handicapped, and the elderly) as well. What we cannot forget is that the basic issue remains the classic one of individual differences and their significance for counselors. For that reason, this analysis is also helpful in comparing the appropriateness of counseling for different individuals within a single culture.

GENERIC CHARACTERISTICS OF COUNSELING

Within the Western framework, counseling and psychotherapy is a white middle-class activity that holds many values and characteristics different from those of Third World groups. Schofield (1964) has noted that therapists tend to prefer clients exhibiting the YAVIS syndrome: young, attractive, verbal, intelligent, and successful. This preference tends to discriminate against people from different minority groups or those from lower-socioeconomic classes. Likewise, D.W. Sue & S. Sue (1972a) have identified three major characteristics of counseling that may act as a source of conflict for Third World groups.

First, counselors often expect their counselee to exhibit some degree of openness, psychological mindedness, or sophistication. Most theories of counseling place a high premium on verbal, emotional, and behavioral expressiveness and the obtaining of insight. These are either the end goals of counseling or are the medium by which "cures" are effected. Second, counseling is traditionally a one-to-one activity that encourages clients to talk about or discuss the most intimate aspects of their lives. Individuals who fail or resist doing this may be seen as resistant, defensive, or superficial. Third, the counseling or therapy situation is often an ambiguous one. The client is encouraged to discuss problems, while the counselor listens and responds. Relatively speaking, the counseling situation is unstructured and forces the client to be the primary active participant. Patterns of communication are generally from client to counselor.

Four other factors identified as generally characteristic of counseling are (a) monolingual orientation, (b) emphasis on long-range goals, (c) distinction between physical and mental well-being, and (d) emphasis on cause-effect relationships. With respect to the former, the use of "good" standard English is predominantly the vehicle by which communication occurs. To individuals who may not speak or use English well, the lack of bilingual counselors is a serious handicap to accurate communication. Furthermore, since counseling is generally isolated from the client's environment and contacts are brief (50 minutes, once a week), it is by nature aimed at seeking long-range goals and solutions.

Another important and often overlooked factor in counseling is the implicit assumption that a clear distinction can be made between mental and physical illness or health. Contrary to this Western view, many cultures may not make a clear distinction between the two. Such a separation may be confusing to Third World clients and cause problems in counseling.

Recent work by Ornstein (1972) in which he identifies the dual hemispheric functioning of the brain also has intriguing implications for counseling. While the left hemisphere of the brain is involved with linear, rational, and cognitive processes, the right half tends to be intuitive, feeling, and experientially oriented. When both hemispheres are operating in a mutually interdependent fashion, they facilitate our functioning as human beings. Ornstein points out that the linear/logical/analytic/verbal mode of the left brain dominates Western thinking. The functioning of the right brain that is intuitive/holistic/creative/nonverbal has been neglected in Western culture and seen as a less legitimate mode of expression.

An analysis of the various American schools of counseling leads to

the inevitable conclusion that Western counseling is left brain oriented.
Such an approach or world view may definitely clash with Eastern and
American Indian philosophy. Thus a left brain orientation means a
linear emphasis on cause-effect approaches and a linear concept of time.
We deal with these concepts in greater detail in the next chapter.

In summary, the generic characteristics of counseling can be seen to
fall into three major categories: (a) language variables—use of standard English and emphasis on verbal communication; (b) class-bound
values—strict adherence to time schedules (50 minutes, once or twice a
week meeting), ambiguous or unstructured approach to problems, and
the seeking of long-range goals or solutions; (c) culture-bound values—
individual centered, verbal/emotional/behavioral expressiveness, communication pattern from client to counselor, openness and intimacy,
analytic/linear/verbal (cause-effect) approach, and clear distinctions
between mental and physical well-being. Tables 2.1 and 2.2 summarize
these generic characteristics and compare their compatibility to those of
four Third World groups.

SOURCES OF CONFLICT AND MISINTERPRETATIONS IN COUNSELING

While an attempt has been made to clearly delineate three major
variables that influence effective counseling, these variables are often

Table 2.1   Generic Characteristics of Counseling

Language	Middle Class	Culture
Standard English	Standard English	Standard English
Verbal communication	Verbal communication	Verbal communication
	Adherence to time schedules (50-minute session)	Individual centered
	Long-range goals	Verbal/emotional/behavioral expressiveness
	Ambiguity	Client-counselor communication
		Openness and intimacy
		Cause-effect orientation
		Clear distinction between physical and mental well-being

Table 2.2   Third World Group Variables

Language	Lower Class	Culture
	Asian Americans	
Bilingual background	Nonstandard English Action oriented Different time perspective Immediate, short-range goals Concrete, tangible, structured approach	Asian language Family centered Restraint of feelings One-way communication from authority figure to person. Silence is respect. Advice seeking Well-defined patterns of interaction (concrete structured) Private versus public display (shame/disgrace/pride) Physical and mental well-being defined differently.
	Blacks	
Black language	Nonstandard English Action oriented Different time perspective Immediate, short-range goals Concrete, tangible, structured approach	Black language Sense of "peoplehood" Action oriented Paranorm due to oppression Importance placed on nonverbal behavior
	Hispanics	
Bilingual background	Nonstandard English Action oriented Different time perspective Immediate short-range goals Concrete, tangible, structured approach	Spanish speaking Group-centered cooperation Temporal difference Family orientation Different pattern of communication A religious distinction between mind/body
	American Indians	
Bilingual background	Nonstandard English Action oriented Different time perspective Immediate, short-range goals Concrete, tangible, structured approach	Tribal dialects Cooperative not competitive individualism Present-time orientation Creative/experiential/intuitive/ nonverbal Satisfy present needs Use of Folk or supernatural explanations

inseparable from one another. For example, use of standard English in counseling definitely places those individuals who are unable to use it fluently at a disadvantage. However, cultural and class values that govern conversation conventions can also operate via language to cause serious misunderstandings. Furthermore, the fact that many Blacks, Chicanos, and American Indians come from a predominantly lower-class background often compounds class and culture variables. Thus it is often difficult to tell which are the sole impediments in counseling. Nevertheless, this distinction is valuable in conceptualizing barriers to effective cross-cultural counseling.

Language Barriers

Western society is definitely a monolingual one. Use of standard English to communicate with one another may unfairly discriminate against those from a bilingual or lower-class background. Not only is this seen in our educational system, but also in the counseling relationship as well. The bilingual background of many Asian Americans (D. W. Sue & Kirk, 1972, 1973; D. W. Sue & Frank, 1973), Chicanos (Padilla, Ruiz, & Alvarez, 1975), and American Indians (Attneave, 1972) may lead to much misunderstanding. This is true even if the Third World person cannot speak his/her own native tongue. Studies (M. Smith, 1957; M. Smith & Kasdon, 1961) indicate that simply coming from a background where one or both of the parents have spoken their native tongue can impair proper acquisition of English.

Even Blacks who come from a different subcultural environment may use words and phrases (Black Language) not entirely understandable to the counselor. E. Smith (1973) points out that Black clients are expected to communicate their feelings and thoughts to counselors in standardized English. For the ghetto student, this is a difficult task, since the use of nonstandard English is the norm. The lower-class language code involves a great deal of implicitness in communication—such as shorter sentences and less grammatical elaboration (but greater reliance on nonverbal cues). On the other hand, the language code of the middle and upper classes is much more elaborate with less reliance on nonverbal cues and entails greater knowledge of grammar and syntax.

In counseling, heavy reliance is placed on verbal interaction to build rapport. The presupposition is that participants in a counseling dialogue are capable of understanding each other. Vontress (1971) points out how counselors, oftentimes fail to understand Black client's language and its nuances for rapport building. Furthermore, those who have not been given the same educational or economic opportunities may lack the prerequisite verbal skills to benefit from "talk therapy" (Calia, 1968).

A minority client's brief, different, or "poor" verbal responses may lead many counselors to impute inaccurate characteristics or motives to him/her. A counselee may be seen as uncooperative, sullen, negative, nonverbal, or repressed on the basis of language expression alone. The problems in understanding and misinterpreting a Black client's verbal presentation of his/her problems in counseling can be seen in the following hypothetical example given by Wesson (1975):

(Brother enters office of white clinician. He is 19 years old, comes from a family of seven, the third oldest child. He is dressed in a longsleeved purple shirt with a ruffled front, sky blue knickers, black lace-up knee boots, a brown double-breasted suede jacket, a black Don Juan hat with a purple band and edging, with a small gold earring. And he is sharp!).

BROTHER: What it is, man!

(White clinician immediately jots down in notebook, "Speaks in 'word hash.' ")

WHITE CLINICIAN: What seems to be your problem, Joe?

BROTHER: Well, you see, I was in love with this stone fox, but I just couldn't get my shit together. My shit was raggedy.

(W.C. pictures in his mind's eye, a stone—that is concrete—fox, jots, "Fetishism and perversion. Also, has past history of diarrhea.")

WHITE CLINICIAN: Yes, go on, boy.

BROTHER: See, last Friday the eagle flew (and cut that boy shit out), so I took my hog down the boulevard 'cause I decided to get myself a new slave.

(W.C. jots down, "Claims to bird watch, and to have ridden a hog down the street in a metropolitan community en route to purchasing a slave.")

WHITE CLINICIAN: (Whispers softly) This boy is definitely experiencing delusions!

BROTHER: Anyway, I ran into my old lady and she laid a nickle on me—I bought this shirt I have on with it, come to think of it. Then me and my partner, Sweat, slid on over to his woman's place to pick up a bag of weed for a dime.

WHITE CLINICIAN: (Whispers) A nickle for a shirt? Sliding to someone's home? Buying weeds? (Louder) Yes, I see.

BROTHER: See, I'm a bad mother, and I like to hold down a corner every now and then.

(W.C. quickly jots down, "Inferiority complex, claims to be bad and unworthy. Low self-esteem, also claims to hold corners in—already—secure positions. Also shows improper sex identification, as he believes that he is a woman and, in addition, a mother.")

BROTHER: We just laid dead there 'til the hawk kept doing a job on us.

(W.C. jots down, "Hallucinates about being deceased. Persecutory complex centered around being repeatedly attacked by a hawk.")

While this particular example may be extended to the point of hilarity, it illustrates how sentence constructions and "in-group" vocabulary phrases may pose problems for the counselor. Since Western society places such a high premium on one's use of English, it is a short step to conclude that minorities are inferior, lack awareness or lack conceptual thinking powers. Such misinterpretations can also be seen in the use and interpretation of psychological tests. So-called IQ and achievement tests are especially notorious for their language bias.

Class-Bound Values

As mentioned previously, class values are important to consider in counseling because Third World people are disproportionately represented in the lower classes. Traditional guidance practices that emphasize assisting the client in self-direction through the presentation of the results of assessment instruments and self-exploration via verbal interactions between client and counselor are seen as meaningful and productive. However, the values underlying these activities are permeated by middle-class ones that do not suffice for those living in poverty. We have already seen how this operates with respect to language. Bernstein (1964) has investigated the suitability of English for the lower-class poor in psychotherapy and has concluded that it works to the detriment of those individuals.

For the counselor who generally comes from a middle- to upper-class background, it is often difficult to relate to the circumstances and hardships affecting the client who lives in poverty. Lewis (1966) vividly described the phenomenon of poverty and its effects on individuals and institutions. For the individual, his/her life is characterized by low wages; unemployment, underemployment, little property ownership, no savings, and lack of food reserves. Meeting even the most basic needs of hunger and shelter are in constant day-to-day jeopardy. Pawning personal possessions and borrowing money at exorbitant interest rates only leads to greater debt. Feelings of helplessness, dependence, and inferiority are easily fostered under these circumstances. Pollack and Menacker (1971) point out how many counselors may unwittingly attribute attitudes that result from physical and environmental adversity to the cultural or individual traits of the person.

For example, note the clinical description of a 12-year-old child written by a school counselor.

Jimmy Jones is a 12-year-old Black male student who was referred by Mrs. Peterson because of apathy, indifference and inattentiveness to classroom activities. . . . Other teachers have also reported that Jimmy "does not pay attention," "daydreams often" and "frequently falls asleep" during class. . . . There is a strong possibility that Jimmy is harboring repressed rage that needs to be ventilated and dealt with. His inability to directly express his anger had led him to adopt passive aggressive means of expressing hostility, i.e., inattentiveness, daydreaming, falling asleep. It is recommended that Jimmy be seen for intensive counseling to discover the basis of the anger.

It was not until after six months of counseling that the counselor finally realized the basis of Jimmy's problem. He came from a home life of extreme poverty, where hunger, lack of sleep, and overcrowding served to severely diminish his energy level and motivation. The fatigue, passivity, and fatalism evidenced by Jimmy were more a result of poverty than some innate trait.

Likewise, Menacker (1971) points out how poverty may bring many parents to encourage children to seek employment at an early age. Delivering groceries, shining shoes, and hustling other sources of income may sap the energy of the schoolchild, leading to truancy and poor performance. Teachers and counselors may view such students as unmotivated and potential "juvenile delinquents."

Research documentation concerning the inferior and biased quality of treatment to lower-class clients are legend (Yamamoto, James, & Palley, 1968; Lee & Tamerlin, 1968; Lerner, 1972; Lorion, 1973). In the area of diagnosis (Lee & Tamerlin, 1968), it has been found that the attribution of mental illness was more likely to occur when the person's history suggested a lower-class rather than higher-socioeconomic class origin. Haase (1956) was able to demonstrate that clinicians given identical Rorschach protocols made more negative prognostic statements and judgments of greater maladjustment when the individual was said to come from a lower- rather than middle-class background.

In the area of treatment, Garfield, Weiss, & Pollock (1973) gave counselors identical descriptions (except for social class) of a nine-year-old boy who engaged in maladaptive classroom behavior. When the boy was assigned upper-class status, more counselors expressed a willingness to become ego-involved with the student than when lower-class status was assigned. Likewise, Habemann & Thiry (1970) found that doctoral degree candidates in counseling and guidance more frequently programmed students from low-socioeconomic backgrounds into a noncollege-bound track than a college-preparation one.

In an extensive review of services delivered to minorities and low-socioeconomic clients, Lorion (1973) found that psychiatrists refer to therapy persons who are most like themselves: white rather than non-white and those from upper Socioeconomic Status (SES). Lorion (1974) also points out that the expectations of lower-class clients are often different from those of psychotherapists. For example, lower-class clients who are concerned with "survival" or making it through on a day-to-day basis expect advice and suggestions from the counselor. Appointments made weeks in advance with short, weekly 50-minute contacts are not consistent with the need to seek immediate solutions. Additionally, many lower-class people, through multiple experiences with public agencies, operate under what is called "minority standard time" (Schindler-Rainman, 1967). This is the tendency of poor people to have a low regard for punctuality. Poor people have learned that endless waits are associated with medical clinics, police stations, and U.S. Department of Health, Education and Welfare (HEW) institutions. One usually waits hours for a 10 to 15-minute appointment. Arriving on time does little good and can be a waste of valuable time. Counselors, however, rarely understand this aspect of life and are prone to see this as a sign of indifference or hostility.

People from a lower SES may also view counseling orientations toward reflection of feelings, concern with insight, and attempts to discover underlying intrapsychic problems as inappropriate. Many lower-class clients expect to receive advice or some form of concrete tangible treatment. When the counselor attempts to explore personality dynamics or to take a historical approach to the problem, the client often becomes confused, alienated, and frustrated. Abad, Ramos, & Boyce (1974) use the case of Puerto Ricans to illustrate this point. They feel the passive psychiatric approach that requires the client to talk about problems introspectively and to take initiative and responsibility for decision making is not what is expected by the Puerto Rican client. Several writers (Bloom, Davis, Hess, 1965; Amos & Grambs, 1968; Schindler-Rainman, 1967; Menacker, 1971) have taken the position that poor people are best motivated by rewards which are immediate and concrete. A harsh environment in which the future is uncertain and where immediate needs must be met make long-range planning of little value. Many lower SES clients are unable to relate to the future orientation of counseling. To be able to sit and talk about things is perceived to be a luxury of the middle and upper classes.

Because of the lower-class client's environment and past inexperience with counseling, the expectations of the minority individual may be quite different or even negative. The client's unfamiliarity with the counseling role may hinder its success and cause the counselor to blame the failure on the client. Thus the minority client may be perceived as hostile and resistant. The result of this interaction may be a premature termination of counseling. Ryan & Gaier (1968) conclude that students from upper-socioeconomic backgrounds have significantly more exploratory interviews with their counselors. Winder & Hersko (1962) pointed out that middle-class patients tend to remain in treatment longer than lower-class patients. Furthermore, the now-classic study of Hollingshead & Redlich (1968) found that lower-class patients tend to have fewer ego-involving relationships and less intensive therapeutic relationships than members of higher-socioeconomic classes.

Culture-Bound Values

In simple terms, "culture" consists of all those things that people have learned to do, believe, value, and enjoy in their history. It is the ideals, beliefs, skills, tools, customs, and institutions into which each member of society is born. While D. W. Sue & S. Sue (1972b) have stressed the need for social scientists to focus on the positive aspects of being bicultural, such dual membership may cause problems for many minorities. The term "marginal" person was coined by Stonequist (1937) and refers to a person's inability to form dual ethnic identification because of bicultural membership. Third World people are placed under strong pressures to adopt the ways of the dominant culture. Third World people's own enthnicity or cultural heritage is seen as a handicap to be overcome, something to be ashamed of and to be avoided. In essence, Third World people may be taught that to be different is to be deviant, pathological, or sick.

Many social scientists (Tedeschi & O'Donovan, 1971; Halleck, 1971) believe that psychology and therapy may be viewed as encompassing the use of social power and that therapy is a "handmaiden of the status quo." The counselor may be seen as an agent of society transmitting and functioning under Western values. An outspoken critic, Szasz (1970), believes the psychiatrists are like slave masters using therapy as a powerful political ploy against people whose ideas, beliefs, and behaviors differ from the dominant society. Several cultural characteristics of counseling may be responsible for these negative beliefs.

First, counselors who believe that having clients obtain insight into their personality dynamics and who value verbal, emotional, and behavioral expressiveness as goals in counseling are transmitting their own cultural values. This generic characteristic of counseling is not only antagonistic to lower-class values, but also to different cultural ones. For example, statements by some mental health professionals that Asian Americans are the most repressed of all clients indicate that they expect their counselees to exhibit openness, psychological mindedness, and assertiveness. Such a statement may indicate a failure on the part of the counselors to understand the background and cultural upbringing of many Asian American clients. Traditional Chinese and Japanese culture may value restraint of strong feelings and subtleness in approaching problems. Intimate revelations of personal or social problems may not be acceptable, since such difficulties reflect not only on the individual, but also the whole family. Thus the family may exert strong pressures on the Asian American client not to reveal personal matters to "strangers" or "outsiders." Similar conflicts have been reported for Chicanos (Cross & Maldonado, 1971) and American Indian clients (Trimble, 1976). A counselor who works with a client from a minority background may erroneously conclude that the person is repressed, inhibited, shy, or passive. Note that all these terms are seen as undesirable by Western standards.

Related to this example is the belief in the desirability of self-disclosure by many mental health practitioners. "Self-disclosure" refers to the client's willingness to tell the counselor what he/she feels, believes, or thinks. Journard (1964) suggests that mental health is related to one's openness in disclosing. While this may be true, the parameters need clarification. In Chapter 1, the example of Grier & Cobbs' (1968) paranorm was given. Vontress (1976) feels that people of African descent are especially reluctant to disclose to Caucasian counselors because of the hardships they have experienced via racism. Few Blacks initially perceive a white counselor as a person of goodwill but rather as an agent of society who may use the information against them. From the Black perspective, uncritical self-disclosure to others is not healthy. We say more about this topic in Chapter 3.

The actual structure of the counseling situation may also work against intimate revelations of a culturally different person's thoughts and feelings. Among many American Indians and Chicanos, intimate aspects of life are only shared with one's close friends. Relative to white middle-class standards, deep friendships are developed only after prolonged contacts. Once friendships are formed, they tend to be lifelong in nature. In contrast, white Americans form relationships quickly, but the relationships do not necessarily persist over long periods of time. Counseling seems to also reflect these values. Clients talk about the most intimate aspects of their lives with a relative stranger once a week for a 50-minute session. To many of the culturally different who stress friendship as a precondition to self-disclosure, the counseling process seems utterly inappropriate and absurd. After all, how is it possible to develop a friendship with brief contacts once a week?

Second, the ambiguous and unstructured aspect of the counseling situation may create discomfort in Third World clients. The culturally different may not be familiar with counseling and may perceive it as an unknown and mystifying process. Some groups, like Chicanos, may have been reared in an environment that actively structures social relationships and patterns of interaction. Anxiety and confusion may be the outcome in an unstructured counseling setting. The following example of a Chicana undergoing vocational counseling illustrates this confusion:

> Maria W. was quite uncomfortable and anxious during the first interview dealing with vocational counseling. This anxiety seemed more related to ambiguity of the situation than anything else. She appeared confused about the direction of the counselor's comments and questions. At this point, the counselor felt that an explanation of vocational counseling would facilitate the process.

COUNSELOR: Let me take some time to explain what we do in vocational counseling. Vocational counseling is an attempt to understand the whole person. Therefore, we are interested in your likes and dislikes, what you do well in, your skills, and what they mean with respect to jobs and vocations. The first interview is usually an attempt to get to know you . . . especially your past experiences and reactions to different courses you've taken, jobs you've worked at, and so forth. Especially important are your goals and plans. If testing seems indicated, as in your case, you'll be asked to complete some tests. After testing we'll sit down and talk about what they mean. When we arrive at possible vocations, we'll use the vocational library and find out what these jobs require in terms of background, training, etc.

CLIENT: Oh! I see . . .

COUNSELOR: That's why we've been talking about your high school experiences . . . sometimes the hopes and dreams can tell us much about your interests.

After this explanation, Maria participated much more in the interviews.

Third, the cultural upbringing of many minorities dictates different patterns of communication that may place them at a disadvantage in counseling. Counseling initially demands that communication move from client to counselor. The client is expected to take the major responsibility for initiating conversation in the session, while the counselor plays a less active role. Asian Americans, Chicanos, and American Indians, however, function under different cultural imperatives that may make this difficult. These three groups may have been reared to respect elders and authority figures and "not to speak until spoken to." Clearly defined roles of dominance and deference are established in the traditional family. Furthermore, in the case of Asians, there is evidence to indicate that mental health is associated with exercising will power, avoiding unpleasant thoughts, and occupying one's mind with positive thoughts. Counseling is seen as an authoritative process in which a good counselor is more direct and active while portraying a father figure (Arkoff, Thaver, & Elkind, 1966). A minority client who may be asked to initiate conversation may become uncomfortable and respond with only short phrases or statements. The counselor may be prone to interpret the behavior negatively, when in actuality it may be a sign of respect.

Fourth, many Latinos, American Indians, Asian Americans, and Blacks also hold a different concept of what constitutes mental health, mental illness, and adjustment. Among the Chinese, the concept of mental health or psychological well-being is not clearly understood. Padilla, Ruiz, & Alvarez (1975) argue that the Spanish-speaking surnamed do not make the same Western distinction between mental and physical health. Thus nonphysical problems are most likely to be referred to a physician, priest, or minister. Third World persons operating under this orientation may enter counseling expecting to be treated by counselors in the manner they expect doctors or priests to behave. Immediate solutions and concrete tangible forms of treatment (advice, confession, consolation, and medication) are expected.

Last, theories of counseling tend to emphasize left brain functioning. That is, they are distinctly analytical, rational, verbal, and strongly stress discovering cause-effect relationships. This emphasis on Aristotelian logic is in marked contrast to the philosophy of many cultures. For example, American Indian world views emphasize the harmonious aspects of the world, intuitive functioning, and a wholistic approach—a world view characterized by right brain activity (Ornstein, 1972) and devoid of analytical/reductionistic inquiries. Thus when Native Americans undergo counseling, the analytic approach may violate their basic philosophy of life.

NONVERBAL COMMUNICATION

Although language, class, and culture factors all interact to create problems in communication between the minority client and counselor, another often-neglected area is nonverbal behavior and conversation conventions. What people say and do are usually qualified by other things they say and do. A gesture, tone, inflection, posture, or eye contact may enhance or negate a message. Reared in a white middle-class society, counselors may assume that certain behaviors or rules of speaking are universal and have the same meaning. Personal space, eye contact, and conventions regarding interaction are prime examples of possible barriers to counseling.

Personal Space

The study of "proxemics" refers to perception and use of personal and interpersonal space. Hall (1966) has identified four interpersonal distance zones characteristic of Anglo culture: intimate, from contact to 18 inches; personal, from 1½ feet to 4 feet; social, from 4 to 12 feet; and public (lectures and speeches), greater than 12 feet. However, different cultures dictate different distances in personal space. For Latin Americans, Africans, Black Americans, and Indonesians, conversing with a person dictates a much closer stance than normally comfortable for Anglos. A Latin American client may cause the counselor to back away. The client may interpret the counselor's behavior as indicative of aloofness, coldness, or a desire not to communicate. On the other hand, the counselor may misinterpret the client's behavior as an attempt to become inappropriately intimate or of being pushy. Thus how furniture in an office is arranged, where the seats are located, and where you seat the client may have meanings and implications that enhance or retard the client-counselor relationship (Boucher, 1972; Graves & Robinson, 1976; Hackney, 1974; Mehrabian, 1968, 1969; Mehrabian & Diamond, 1971). Eskimos, for example, when talking about intimate aspects of their life, may sit side by side rather than across from one another.

Eye Contact

Another important aspect of nonverbal communication is the meaning ascribed to eye contact (gazeholding and directness of stare). Knapp (1972) and Kendon (1967) found that Anglo Americans rely heavily on eye contact as indicating whether a person is listening or tuned out. In Black culture, it is often assumed that being in the same room or in close proximity to another person is enough to indicate attentiveness. Going through the motions of looking at the person and nodding your head is not necessary (Hall, 1954). White middle-class people when speaking to others, look away (eye avoidance) approximately 50% of the time. However, when whites listen, they make eye contact with the speaker over 80% of the time. This is in marked contrast to Black Americans who when speaking make greater eye contact and when listening make infrequent eye contact. The fact that Blacks also have a shorter conversing distance and greater body activity when speaking may have lead many teachers, counselors, and mental health professionals to make unconscious interpretations. For example, counselors who work with Blacks often feel that their clients are hostile and angry. While such a conclusion may be correct, in some cases it is also possible that (*a*) the intense "stare" of Blacks, (*b*) the shorter personal space, and (*c*) greater body activity when speaking may be misread by the counselor. Likewise, when Blacks do not make eye contact with a speaker (teacher or counselor) an interpretation that the person is disinterested or inattentive may be made. The power of nonverbal cues is that they occur outside our awareness and we cannot consciously check what it is which gives us that "feeling."

Different cultures have different meanings for the directness of a gaze. Traditional Navajos use much more peripheral vision and avoid eye contact if possible. Knapp (1972) states that some Navajos believe that direct stares are considered hostile and this technique is used to chastise children. Among Mexican Americans and the Japanese, avoidance of eye contact may be a sign of respect or deference. For the counselor to unknowingly ascribe motives such as inattentiveness, rudeness, aggressiveness, shyness, or low intelligence is extremely hazardous. This warning is emphasized because mental health professionals often use eye contact as a diagnostic sign.

Conversation Conventions

Applegate (1975) believes that the rules of speaking, those that govern how we greet, address, and take turns in speaking, differ from culture to culture. In Anglo society, handshaking in many cases is optional in greeting and not obligatory. Jaramillo (1973) observes that Latin Americans never greet one another without some form of body contact. Padilla, Ruiz, & Alvarez (1955) also find this to be true for American Latinos and recommend some form of body contact in greeting Chicano clients. Likewise, physical expressions of greeting also vary across cultures (kissing, bowing, handshaking, etc.).

There are also complex rules regarding when to speak or yield to another person. Dubin (1973) points out how Americans frequently feel uncomfortable with a pause or silent stretch in the conversation, feeling obligated to fill it in with more talk. While silence may be viewed negatively by many Americans, other cultures interpret and use silence much differently. The English and Arabs use silence for privacy (Hall, 1966), while the Russians, French, and Spanish read it as agreement among the parties. In Asian culture (D.W. Sue & D. Sue, 1973), silence is traditionally a sign of respect for elders. Furthermore, silence by many Chinese and Japanese is not a floor-yielding signal inviting others to pick up the conversation. Rather it may indicate a desire to continue speaking after making a particular point. Oftentimes, silence is a sign of politeness and respect rather than a lack of a desire to continue speaking. A counselor uncomfortable with silence may fill in and prevent the client from elaborating further. Even greater danger is to impute false motives to the client's apparent reticence.

Volume of speed and directness in conversation is also influenced by cultural values. The overall loudness of speech displayed by many American visitors to foreign countries have earned them the reputation as being boisterous and shameless. Likewise, lower volume on the part of clients may be interpreted by the counselor as weakness or shyness. Additionally, indirectness in speech is a prized art in many cultures. The American emphasis on "getting to the point" and "not beating around the bush" may alienate others. Asian Americans may see this behavior as immature, rude, and lacking in finesse. On the other hand, counselees from different cultures may be negatively labeled as evasive and afraid to confront the problem.

GENERALIZATIONS AND STEREOTYPES: SOME CAUTIONS

As can be seen in Table 2.1, the generic characteristics of counseling tend to fall into three major categories. These characteristics are summarized and can be compared with the values of Four Third World groups: Asian Americans, Blacks, Latinos, and American Indians (see

Table 2.2). Although it is critical for counselors to have a basic understanding of counseling characteristics and Third World life values, there is the ever-present danger of overgeneralizing and stereotyping. For example, the listing of Third World group variables does not indicate that all persons coming from a minority group will share all or even some of these traits. Furthermore, emerging trends such as short-term and crisis counseling approaches and other less verbally oriented techniques differ from the generic traits listed. Yet it is highly improbable that any of us can enter a situation or encounter people without forming impressions consistent with our own experiences and values. The fact that a client is dressed neatly in a suit or wears blue jeans, a man or a woman, or of a different race will likely affect our assumptions about him/her. First impressions will be formed that fit our own interpretations and generalizations of human behavior. Generalizations are necessary for us to use. Without them we would become inefficient creatures. They are guidelines for our behaviors that are tentatively applied in a new situation but open to change and challenge.

It is exactly at this stage that generalizations remain generalizations or become stereotypes. *Stereotypes* may be defined as rigid preconceptions we hold about *all* people who are members of a particular group whether it be defined along racial, religious, sexual, or other lines. The belief in a perceived characteristic of the group is applied to all members without regard for individual variations. The danger of stereotypes is that they are impervious to logic or experience. All incoming information is distorted to fit our preconceived notions. For example, people who are strongly anti-Semitic will accuse Jews of being stingy and miserly and then, in the same breath, accuse them of flaunting their wealth by conspicuous spending.

In using tables 2.1 and 2.2 the information should act as guidelines rather than absolutes. These generalizations should serve as the background from which the "figure" emerges. For example, belonging to a particular group may mean sharing common values and experiences. Individuals within a group, however, also differ. The background offers a contrast for us to see more clearly individual differences. It should not submerge but increase the visibility of the figure. This is the figure-ground relationship that should aid us to recognize the uniqueness of people more readily.

REFERENCES

Abad, V., Ramos, J., & Boyce, E. A model for delivery of mental health services to Spanish-speaking minorities. *American Journal of Orthopsychiatry,* 1974, **44,** 584–595.

Amos, W. E., & Grambs, J. D. (Eds.) *Counseling the Disadvantaged Youth.* Englewood Cliffs, N.J.: Prentice-Hall, 1968.

Applegate, R. B. The language teacher and the rules of speaking. *TESOL Quarterly,* 1975, **9,** 271–281.

Arkoff, A., Thaver, F., & Elkind, L. Mental Health and counseling ideas of Asian and American students. *Journal of Counseling Psychology,* 1966, **13,** 219–228.

Attneave, C. Mental health of American Indians: Problems, perspectives and challenge for the decade ahead. Paper presented at the meeting of the American Psychological Association, Honolulu, August 1972.

Bernstein, B. Social class, speech, systems and psychotherapy. In R. Riessman, J. J. Cohen, & A. Pearl (Eds.), *Mental Health of the Poor.* New York: Free Press of Glencoe, 1964.

Bloom, B., Davis, A., & Hess, R. *Compensatory Education for Cultural Deprivation.* New York: Holt, Rinehart & Winston, 1965.

Boucher, M. L. Effect of seating distance on interpersonal attraction in an interview situation. *Journal of Consulting and Clinical Psychology,* 1972, **38,** 15–19.

Calia, V. F. The culturally deprived client: A reformulation of the counselor's role. In J. C. Bentley (Ed.), *The Counselor's Role: Commentary and Readings.* Boston: Houghton Mifflin, 1968.

Carkhuff, R. R., & Pierce, R. Differential effects of therapist race and social class upon patient depth of self-exploration in the initial clinical interview. *Journal of Consulting Psychology,* 1965, **31,** 632–634.

Cobb, C. W. Community mental health services and the lower socioeconomic class: A summary of research literature on outpatient treatment (1963–1969). *American Journal of Orthopsychiatry,* 1972, **42,** 404–414.

Cross, W. C., & Maldonado, B. The counselor, the Mexican-American, and the stereotype. *Elementary School Guidance and Counseling,* 1971, **6,** 25–31.

Dubin, F. *The problem, Who speaks next? considered cross-culturally.* Paper presented at the meeting of (TESOL) Teachers of English to Speakers of Other Languages, San Juan, Puerto Rico, May 1973

ERIC Document Reproduction Service No. Ed. 082–569;.

Garfield, J. C., Weiss, S. L., & Pollock, E. A. Effects of a child's social class on school counselors' decision making, *Journal of Counseling Psychology,* 1973 **20,** 166–168.

Graves, J. R., & Robinson, J. D. Proxemic behavior as a function of inconsistent verbal and nonverbal messages. *Journal of Counseling Psychology,* 1976, **23,** 333–338.

Grier, W., & Cobbs, P. *Black Rage.* New York: Basic Books, 1968.

Haase, W. *Rorchach diagnosis, socioeconomic class and examiner bias.* Unpublished doctoral dissertation, New York University, 1956.

Habemann, L., & Thiry, S. *The effect of socio-economic status variables on counselor perception and behavior.* Unpublished master's thesis, University of Wisconsin, 1970.

Hackney, H. Facial gestures and subject expression of feelings. *Journal of Counseling Psychology,* 1974, **21,** 173–178.

Hall, E. T. *Handbook for Proxemic Research*. Washington, D.C.: Society for the Ontology of Visual Communications, 1974.

Hall, E. T. *The Hidden Dimension*. Garden City, N.Y.: Doubleday, 1966.

Halleck, S. J. Therapy is the handmaiden of the status quo. *Psychology Today*, April 1971, 30–34; 98–100.

Hollingshead, A. R., & Redlich, F. C. *Social Class and Mental Health*. New York: Wiley, 1968

Jaramillo, J. L. Cultural differences in the TESOL classroom. *TESOL Quarterly*, 1973, 7, 51–60.

Journard, S. M. *The Transparent Self*. Princeton, N.J.: D. Van Nostrand, 1964.

Kendon, A. Some functions of gaze-direction in social interaction. *Aeta Psychologica*, 1965, **26**, 22–63.

Knapp, M. I. *Nonverbal communication in human interaction*. New York: Holt, Rinehart & Winston, 1972.

Lee, S., & Tamerlin, M. K. *Social class status and mental illness*. Unpublished doctoral dissertation, University of Oklahoma, 1968.

Lerner, B. *Therapy in the Ghetto*. Baltimore: Johns Hopkins University Press, 1972.

Lewis, O. *La Vida: A Puerto Rican Family in the Context of Poverty—San Juan and New York*. New York: Random House, 1966.

Lorion, R. P. Patient and therapist variables in the treatment of low-income patients. *Psychological Bulletin*, 1974, **81**, 344–364.

Lorion, R. P. Socioeconomic status and treatment approaches reconsidered. *Psychological Bulletin*, 1973, **79**, 263–250.

Mehrabian, A. Relationship of attitude to seated posture, orientation, and distance. *Journal of Personality and Social Psychology*, 1968, **10**, 26–30.

Mehrabian, A. Significance of posture and position in the communication of attitude and status relationships. *Psychological Bulletin, 1969*, **71**, 359–352.

Mehrabian, A., & Diamond, S. G. Effects of furniture arrangement, props, and personality on social interaction. *Journal of Personality and Social Psychology*, 1971, **20**, 18–30.

Menacker, J. *Urban Poor Students and Guidance*. Boston: Houghton Mifflin, 1971.

Ornstein, R. E. *The Psychology of consciousness*. San Francisco: Freeman, 1972.

Padilla, A. M., Ruiz, R. A., & Alvarez, R. Community mental health services for the Spanish-speaking/surnamed population. *American Psychologist*, 1975, **30**, 892–905.

Pollock, E., & Menacker, J. *Spanish-speaking students and guidance*. Boston: Houghton Mifflin, 1971.

Ruiz, R. A., & Padilla, A. M. Counseling Latinos. *Personnel and Guidance Journal*, **55**, 1977.

Ryan, D. W., & Gaier, E. L. Student socioeconomic status and counselor contact in junior high school. *Personnel and Guidance Journal, 1968*, **46**, 466–452.

Schindler-Rainman, E. The poor and the PTA. *PTA Magazine*, 1965, **61**(8), 4–5.

Schofield, W. *Psychotherapy: The Purchase of Friendship*. Englewood Cliffs, N.J.: Prentice-Hall, 1964.

Smith, E. J. *Counseling the Culturally Different Black Youth*. Columbus, O.: Charles E. Merrill, 1973.

Smith, M. E. Progress in the use of English after twenty-two years by children of Chinese ancestry in Honolulu. *Journal of Genetic Psychology,* 1957, **90**, 255–258.

Smith, M. E., & Kasdon, L. M. Progress in the use of English after twenty-two years by children of Filipino and Japanese ancestry in Hawaii. *Journal of Genetic Psychology,* 1961, **99**, 129–138.

Stonequist, E. V. *The Marginal Man: A Study in Personality and Culture Conflict.* New York: Russell & Russell, 1937.

Sue, D. W. Asian Americans: Social-psychological forces affecting their life styles. In S. Picou & R. Campbell (Eds.), *Career Behavior of Special Groups.* Columbus, O.: Charles E. Merrill, 1975.

Sue, D. W., & Frank, A. C. A typological approach to the study of Chinese and Japanese American college males. *Journal of Social Issues,* 1973, **29**, 129–148.

Sue, D. W., & Kirk, B. A. Psychological Characteristics of Chinese-American college students. *Journal of Counseling Psychology,* 1972, **19**, 451–458.

Sue, D. W., & Kirk, B. A. Differential charcteristics of Japanese-American and Chinese-American college students. *Journal of Counseling Psychology,* 1953, **20**, 142–148.

Sue, D. W., & Sue, D. Understanding Asian-Americans: The neglected minority. *Personnel and Guidance Journal,* 1973, **51**, 386–389.

Sue, D. W., & Sue, S. Counseling Chinese-Americans. *Personnel and Guidance Journal,* 1972a, **50**, 635–644.

Sue, D. W., & Sue, S. Ethnic minorities: Resistance to being researched. *Professional Psychology,* 1972b, **2**, 11–15.

Sue, S., Allen, D., & Conaway, L. The responsiveness and equality of mental health care to Chicanos and Native Americans. *American Journal of Community Psychology,* 1975.

Sue, S., & McKinney, H. Asian Americans in the community mental health care system. *American Journal of Orthopsychiatry,* 1974, **45**, 111–118.

Sue, S., McKinney, H., Allen, D., & Hall, J. Delivery of community mental health services to black and white clients. *Journal of Consulting and Clinical Psychology,* 1974, **42**, 594–901.

Szasz, T. S. The crime of commitment. *Readings in Clinical Psychology Today.* Del Mar, Calif.: CRM Books, 1970.

Tedeschi, J. T., & O'Donovan, D. Social power and the psychologist. *Professional Psychology,* 1971, **2**, 59–64.

Trimble, J. E. Value differences among American Indians: Concerns for the concerned counselor. In P. Pedersen, W. J. Lonner, & J. G. Draguns (Eds.), *Counseling Across Cultures.* Honolulu: East-West Center, 1976.

Vontress, C. E. Racial and ethnic barriers in counseling. In P. Pedersen, W. J. Lonner, & J. G. Draguns (Eds.), *Counseling Across Cultures.* Honolulu: East-West Center, 1976.

Vontress, C. E. Racial differences: Impediments to rapport. *Journal of Counseling Psychology,* 1971, **18**, 7–13.

Wesson, K. A. The Black man's burden: The white clinician. *Black Scholar,* 1975, **6**, 13–18.

Winder, A. E., & Hersko, M. The effects of social class on the length and type of psychotherapy in a Veterans Administration mental hygiene clinic. *Journal of Clinical Psychology,* 1962, **11**, 75–79.

Yamamoto, J., James, Q. C., & Palley, N. Cultural problems in psychiatric therapy. *Archives of General Psychiatry,* 1968, **19**, 45–49.

3

Credibility and Racial/Cultural Similarity in Cross-Cultural Counseling

In the previous two chapters, we have discussed and analyzed some very important conditions/variables that contribute to effective and ineffective cross-cultural counseling. We have mentioned several times that the inability of a counselor to establish rapport and a relationship of trust with a culturally different client is a major counseling barrier. A basic assumption underlying counseling is that the relationship the counselor establishes with a client can either enhance or negate the process. When the emotional climate is negative, and when little trust or understanding exists between the counselor and client, counseling can be both ineffective and destructive. Yet if the emotional climate is realistically positive and if trust and understanding exist between the parties, the two-way communication of thoughts and feelings can proceed with optimism. This latter condition is often referred to as "rapport" and sets the stage in which other essential conditions can become effective. One of these, self disclosure, is particularly crucial to the process and goals of counseling because it is the most direct means by which an individual makes himself/herself known to another (Rogers, 1962; Jourard & Lasakow, 1971; Vontress, 1973; Williams, 1974). This chapter attempts to discuss the issue of trust as it relates to minority clients. Our discussion does not deal with cultural variables among certain groups (Asian Americans, Native Americans, etc.) that dictate against self-disclosure to strangers. This has already been presented in the last chapter. First, a brief discussion of the sociopolitical situation as it affects the trust-mistrust dimension of the culturally different is presented. Second, we look at factors that enhance or negate the cross-cultural counselor's effectiveness as it relates to the theory of social influence. Last, we systematically examine how counselor credibility and similarity affect a culturally different client's willingness to work with a counselor from another race/culture.

SOCIOPOLITICAL CONSIDERATIONS OF TRUST-MISTRUST

The history of race relations in the United States has influenced us to the point of being extremely cautious in revealing our feelings and attitudes about race to strangers. In an interracial encounter with a stranger, each party will attempt to discern gross or subtle racial attitudes of the other while minimizing vulnerability. For minorities in the United States, this lesson has been learned well. While white Americans may also exhibit cautiousness similar to their minority counterparts, the structure of society places more power to injure and damage in the hands of the majority culture. In most situations, white Americans are less vulnerable than their minority counterparts.

As we have seen in the last two chapters, and as you shall shortly be introduced to the individual chapters on American Indians, Asian Americans, Blacks, and Hispanics, the history and experiences of the culturally different have been those of oppression, discrimination, and racism. Institutional racism has created psychological barriers among minorities that are likely to interfere with the counseling process. Ladner (1971) had aptly defined the crucial components of institutional racism. Institutional racism is a set of policies, priorities, and accepted normative patterns designed to subjugate, oppress, and force dependence of individuals and groups to the larger society. It does this by sanctioning unequal goals, unequal status, and unequal access to goods and services. Institutional racism has fostered the enactment of discriminatory statutes, the selective enforcement of laws, the blocking of economic opportunities and outcomes, and the imposition of forced assimilation/acculturation toward the culturally different. The sociopolitical system thus attempts to define the prescribed role occupied by minorities. Feelings of powerlessness, inferiority, subordination, deprivation, anger and rage, and overt/covert resistance to factors in interracial relationships are likely to result.

Several writers (Harrison, 1975; Thomas, 1969; Willie, Kramer & Brown, 1973) have pointed out how Blacks in responding to their slave heritage, history of discrimination, and America's reaction to their skin color have adopted behavior patterns toward whites important for survival in a racist society. These behavior patterns may include indirect expressions of hostility, aggression, distrust, and fear. During slavery, Black mothers in order to rear children who would fit into a segregated system and who could physically survive were forced to teach them (*a*) to express aggression indirectly, (*b*) to read the thoughts of others while hiding their own, and (*c*) to engage in ritualized accommodating-subordinating behaviors designed to create as few waves as possible (Willie, Kramer & Brown, 1973). This process involves a "mild dissociation," where Blacks may separate their true selves from their role as "Negros" (Pinderhughes, 1973). A dual identity is often used, where the true self is revealed to fellow Blacks, while the dissociated self is revealed to meet the expectations of prejudiced whites. From the analysis of Black history, the dissociative process may be manifested in two major ways.

First, "playing it cool" has been identified as one means by which Blacks or other minorities may conceal their true feelings (Grier & Cobbs, 1971; Vontress, 1970; Wolkon Moriwaki, & Williams). The intent of this manner of behavior is to prevent whites from knowing what the minority person is thinking/feeling and to express feelings/behaviors in such a way as to prevent offending or threatening whites. Thus a culturally different individual who may be experiencing conflict, explosive anger, and suppressed feelings will appear serene and composed on the surface. It is a defense mechanism aimed at protecting minorities from harm and exploitation.

Second, the "Uncle Tom syndrome" may be used by minorities to appear docile, nonassertive, and happy-go-lucky. Among Blacks, some have learned, especially during slavery, that passivity is a necessary survival technique. To retain the most menial jobs, to minimize retaliation, and to maximize survival of the self and loved ones, many minorities have learned to deny their aggressive feelings toward their oppressors.

In summary, it becomes all too clear that past and continuing discrimination against the culturally different is a tangible basis for minority distrust of the majority society (Mitchell, 1970; Grier & Cobbs, 1968). White people are perceived as potential enemies unless proved otherwise, and the social system is against them unless the culturally different personally experiences otherwise. Under such a sociopolitical atmosphere, minorities may use several adaptive devices to prevent whites from knowing their true feelings. As cross-cultural counseling may mirror the sentiments of the larger society, these modes of behavior and their detrimental effects may be reenacted in the sessions.

The fact that many minority clients are suspicious, mistrustful, and guarded in their interactions with white counselors is certainly understandable in light of the foregoing analysis. In spite of their conscious desires to help, white counselors are not immune to inheriting racist attitudes, beliefs, myths, and stereotypes about Asian American, Black, Chicano, Native American, and Puerto Rican clients. For example, white counselors often believe that Blacks are nonverbal, paranoid, and angry and most likely have character disorders (Willie, Kramer & Brown, 1973). As a result, they view Blacks as unsuitable for counseling and psychotherapy. Counselors and social scientists who hold to this belief fail to understand the facts listed next.

1. As a group, Black Americans tend to communicate and feel that nonverbal communication is a more accurate barometer of one's true feelings and beliefs (Hall, 1976; Willie, Kramer, & Brown, 1973). Blacks have learned that intellectual interactions are less trustworthy than the nonverbal messages sent by participants. Hall (1976) observes that Blacks are better able to read nonverbal messages than their white counterparts and rely less on intellectual verbalizations than nonverbal communication to make a point. Whites, on the other hand, tune in more to verbal than nonverbal messages. Because of their less reliance on nonverbal cues, greater verbal elaborations are needed to get a point across. Being ignorant and insensitive to these differences, white counselors are prone to feel that Blacks are unable to communicate in "complex" ways. This judgment is based on the high value counseling places on intellectual/verbal activity.

2. Rightfully or not, white counselors are often perceived as symbols of the Establishment, and the minority client is likely to impute all the negative experiences of oppression to the counselor (Vontress, 1971; Russell, 1970). This may prevent the minority client from responding to the counselor as an individual. While the counselor may be possessed of the most admirable motives, the client may reject the counselor simply because he/she is white (Vontress, 1971). Thus communication may be directly or indirectly shut off.

3. Some minorities may lack confidence in the counseling process because the white counselor often proposes white solutions to their concerns (A. Thomas & Sillens, 1969). Much pressures are placed in trying to have the culturally different client accept an alien value system and reject his/her own.

4. The "playing it cool" and "Uncle Tom" responses of many minor-

ities are also present in the counseling session. As pointed out earlier, these mechanisms are attempts to conceal true feelings, to effectively prevent the client from self-disclosure, and to prevent the counselor from getting to know the client.

To summarize, the culturally different client entering cross-cultural counseling is likely to experience considerable anxiety about ethnic/racial/cultural differences. Suspicion, apprehension, verbal constriction, unnatural reactions, open resentment and hostility, and "passive" or "cool" behaviors may all be expressed. Self-disclosure and the possible establishment of a working relationship can be seriously delayed and/or prevented from occurring. In all cases, the counselor may be put to severe tests about his/her trustworthiness. A culturally effective counselor is one who is able to adequately resolve challenges to his/her credibility. We now turn our attention to an analysis of those dimensions that may enhance or diminish the minority client's receptivity to self-disclosure.

CREDIBILITY AND ATTRACTIVENESS IN CROSS-CULTURAL COUNSELING

In the last section, we presented a case to explain how the political atmosphere of the larger society affects the minority client's perception of a cross-cultural counseling situation. Minorities in the United States have solid reasons for not trusting white Americans. Lack of trust often leads to guardedness, inability to establish rapport, and lack of self-disclosure on the part of culturally different clients. What a counselor says and does in the sessions can either enhance or diminish his/her credibility and attractiveness. A counselor who is perceived by clients as highly credible and attractive is more likely to elicit (*a*) trust, (*b*) motivation to work/change, and (*c*) self-disclosure. These appear to be important conditions for effective counseling to occur.

Theories of counseling and psychotherapy attempt to outline an approach designed to make them effective. It is my contention that cross-cultural helping cannot be approached through any one theory of counseling. There are several reasons for such a statement. First, theories of counseling are composed of philosophical assumptions regarding the nature of "man" and a theory of personality (London, 1964; Corsini, 1979; Patterson, 1973). These characteristics, as pointed out earlier, are highly culture bound. What is the "true" nature of people is a philosophical question. What constitutes the healthy and unhealthy personality is also debatable and varies from culture to culture and class to class.

Second, theories of counseling are also composed of a body of therapeutic techniques and strategies. These techniques are applied to clients with the hope of effecting change in either behaviors or attitudes. A counseling theory dictates what techniques are to be used and, implicitly, in what proportions. For example, it does not take much training to see that client-centered counselors behave differently from rational-emotive ones. Using Ivey & Authier's (1979) microcounseling paradigm, it is possible to characterize the former as using mostly attending skills (paraphrasing and reflecting of feelings), while the latter uses more influencing skills (expression of content, interpretation, giving advice, etc.). The fact that one school of counseling can be distinguished from another has implications: it suggests a certain degree of rigidity in working with culturally different clients who might find such techniques offensive or inappropriate. The implicit assumption is that these techniques are applicable to all populations, situations, and problems. The techniques are imposed according to the theory and not based on client needs and values.

Third, theories of counseling have, oftentimes, failed to agree among themselves about what constitutes desirable "outcomes" in counseling. This makes it extremely difficult to determine the effectiveness of counseling and therapy (Patterson, 1973). For example, the psychoanalytically oriented counselor uses "insight," the behaviorist uses "behavior change," the client-centered person uses "self-actualization," and the rational-emotive person uses "rational cognitive processes." The potential for disagreement over appropriate outcome variables is increased even further when the counselor and client come from different cultures. While the counseling outcome is extremely important, we attempt to concentrate our discussion on "process" elements. We are here more concerned with *how* change occurs (process) during counseling rather than *what* change (outcome) results from counseling.

COUNSELING AS INTERPERSONAL INFLUENCE

When people engage in interactions with one another, they inevitably attempt to exert influence. These social influence attempts may be overt/covert or conscious/unconscious. Whether the intent is to create a favorable impression when meeting people, toilet training a young child, convincing people that cigarette smoking is harmful, gaining acceptance from a desired group, or selling goods, these social influence attempts are all aimed at changing attitudes and/or behaviors.

Likewise, counseling may be conceptualized as an interpersonal influence process in which the counselor uses his/her social power to influence the client's attitudes and behaviors (Strong, 1968). In reviewing the literature in social psychology on opinion change, Strong (1968) found parallels between this field and the counseling process. Specifically, attributes of communicators that had been established as important determinants of attitude change seemed similar to those that make an effective counselor. Counselors who are perceived by their clients as credible (expert and trustworthy) and attractive are able to exert greater influence than those perceived as lacking in credibility and attractiveness. There is a sufficient number of counseling analogue studies that support this contention (Strong & Schmidt, 1970; Schmidt & Strong, 1971; Atkinson & Carskaddon, 1975; Barak & La Crosse, 1975; Spiegel, 1976; Merluzzi, Merluzzi, & Kaul, 1977). Using social influence theory as a means to analyze counseling not only has empirical validity and concentrates on process variables, but also seems to be equally applicable to all approaches. Regardless of the counseling orientation (client centered, psychoanalytic, behavioral, transactional analysis (TA), etc.), the counselor's effectiveness tends to depend on his/her perceived expertness, trustworthiness, and attractiveness (Barak & La Crosse, 1975; Barak & Dell, 1977).

Most of the studies mentioned have dealt exclusively with a white population. Thus findings that certain attributes contribute to a counselor's credibility and attractiveness may not be so perceived by culturally different clients. It is entirely possible that credibility as defined by credentials indicating specialized training may only mean to a Black client that the white counselor has no knowledge or expertise in working with Blacks. This assumption is based on the fact that most training programs are geared for white middle-class clients and are culturally exclusive.

Our focus in this section is twofold: (a) we outline the various ways clients perceive their counselor's attempts to influence them, and (b) we discuss the dimensions of counselor expertness, trustworthiness, and similarity as they relate to the culturally different client. Hopefully, we will be able to lay the foundations for a theory of cross-cultural counseling to be presented and discussed later.

Psychological Sets of Clients

Credibility and attractiveness of the counselor is very much dependent on the psychological set or frame of mind of the culturally different client. We all know individuals who tend to value rational approaches to solving problems and others who value a more affective (attractiveness) approach. It would seem reasonable that a client who values rationality might be more receptive to a counseling approach that emphasizes the counselor's credibility. Thus understanding a client's psychological set may facilitate the counselor's ability to exert social influence in counseling. Collins (1970) has proposed a set of conceptual categories that we can use to understand people's receptivity to pressures for conformity (change). We apply those categories here with respect to the counseling situation. These five hypothetical "sets" or "frames of mind" are elicited in clients for several different reasons. Race, ethnicity, and the experience of discrimination often affect the type of "set" that will be operative in a minority client.

1. **The Problem-Solving Set: Information Orientation:** In the problem-solving set, the client is concerned about obtaining correct information (solutions, outlooks, and skills) that has adaptive value in the real world. The client accepts or rejects information from the counselor on the basis of its perceived truth or falsity; is it an accurate representation of reality? The processes tend to be rational and logical in analyzing and attacking the problem: (*a*) The client may apply a consistency test and compare the new facts with information he./she already possesses. (*b*) The person may apply a corroboration test by actively seeking information from others for comparison purposes. The former test makes use of information the individual already has, while the latter requires him/her to seek out new information.

    Through socialization and personal experiences, we have learned that some people are more likely to provide accurate/ helpful information (credible) than others. Sources that have been dependable in the past, have high status, possess good reputations, occupy certain roles, and are motivated to make accurate representations are more likely to influence us. Minorities may have learned that many whites have little expertise when it comes to their life-styles and that the information/suggestions they give are white solutions/labels.

2. **The Consistency Set:** People are operating under the consistency set whenever they change an opinion, belief, or behavior in such a way as to make it consistent with other opinions, beliefs, and behaviors. This principle is best illustrated in Festinger's *A Theory of Cognitive Dissonance* (1957). Stated simply, the theory says that when a person's attitudes, opinions, or beliefs are met with disagreement

(inconsistencies), cognitive imbalance or dissonance will be created. The existence of dissonance is psychologically uncomfortable and produces tension with drive characteristics. The result is an attempt to reduce the dissonance. Collins (1970) asserts that the consistency set may really be a by-product of the problem-solving set. This is so because we assume that the real world is consistent. For example, since counselors are supposed to help, we naturally believe that they would not do things to hurt us. If they do, then it creates dissonance. To reduce this inconsistency, we may discredit or derogate the counselor (he/she is not a good person after all!) or in some way excuse the act (he/she did it unintentionally). The rules of the consistency set specify that "good people do good things" and "bad people do bad things." It is important to note that the consistency set states that people are not necessarily *rational* beings but *rationalizing* ones. A counselor who is not in touch with his/her prejudices/biases may send out conflicting messages to a minority client. The counselor may verbally state, "I am here to help you," but at the same time, nonverbally indicate racist attitudes/feelings. This can destroy the credibility of the counselor very quickly in the case of a minority client who accurately applies a consistency set: "White people say one thing but do another. You can't believe what they tell you."

3.   **The Identity Set:** In the identity set, the individual generally desires to be like or similar to a person or group he/she holds in high esteem. Much of our identity is formed from those reference groups to which we aspire. We attempt to take on the reference groups, characteristics, beliefs, values, and behaviors because they are viewed as favorable. An individual who strongly identifies with a particular group is likely to accept the group's beliefs and conform to behaviors dictated by the group. If race or ethnicity constitutes a strong reference group for a client, then a counselor of the same race/ethnicity is likely to be more influential than one who is not.

4.   **The Economic Set:** In the economic set, the person is influenced because of perceived rewards and punishments the source is able to deliver. In this set, a person performs a behavior or states a belief in order to gain rewards and avoid punishments. In the case of the counselor, he/she controls important resources that may affect the client. For example, a counselor may decide to recommend the expulsion of a student from the school. In less subtle ways, the counselor may ridicule or praise a client during a group counseling session. In these cases, the client may decide to change his/her

behavior because the counselor holds greater power. The major problem with the use of rewards and punishment to induce change is that while it may assure "behavioral compliance," it does not guarantee "private acceptance." Furthermore, for reward and coercive power to be effective, the counselor must maintain constant surveillance. Once the surveillance is removed, the client is likely to revert back to previous modes of behavior. For culturally different clients, counseling that primarily operates on the economic set is more likely to prevent trust, rapport, and self-disclosure.

5. **The Authority Set:** Under this set, some individuals are thought to have a particular position that gives them a legitimate right to prescribe attitudes and/or behaviors. In our society, we have been conditioned to believe that certain authorities (police officers, chairpersons, designated leaders, etc.) have the right to demand compliance. This occurs via training in role behavior and group norms. Mental health professionals, like counselors, are thought to have a legitimate right to recommend and provide psychological treatment to disturbed or troubled clients. It is this psychological set that legitimizes the counselor's role as a helping professional. Yet, for many minorities, it is exactly the roles in society that are perceived to be instruments of institutional racism.

None of the five sets or frames of reference are mutually exclusive. These sets frequently interact, and any number of them can operate at the same time. For example, it is possible that you are influenced by a counselor you find highly credible. It is also possible that you like the counselor or find him/her very attractive. Are you accepting his/her influence because the counselor is credible (problem-solving set), attractive (identification set), or both?

It should be quite clear at this point that characteristics of the influencing source (counselor) are all important in eliciting types of changes. In addition, the type of set placed in operation, oftentimes, dictates the permanency and degree of attitude change. For example, the primary component in getting compliance (economic and authority set) is the power that the person holds over you: the ability to reward or punish. In identification (identity set), it is the attractiveness or liking of the counselor, and in internalization (problem-solving and consistency set), credibility or truthfulness is important.

While these sets operate similarly for both majority and minority clients, their manifestations may be quite different. Obviously, a minority client may have great difficulty identifying (identification set) with a counselor from another race or culture. Also, what constitutes credibility to a minority client may be far different from that of a majority client. We now focus on how counselor characteristics affect these sets as they apply to the culturally different.

Counselor Credibility

Credibility (that elicits the problem-solving, consistency, and identification sets) may be defined as the constellation of characteristics that make certain individuals appear worthy of belief, capable, entitled to confidence, reliable, and trustworthy. Hovland, Janis, & Kelley (1953) identified two components of credibility: expertness and trustworthiness. Expertness is an "ability" variable, while trustworthiness is a "motivation" one. Expertness depends on how well informed, capable, or intelligent others perceive the communicator (counselor). Trustworthiness is dependent on the degree to which people perceive the communicator (counselor) as motivated to make nonvalid assertions. In counseling, these two components have been the subject of much research and speculation (Strong, 1968; Strong & Schmidt, 1970; Sprafkin, 1970; Dell, 1973; Barak & La Crosse, 1975; La Crosse & Barak, 1976; Spiegel, 1976; Barak & Dell, 1977). The weight of evidence supports our commonsense beliefs that the counselor who is perceived as expert and trustworthy can influence clients more than one who is lower on these traits.

Expertness   Clients often go to a counselor not only because they are in distress and in need of relief, but also because they believe the counselor is an expert; he/she has the necessary knowledge, skills, experience, training, and tools to help (problem-solving set). Perceived expertness is typically a function of (*a*) reputation, (*b*) evidence of specialized training, and/or (*c*) behavioral evidence of proficiency/competency. For culturally different clients, the issue of counselor expertness seems to be raised more often than in going to a counselor of one's own culture and race. As mentioned previously, the fact that counselors have degrees and certificates from prestigious institutions (authority set) may not enhance perceived expertness. This is especially true of clients who are culturally different and aware that institutional racism exists in training programs. Indeed, it may have the opposite effect by reducing credibility! Neither is reputation-expertness (authority set) likely to impress a minority client unless the favorable testimony comes from someone of his/her own group.

Thus behavior-expertness or demonstrating your ability to help a client becomes the critical form of expertness in cross-cultural counseling (problem-solving set). And, as we discussed in Chapter 2, using counseling skills and strategies appropriate to the life values of the culturally different client is crucial. We have already mentioned that there is evidence to suggest that certain minority groups prefer a much more active approach in counseling. A counselor playing a relatively inactive role may be perceived as being inexpert (Peoples & Dell, 1975). The example presented next shows how the counselor's approach lowers perceived expertness:

ASIAN AMERICAN MALE CLIENT:	"It's hard for me to talk about these issues. My parents and friends . . . they wouldn't understand . . . if they ever found out I was coming here for help . . . "
WHITE MALE COUNSELOR:	"I sense that it's difficult to talk about personal things. How are you feeling right now?"
ASIAN AMERICAN CLIENT:	"Oh, all right."
WHITE COUNSELOR:	"That's not a feeling. Sit back and get in touch with your feelings (pause). Now tell me, how are you feeling right now?"
ASIAN AMERICAN CLIENT:	"Somewhat nervous."
WHITE COUNSELOR:	"When you talked about your parents and friends not understanding and the way you said it, made me think you felt ashamed and disgraced at having to come. Was that what you felt?"

While this exchange appears to indicate that the counselor (a) was able to see the client's discomfort and (b) interpret his feelings correctly, it also points out the counselor's lack of understanding and knowledge of Asian cultural values. While we do not want to be guilty of stereotyping Asian Americans, many do have difficulty, at times, dealing with feelings. The counselor's persistent attempts to focus on feelings and his direct and blunt interpretation of them may indicate to the client that the counselor lacks the more subtle skills of dealing with a sensitive topic and/or is shaming the client (see Chapter 7).

In many ways, behavioral manifestations of counselor expertness overrides other considerations. For example, many counselor educators claim that specific counseling skills are not as important as the attitude one brings into the counseling situation. Behind this statement is the belief that universal attributes of genuineness, love, unconditional acceptance, and positive regard are the only things needed. Yet the question remains, how does a counselor communicate these things to a culturally different client? While a counselor might have the best of intentions, it is possible that his/her intention might be misunderstood. Let us use another example with the same Asian American client.

ASIAN AMERICAN CLIENT: "I'm even nervous about others seeing me come in here. It's so difficult for me to talk about this."

WHITE COUNSELOR: "We all find some things difficult to talk about. It's important that you do."

ASIAN AMERICAN CLIENT: "It's easy to say that. But, do you really understand how awful I feel, talking about my parents?"

WHITE COUNSELOR: "I've worked with many Asian Americans, and many have similar problems."

In this sample dialogue, we find a distinction between the counselor's intentions and the effects of his comments. The counselor's intentions were to reassure the client that he understood his feelings, to imply that he had worked with similar cases, and to make the client not feel isolated (others have the same problems). The effects, however, were to dilute and dismiss the client's feelings and concerns, to take the uniqueness out of the situation.

Likewise, a counselor who adheres rigidly to a particular school of counseling or who relies primarily on a few counseling responses is seriously limited in his/her ability to help a wide range of clients. While counseling theories are important, counselor training programs have an equally strong responsibility to teach helping skills that cut across schools of counseling. Only in this way, will future counselors be better able to engage in a wide variety of counseling behaviors when working with culturally diverse groups.

Trustworthiness   Perceived trustworthiness encompasses such factors as sincerity, openness, honesty, or perceived lack of motivation for personal gain. A counselor who is perceived as trustworthy is likely to exert more influence over a client than one who is not. In our society, certain roles like ministers, doctors, psychiatrists, and counselors are presumed to exist to help people. This assumption is accepted until proved otherwise. With respect to minorities, self-disclosure is very much dependent on this attribute of perceived trustworthiness. Because counselors are often perceived by minorities to be "agents of the Establishment," trust is something that does not come with the role (authority set). Indeed, it may be the perception of many minorities that counselors cannot be trusted unless otherwise demonstrated. Again, the role and reputation you have as being trustworthy must be demonstrated in behavioral terms. More than anything, challenges to the counselor's trustworthiness will be a frequent theme blocking further exploration/movement until it is resolved to the satisfaction of the client. These verbatim transcripts illustrate the trust issue:

WHITE MALE COUNSELOR: "I sense some major hesitations . . . it's difficult for you to discuss your concerns with me."

BLACK MALE CLIENT: "You're damn right! If I really told you how I felt about my coach [white], what's to prevent you from telling him? You whities are all of the same mind."

WHITE COUNSELOR: "Look . . . it would be a lie for me to say I don't know your coach [angry voice]. He's an acquaintance, but not a personal friend. Don't put me in the same bag with all whites! Anyway, even if he was, I hold our discussions in strictest confidence. Let me ask you this question . . . What can I do that would make it easier for you to trust me?"

BLACK CLIENT: "You're on your way man!"

This verbal exchange illustrates several issues related to trustworthiness. First, the minority client is likely to constantly test the counselor regarding issues of confidentiality. Second, the onus of responsibility for proving trustworthiness falls on the counselor. Third, to prove one is trustworthy requires, at times, self-disclosure on the part of the counselor. That the counselor did not hide the fact that he knew the coach (openness), became angry about being lumped with all whites (sincerity), assured the client he would not tell the coach or anyone about their sessions (confidentiality), and asked the client how he could work to prove he was trustworthy (genuineness) were all elements which enhanced his trustworthiness.

The "prove to me that you can be trusted" ploy is a most difficult one for counselors to handle. It is difficult because it demands self-disclosure on the part of counselors, something counselor training programs have taught us to avoid. It places the focus on the counselor rather than the client and makes many uncomfortable. It is likely to evoke defensiveness on the part of many counselors. Here is another verbatim exchange in which defensiveness is evoked, destroying the counselor's trustworthiness.

BLACK FEMALE CLIENT:	"Students in my drama class expect me to laugh when they do 'steppin fetchin' routines and tell Black jokes . . . I'm wondering whether you've ever laughed at any of those jokes."
WHITE MALE COUNSELOR:	(long pause) "Yes, I'm sure I have . . . Have you ever laughed at any white jokes?"
BLACK CLIENT:	"What's a white joke?"
WHITE COUNSELOR:	"I don't know (nervous laughter); I suppose one making fun of whites . . . Look, I'm Irish, have you ever laughed at Irish jokes?"
BLACK CLIENT:	"People tell me many jokes, but I don't laugh at racial jokes. I feel we're all minorities and should respect each other."

Again, the client tested the counselor indirectly by asking him if he ever laughed at racial jokes. Since most of us probably have, to say no would be a blatant lie. The client's motivation for asking this question was (a) to find out how sincere and open the counselor was and (b) whether the counselor could recognize his racist attitudes without letting it interfere with counseling. While the counselor admitted to having laughed at such jokes, he proceeded to destroy his trustworthiness by becoming defensive. Rather than simply stopping with his statement of "Yes, I'm sure I have" or making some other similar one such as "Yes, I have, but I don't anymore," he defends himself by trying to get the client to admit to similar actions. Thus the counselor's trustworthiness is seriously impaired. He is perceived as motivated to defend himself rather than help the client.

To summarize, expertness and trustworthiness are important components of any counseling relationship. In cross-cultural counseling, however, the counselor may not be presumed to possess either. The counselor working with a minority client is likely to experience severe tests of his/her expertness and trustworthiness before serious counseling can proceed. The responsibility for proving to the client that you are a credible counselor is likely to be greater when working with a minority than a majority counselee. How you meet the challenge is important in determining your effectiveness as a cross-cultural counselor.

Similarity   Social psychological (Dabbs, 1964; Brock, 1965; Byrne & Nelson, 1965; Mills & Aronson, 1965) and counseling analogue studies (Schmidt & Strong, 1971; Barak & La Crosse, 1975; Barak & Dell, 1977) suggest that communicators (counselors) are able to influence others more effectively if they appear attractive to them. It is important to note that attractiveness and credibility are often associated with one another. For example, I might like a person or find him/her attractive because he/she is logical and trustworthy. However, interpersonal attraction is more likely to be the result of similarity.

Why does similarity cause increased interpersonal attraction? It appears that interactions with people who are similar to us tend to be rewarding because it validates our convictions (identification and consistency set). Likewise, if we are strongly attracted to someone (liking), this person is more likely to have influence over us. When people are dissimilar to us there is the possibility that they will disagree with our beliefs, attitudes, and/or opinions (consistency set). Not only may this fear be present in counseling, but also there is the real possibility that the counselor will not understand or will misinterpret the motives/beliefs/behaviors of the culturally different client.

Belief Similarity versus Race Similarity.   Schmedinghoff (1977) raises this issue directly with respect to cultural, racial, and class dissimilarity in working with Black clients. Does the counselor have to share the cultural, racial, and class backgrounds of his/her clients to be effective? This is a difficult question to answer, and even the research in this area is inconclusive. Several authors (Banks, 1971; Kincaid, 1969; Vontress, 1971, 1972) argue strongly that successful interracial counseling is highly improbable because of the cultural/racial barriers involved. Studies which indicate that (*a*) Black clients prefer Black counselors (Wolkon, Moriwaki, & Williams, 1973; Harrison, 1975) and Asian-Americans prefer Asian Americans (Atkinson, Marujama, & Matsui, 1978), (*b*) there is a high rate of return of Black clients to Black counselors (Heffernon & Bruehl, 1971), (*c*) a greater understanding of Black clients by Black counselors is often exhibited (Bryson & Cody, 1973), (*d*) there is greater depth of self-exploration of Black patients treated by Black therapists (Carkhuff & Pierce, 1967), (*e*) higher ratings of counselor effectiveness is given to Black counselors by Black counselors (Banks, Berenson, & Carkhuff, 1967; Gardner, 1972), and (f) greater behavioral change follows counseling of Black students by Black counselors seem to support the proposition that counselor-client racial similarity enhances the likelihood of success in counseling. While nearly all these studies deal with Blacks, similar claims may be made for other racial groups as well. Yet others (Arbuckle, 1972; Aspy, 1970; Jones & Jones, 1972, P. T. Cimbolic, 1973) claim that well-trained and sensitive counselors of another race may be able to establish effective counseling relationships with their clients. For example, type of issue (educational/vocational vs. personal problems) operating (Johnson, 1977), sex of counselor (Bryson, Bardo, & Johnson, 1975), counselor experience (P. Cimbolic, 1972), and counselor style (Peoples & Dell, 1975) may be more important than race.

Schmedinghoff (1977) suggests that racial composition of the client-counselor dyad may be of little significance. Citing studies conducted by Rokeach (1968, 1973), he implies that belief similarity-dissimilarity is more important than racial ones. Stating this in its negative form, one would say that belief prejudice is more important in counseling than race prejudice. There is empirical support for the proposition that as perceived dissimilarity of attitudes increases, dislike or prejudice increases (Insko & Robinson, 1967; Rokeach, Smith, & Evans, 1960; Rokeach & Mezei, 1966). In all these studies, belief and race similarity-dissimilarity were pitted against one another. If we accept this proposition, it suggests that racial similarity may be less important in forming counseling rapport than genuine acceptance of another's beliefs. The importance of race or belief as determinants of interpersonal evaluation, however, is not all that clear. Schmedinghoff (1977) fails to mention several methodological problems pointed out by Collins (1970) about these studies.

1. First, most of the forementioned studies used hypothetical stimulus persons introduced by brief descriptions: a white boy who believes in God, a Black boy who believes in God, and a white boy who is an atheist. The results might have been different if the choices were based on real flesh-and-blood people.

2. Second, the manipulation of race and belief might not have been equal. For example, a one-word description of race might not be as powerful as a more elaborated description of a belief system. This criticism is supported by a study which shows that when a belief system was manipulated with just one sentence instead of many, race was more potent than belief (Triandis, 1961).

3.   Third, many of these studies fail to take into account the issue of social distance. As the relationship increases in intimacy and publicness, race as a criterion increases in importance. Similarity of beliefs may be more important for less intimate forms of friendship, but on behavioral contact measures (Sears & Abeles, 1969) that involve issues such as "invite home to dinner," "go on a date," and "get married," race seems much more potent.

Let us summarize what we have here. The belief similarity-dissimilarity hypothesis explains interpersonal attraction in the following manner: (a) A child grows up and learns to distinguish between various social groups; (b) the child learns that these social groups may have values and beliefs dissimilar to his/her own group; (c) on the basis of this assumed difference, negative reactions in the form of liking someone less, turning away from social contact, or even prejudice develops.

While prejudice seems correlated with assumed incongruence of beliefs, little evidence exists for this hypothesis (Collins, 1970). The literature on how prejudice is acquired indicates that prejudice causes people to assume that other people's beliefs are dissimilar. In other words, majority group children (a) learn a general good or bad affective reaction toward a distinct social group and (b) acquire specific beliefs about them.

The conclusion that negative affective reactions (prejudice) comes first and the assumed dissimilarity of beliefs comes second is not meant to support the position that only Blacks can counsel Blacks, Asians counsel Asians, Chicanos counsel Chicanos, and Native Americans counsel Native Americans. Just as stating that race similarity is unimportant in counseling and that belief similarity is more so, it represents an oversimplification. We have seen in Chapter 2 how one's implied cultural identity can influence a minority client's receptivity to a culturally different counselor. The way the identification set operates depends very much on the stage of cultural identity in which the minority client finds himself/herself.

Cultural Identity: Similarity versus Dissimilarity.   A question such as "Can a white counselor counsel a Black client?" cannot be easily answered with a yes or no response. Indeed, the question may be too broad and ambiguous to come up with a meaningful answer. We have already discussed a multiplicity of factors that would influence an affirmative or negative response. Cultural identity development seems to be an important variable in clarifying this question. The most highly developed models have dealt with Blacks (Cross, 1971; Jackson, 1975) and Asian Americans (S. Sue, & D. W. Sue, 1971). Atkinson, Morten, & D. W. Sue (1979) feel that many of the basic tenets of these theories can be applied to other minority groups who share an experience of oppression. They have proposed a Minority Identity Development (MID) model in which five stages are defined. At each stage, there are four corresponding attitudes that form the minority person's identity. How a person views (*a*) the self, (*b*) others of the same minority, (*c*) others of another minority, and (*d*) majority individuals are correlated with a particular stage. Table 3.1 summarizes the MID model, its five stages and their resultant attitudes.

1. **Stage one—The Conformity Stage:** This stage is characterized by a preference for dominant cultural values over one's own culture. The reference group (identification set) is likely to be white America, and feelings of racial self-hatred, negative beliefs of one's own culture and positive feelings toward the dominant culture are likely to be strong.

2. **Stage Two—Dissonance Stage:** Cultural confusion and conflict (consistency set and problem-solving set) are likely to be character- istic of minorities in this stage. Information and/or experiences begin to challenge accepted values and beliefs of the conformity stage. Active questioning of the dominant-held system of minority stratification and a need to resolve conflicting attitudes operate strongly.

3. **Stage Three—Resistance and Immersion Stage:** An active rejection of the dominant society and culture and a complete endorsement of minority-held views become evident. Desires to combat oppression and racism become the primary motivation of the person. There is an attempt to get in touch with one's history, culture, and tradi- tions. Distrust and hatred of white society is strong. The reference group is one's own culture.

4. **Stage Four—Introspection Stage:** Again, this stage is characterized by conflict and too-narrow and rigid constraints of the previous stage. Notions of loyalty and responsibility to one's own group and notions of personal autonomy come into conflict. Group-usurped individuality, culturocentrism, and absolute rejection of dominant cultural values become questioned.

5. **Stage Five—Synergetic Articulation and Awareness Stage:** In describing this stage, Atkinson, Morten, & D. W. Sue (1979) state: Minority individuals in this stage experience a sense of self-fulfill- ment with regard to cultural identity. Conflicts and discomforts

Table 3.1 Summary of Minority Identity Development Model

Stages of minority development model	Attitude toward self	Attitude toward others of the same minority	Attitude toward others of different minority	Attitude toward dominant group
Stage 1—conformity	Self-depreciating	Group depreciating	Discriminatory	Group appreciating
Stage 2—dissonance	Conflict between self-depreciating and appreciating	Conflict between group depreciating and group appreciating	Conflict between dominant-held views of minority hierarchy and feelings of shared experience	Conflict between group appreciating and group depreciating
Stage 3—resistance and immersion	Self-appreciating	Group appreciating	Conflict between feelings of empathy for other minority experiences and feelings of culturocentrism	Group depreciating
Stage 4—introspection	Concern with basis of self-appreciation	Concern with nature of unequivocal appreciation	Concern with ethnocentric basis for judging others	Concern with the basis of group depreciation
Stage 5—synergetic articulation and awareness	Self-appreciating	Group appreciating	Group appreciating	Selective appreciating

From D. R. Atkinson, G. Morten & D. W. Sue, *Counseling American Minorities: A Cross-Cultural Perspective*, Dubuque, Iowa: W. C. Brown, 1979, 198.

experienced in the introspection stage have been resolved, allowing greater individual control and flexibility. Cultural values of other minorities as well as those of the dominant group are objectively examined and accepted or rejected on the basis of prior experience gained in earlier stages of identity development. Desire to eliminate *all* forms of oppression becomes an important motivation of the individual's behavior. (p. 197)

The delineation of these five stages sheds light on the question about whether a member from a different race/culture can counsel a minority client. The differences that can exist between members of the same minority group with respect to cultural identity affects our answer. A person at the conformity stage will evidence more preference for a majority member counselor and is likely to find him/her more credible, trustworthy, and attractive. Clients at the dissonance stage are likely to prefer counselors who are familiar with dominant and minority cultures. In most cases, the counselor who would fit these conditions would probably be a minority person. This is so because there is a greater probability that minorities are more familiar with the dominant society's values and workings than whites are familiar with minority cultures. Minorities at the resistance and immersion stage will view members of the dominant society with distrust and hostility. Thus if counselors are sought, they must be members of the minorities' own race and culture. Membership group similarity is all important. Clients at the introspection stage also prefer counselors of their own culture/race but are more receptive to counselors who share their world view. Likewise, minority clients at the synergetic articulation and awareness stage evidence security in their own ethnic/cultural identity and also have acquired a desired level of personal freedom. Again, similar world views attitudinal similarity, and belief similarity are more important than membership group similarity.

Whether a counselor can work effectively with a person from a different culture/race depends on many factors of which racial and attitudinal similarity-dissimilarity are two important ones. The nature of the problem, counselor experience, counseling style, and degree of ethnic/racial consciousness are just a few of the important variables that need to be considered. Yet it cannot be denied that membership group and attitudinal similarity tend to enhance attractiveness (interpersonal attraction) and increase the probability of identification (identity set). In general, a person similar to you may be able to exert greater influence than one who is dissimilar. A counselor's similarity to the client may lead the client to initially view the counselor as an appropriate person to seek assistance from. Yet, as we see in the next chapter, ethnic identity, attitudinal/belief similarity and even counseling styles may be all associated with world views.

CONCLUSIONS

Since counseling is a white middle-class activity, the factors that may enhance the social influence of the majority counselor might, indeed, lower his/her power base when working with a culturally different client. As we have seen, credibility is usually defined in terms of two general dimensions: expertness and trustworthiness. Perceived expertness is typically a function of reputation, behavioral proficiency, or evidence of specialized training (degrees, certificates, and so on). Trustworthiness encompasses such factors as sincerity, openness, honesty, or perceived lack of motivation for personal gain. While majority clients may also be concerned with the counselor's credibility, cultural differences and/or experiences of oppression in U.S. society make the minority client more sensitive to these characteristics of the counselor. Tests of credibility may occur frequently in the counseling session, and the onus of responsibility for proving expertness and trustworthiness lies with the counselor.

In cross-cultural counseling, the counselor may also be unable to use the client's identification set (membership group similarity) to induce change. At times, racial dissimilarity may prove to be so much of a hindrance as to render counseling ineffective. Some have agreed that attitudinal similarity may be more important than racial similarity in counseling. Research in this area is inconclusive. It seems to depend on several factors: (a) the type of presenting problems, (b) degree of racial/ethnic identity, and (c) certain characteristics of the counselor that may override race differences. Indeed, the difficulties in cross-cultural counseling may not stem from race factors, per se, but from the implications of being a minority in the United States that assigns secondary status to them. In any case, a broad general statement on this matter is oversimplistic. Cross-cultural counseling by virtue of definition implies major differences between the client and counselor. How these differences may be bridged and under what conditions will a counselor be able to work effectively with a culturally different client are key questions.

REFERENCES

Arbuckle, D. S. The Counselor: Who? What? *Personnel and Guidance Journal*, 1972, **50,** 585–790.

Aspy, D. N. Empathy–congruence—caring are singular. *Personnel and Guidance Journal, 1970,* **48,** 635–640.

Atkinson, D. R., & Carskaddon, G. A prestigious introduction, psychological jargon, and perceived counselor credibility. *Journal of Counseling Psychology*, 1975, **22,** 180–186.

Atkinson. D. R., Marujama, M., & Matsui, S. The effects of counselor race and counseling approach on Asian Americans' perceptions of counselor credibility and utility. *Journal of Counseling Psychology*, 1978, **25,** 76–83.

Atkinson, D. R., Morten, G., & Sue, D. W. *Counseling American Minorities: A Cross-Cultural Perspective*. Dubuque, Iowa: W. C. Brown, 1979.

Banks, G. The effects of race on the one-to-one helping interviews. *Social Service Review*, 1971, **45,** 137–146.

Banks, G., Berenson, B., & Carkhuff, R. The effects of counselor race and training upon the counseling process with Negro clients in initial interviews. *Journal of Clinical Psychology*, 1967, **23,** 70n72.

Barak, A., & Dell, D. M. Differential perceptions of counselor behavior: Replication and extension. *Journal of Counseling Psychology*, 1977, **24,** 288–292.

Barak, A., & La Crosse, M. B. Multidimensional perception of counselor behavior. *Journal of Counseling Psychology*, 1975, **22,** 471–456.

Brock, T. C. Communicator-recipient similarity and decision change. *Journal of Personality and Social Psychology*, 1965, **1,** 650–654.

Byrne, D., & Nelson, D. Attraction as a linear function of proportion of positive reinforcements. *Journal of Personality and Social Psychology*, 1965, **1,** 659–663.

Bryson, S., Bardo, H., & Johnson, C. Black female counselor and the Black male client. *Journal of Non-White Concerns in Personnel and Guidance*, 1975, **3,** 53–58.

Bryson, S., & Cody, J. Relationship of race and level of understanding between counselor and client. *Journal of Counseling Psychology*, 1973, **20,** 495–498.

Burnstein, E., & McRae, A. V. Some effects of shared threat and prejudice in racially mixed groups. *Journal of Abnormal and Social Psychology*, 1962, **64,** 257–263. Carkhuff, R. R., & Pierce, R. Differential effects of therapist race and social class upon patient depth of self-exploration in the initial clinical interview. *Journal of Consulting Psychology*, 1967, **31,** 632–634.

Cimbolic, P. Counselor race and experience effects on Black clients. *Journal of Consulting and Clinical Psychology*, 1972, **39,** 328–332.

Cimbolic, P. T. Group effects on Black clients' perception of counselors. *Journal of College Student Personnel,* 1973, **14,** 296–302.

Collins, B. E. *Social Psychology*. Reading, Mass.: Addison-Wesley, 1970.

Corsini, R. J. *Current Psychotherapies*. (2nd ed.) Itasca, Ill.: Peacock. 1979.

Cross, W. E. The Negro-to-Black conversion experience. *Black World*, 1971, **20,** 13–25.

Dabbs, J. M. Self-esteem, communicator characteristics, and attitude change. *Journal of Abnormal and Social Psychology*, 1964, **69,** 173–181.

Dell, B. M. Counselor power base, influence attempt, and behavior change in counseling. *Journal of Counseling Psychology*, 1973, **20,** 399–405.

Festinger, L. *A Theory of Cognitive Dissonance*. Evanston, Ill.: Row & Peterson, 1957.

Gardner, W. E. The differential effects of race, education and experience in helping. *Journal of Clinical Psychology*, 1972, **28**, 87–89.

Grier, W. H., & Cobbs, P. *Black Rage*. New York: Basic Books, 1968.

Grier, W. H., & Cobbs, P. *The Jesus Bag*. San Francisco: McGraw-Hill, 1971.

Hall, E. T. *Beyond Culture*. New York: Anchor Books, 1976.

Harrison, D. K. Race as a counselor-client variable in counseling and psychotherapy: A review of the research. *Counseling Psychologist*, 1975, **5**, 124–133.

Heffernon, A., & Bruehl, D. Some effects of race of inexperienced lay counselors on Black junior high school students. *Journal of School Psychology*, 1971, **9**, 35–37.

Hovland, C. I., Janis, I. L., & Kelley, H. H. *Communication and persuasion*. New Haven: Yale University Press, 1953.

Insko, C. A., & Robinson, J. E. Belief similarity versus race as determinants of reactions to Negroes by Southern white adolescents: A further test of Rokeach's theory. *Journal of Personality and Social Psychology*, 1967, **7**, 216–221.

Ivey, A. & Authier, J. *Microcounseling: Innovations in interviewing Training*. Springfield, Ill.: Charles C. Thomas, 1979.

Jackson, B. Black identity development. *MEFORM: Journal of Educational Diversity and Innovation*, 1975, **2**, 19–25.

Johnson, H. N. A survey of students' attitudes toward counseling at a predominantly Black univeristy. *Journal of Counseling Psychology*, 1977, **24**, 162–164.

Jones, M. H., & Jones, M. C. The neglected client. In R. Jones (Ed.), *Black Psychology*. New York: Harper & Row, 1972.

Jourard, S., & Lasakow, P. *Self-Disclosure: An Experimental Analysis of the Transparent Self*. New York: Wiley-Interscience, 1971.

Kincaid, M. Identity and therapy in the Black community. *Personnel and Guidance Journal*, 1969, **47**, 884–890.

La Crosse, M. B., & Barak, A. Differential perception of counselor behavior. *Journal of Counseling Psychology*, 1976, **23**, 170–172.

Ladner, J. A. *Tomorrow's Tomorrows: The Black Women*. Doubleday, 1971.

London, P. *Modes and Morals of Psychotherapy*. New York: Holt, Rinehart & Winston, 1964.

Merluzzi, T. V., Merluzzi, B. H., & Kaul, T. J. Counselor race and power base: Effects on attitudes and behavior. *Journal of Counseling Psychology*, 1977, **24**, 430–436.

Mills, J., & Aronson, E. Opinion change as a function of the communicator's attractiveness and desire to influence. *Journal of Personality and Social Psychology*, 1965, **1**, 173–177.

Mitchell, H. The Black experience in higher education. *Counseling Psychologist*, 1970, **2**, 30–36.

Patterson, C. H. *Theories of Counseling and Psychotherapy* (2nd ed.). New York: Harper & Row, 1973.

Peoples, V. Y., & Dell, D. M. Black and white student preferences for counselor roles. *Journal of Counseling Psychology*, 1975, **22**, 529–534.

Pinderhughes, C. A. Racism in psychotherapy. In C. Willie, B. Kramer, & B. Brown (Eds.), *Racism and Mental Health*. Pittsburg: University of Pittsburg Press, 1973, 61–121.

Rogers, C. R. The interpersonal relationship: the core of guidance. *Harvard Educational Review*, 1962, **32**, 416–429.

Rokeach, M. *Beliefs, Attitudes and Values*. San Francisco: Jossey-Bass, 1968.

Rokeach, M. *Nature of Human Values*. New York: Free Press, 1973.

Rokeach, M., & Mezei, L. Race and shared belief as factors in social choice. *Science*, 1966, **151**, 167–172.

Rokeach, M., Smith, P. W., & Evans, R. I. Two kinds of prejudice or one? In M. Rokeach (Ed.), *The Open and Closed Mind*. New York: Basic Books, 1960, 132–168.

Russell, R. D. Black perceptions of guidance. *Personnel and Guidance Journal*, 1970, **48**, 721–728.

Schmedinghoff, G. J. Counseling the Black student in higher education. Is it racial, socioeconomic, or human question? *Journal of College Student Personnel*, 1977, **18** 472–477.

Schmidt, L. D., & Strong, S. R. Attractiveness and influence in counseling. *Journal of Counseling Psychology*, 1971, **18**, 348–351.

Sears, D. O., & Abeles, R. P. Attitudes and opinions. *Annual Review of Psychology*, 1969, **20**,253–288.

Spiegel, S. B. Expertness, similarity, and perceived counselor competence. *Journal of Counseling Psychology*, 1976, **23**, 436–441.

Sprafkin, R. P. Communicator expertness and changes in word meaning in psychological treatment. *Journal of Counseling Psychology*, 1970, **17**, 191–196.

Strong, S. R. Counseling: An interpersonal influence process. *Journal of Counseling Psychology*, 1968, **15**, 215–224.

Strong, S. R., & Schmidt, L. D. Expertness and influence in counseling. *Journal of Counseling Psychology*, 1970, **15**, 31–35.

Sue, S., & Sue, D. W. Chinese-American personality and mental health. *Amerasia Journal*, 1971, **1**, 36–49.

Thomas, C. W. Black-white campus and the functions of counseling. *Counseling Psychologist*, 1969, **1**, 70–73.Thomas, A., & Sillens, S. *Racism and Psychiatry*. New York: Brunner/Mazel, 1972.

Triandis, H. C. A note on Rokeach's theory of prejudice. *Journal of Abnormal and Social Psychology*, 1961, **62**, 184–186.

Vontress, C. E. The Black militant as a counselor. *Personnel and Guidance Journal*, 1972, **50**, 576–580.

Vontress, C. E. Counseling Blacks. *Personnel and Guidance Journal*, 1970, **48**, 713–719.

Vontress, C. E. Counseling: Racial and ethnic factors. *Focus on Guidance*, 1973, **5**, 1–10.

Vontress, C. E. Racial differences: Impediments to rapport. *Journal of Counseling Psychology*, 1971, **18**, 7–13.

Williams, B. M. Trust and self-disclosure among Black college students. *Journal of Counseling Psychology*, 1974, **21**, 522–525.

Willie, C. V., Kramer, B. M., & Brown, B. S. *Racism and Mental Health*. Pittsburg: University of Pittsburg Press, 1973.

Wolkon, G. H., Moriwaki, S., & Williams, K. J. Race and social class as factors in the orientation toward therapy. *Journal of Counseling Psychology*, 1973, **20**, 312–316.

4
Dimensions of World Views:
Cultural Identity

The previous three chapters have made a strong case for the fact that the data base and process of counseling have and continue to be damaging to many culturally different clients. For counselors to work effectively with their Third World clients, they must not only understand this major point, but also be able to understand the concept of world views. It has become increasingly clear that many minority persons hold world views different from members of the dominant culture. The issue of understanding a minority client's world view in counseling has not been adequately discussed or stressed. A world view may be broadly defined as how a person perceives his/her relationship to the world (nature, institutions, other people, things, etc.). World views are highly correlated with a person's cultural upbringing and life experiences (D. W. Sue, 1975; Jackson, 1975). Not only are world views composed of our attitudes, values, opinions, and concepts, but also they may affect how we think, make decisions, behave, and define events. For minorities in America, a strong determinant of world views is very much related to racism and the subordinate position assigned to them in society. While the intent of this chapter is to discuss racial and ethnic minorities, it must be kept in mind that economic and social class, religion, and sex are also interactional components of a world view. Thus upper- and lower-socioeconomic class Asian Americans, Blacks, Chicanos, or Native Americans do not necessarily have identical views of the world.

Counselors who hold a world view different from that of their clients

---

Permission granted to reproduce any or all of the following article: D. W. Sue, Eliminating cultural oppression in counseling: Toward a general theory. *Journal of Counseling Psychology,* 1978, **25**, 419–428.

and are unaware of the basis for this difference are most likely to impute negative traits to clients. Constructs used to judge "normality" and "healthy" or "abnormality" and "unhealthy" may be inadvertently applied to clients. In most cases, culturally different clients have a greater probability of holding world views different from those of counselors. Yet many counselors are so "culturally blind" that they respond according to their own conditioned values, assumptions, and perspectives of reality without regard for other views. What is needed for counselors is for them to become "culturally aware," to act on the basis of a critical analysis and understanding of their own conditioning and the conditioning of their clients and the sociopolitical system of which they are both a part. Without this awareness, counselors who work with the culturally different may be engaging in cultural oppression. Since understanding a Third World client's cultural identity development is most likely to lead to the understanding of world views, it seems imperative that we explore this dimension.

In this chapter, an attempt is made to discuss how race and culture-specific factors may interact in such a way as to produce people with different world views. A conceptual model is presented that integrates research findings with the clinical literature on cultural identity development. First, two factors identified as being important in understanding persons with different psychological orientations are discussed: (a) locus of control (Gore & J.B. Rotter, 1963; J. Rotter, 1966; Gurin et. al., 1969; Caplan & Paige, 1968; Caplan, 1970; Forward & Williams, 1970; and (b) locus of responsibility (Gurin et. al., 1969; Forward & Williams, 1970; Abeles, 1976; Turner & Wilson, 1976; Avis & Stewart, 1976). Second, how these variables form four different psychological outlooks in life and their consequent characteristics, dynamics, and implications for counseling are presented. Last, some conclusions and precautions are discussed.

Locus of Control

J. Rotter (1966) first formulated the concept of internal-external control or the internal-external (I-E) dimension. "Internal control" (IC) refers to people's belief that reinforcements are contingent on their own actions and that people can shape their own fate. "External control" (EC) refers to people's belief that reinforcing events occur independently of their actions and that the future is determined more by chance and luck. J. Rotter conceived this dimension as measuring a generalized personality trait that operated across several different situations. Based on past experience, people learn one of two world views: the locus of control rests with the individual or the locus of control rests with some external force. Lefcourt (1966) and J. Rotter (1966, 1975) have summarized the research findings that correlated high internality with (*a*) greater attempts at mastering the environment, (*b*) superior coping strategies, (*c*) better cognitive processing of information, (*d*) lower predisposition to anxiety, (*e*) higher achievement motivation, (*f*) greater social action involvement, and (*g*) placing greater value on skill determined rewards. As can be seen, these attributes are highly valued by U.S. society and constitute the core features of mental health.

Early research on generalized expectancies of locus of control suggests that ethnic group members (Strickland, 1973; Tulkin, 1968; Levenson, 1974; Hsieh, Shybut, & Lotsof, 1969; Wolfgang, 1973), lower-class people (Lefcourt, 1966; Strickland, 1971; Crandall, Katkovsky, & Crandall, 1965; Battle & Rotter, 1963; Garcia & Levenson, 1975), and women (Sanger & Alker, 1972) score significantly higher on the external end of the continuum. Using the I-E dimension as a criterion of mental health would mean that minority, poor, and female clients be viewed as possessing less desirable attributes. Thus a counselor who encounters a minority client with a high external orientation ("it's no use trying," "there's nothing I can do about it," and "you shouldn't rock the boat") may interpret the client as being inherently apathetic, procrastinating, lazy, depressed, or anxious about trying. As we see in the next section, all these statements tend to blame the individual for his/her present condition.

The problem with an unqualified application of the I-E dimension is that it fails to take into consideration the different cultural and social experiences of the individual. This failure may lead to highly inappropriate and destructive applications in counseling. While the social learning framework from which the I-E dimension is derived may be very legitimate, it seems plausible that different cultural groups, women, and lower-class people have learned that control operates differently in their lives as opposed to how it operates for society at large. In the case of Third World groups, the concept of external control takes on a wider meaning.

Some investigators (Crandall, Katkovsky, & Crandall, 1965; Hersch & Scheibe, 1967) argue that the locus of control continuum must make clearer distinctions on the external end. For example, externality related to impersonal forces (chance and luck) is different from that ascribed to cultural forces and those to powerful others. Chance and luck operate equally across situations for everyone. However, the forces that determine locus of control from a cultural perspective may be viewed by the particular ethnic group as acceptable and benevolent. In this case, externality is viewed positively. Two ethnic groups may be used as examples to illustrate this point.

Hsieh, Shybut, & Lotsof (1969) found that Chinese, American-born Chinese and Anglo Americans varied in the degree of internal control they felt. The first group scored lowest in internality followed by the Chinese Americans and finally by Anglo Americans. These investigators felt that the "individual-centered" American culture emphasizes the uniqueness, independence, and self-reliance of each individual. It places a high premium on self-reliance, individualism and status achieved through one's own efforts. In contrast, the "situation-centered" Chinese culture places importance on the group (an individual is not defined apart from the family), tradition, social roles–expectations, and harmony with the universe. Thus the cultural orientation of the more traditional Chinese tends to elevate the external scores. Note, however, that the external orientation of the Chinese is highly valued and accepted.

Likewise, one might expect Native Americans to score higher on the external end of the I-E continuum on the basis of their own cultural values. Several writers (Bryde, 1971; Trimble, 1976) have pointed to Native American concepts of "noninterference" and "harmony with nature" that may tend to classify them as high externals. Anglos are said to be concerned with attempts to control the physical world and to assert mastery over it. To Native Americans, accepting the world (harmony) rather than changing it is a highly valued life-style.

Support for the fact that Rotter's I-E distinction is not a unidimensional trait has also come from other studies (Mirels, 1970; Gurin et al., 1969) that indicate the presence of a political influence (powerful others). For example, a major focus in the literature dealing with locus of control is that of powerlessness. *Powerlessness* may be defined as the expectancy that a person's behavior cannot determine the outcomes or reinforcements he/she seeks. Mirels (1970) feels that a strong possibility exists that externality may be a function of a person's opinions about prevailing social institutions. For example, lower-class individuals and Blacks are not given an equal opportunity to obtain the material rewards in Western culture. Because of racism, Blacks may be perceiving, in a realistic fashion, a discrepancy between their ability and attainment.

In this case, externality may be seen as a malevolent force to be distinguished from the benevolent cultural ones just discussed. Gurin et al. (1969), on the basis of their study, have concluded that while high external people are less effectively motivated, perform poorly in achievement situations, and evidence greater psychological problems, this does not necessarily hold for minorities and low-income persons. Focusing on external forces may be motivationally healthy if it results from assessing one's chances for success against systematic and real external obstacles rather than unpredictable fate! Three factors of importance for our discussion were identified by Gurin et al.

The first factor called "control ideology" was a measure of general belief about the role of external forces in determining success and failure in the larger society. It represents a cultural belief in the Protestant ethic; success is the result of hard work, effort, skill, and ability. The second factor, "personal control," reflected a person's belief about his/her own sense of personal efficacy or competence. While the former represents an ideological belief, the latter was more related to actual control. Gurin et al. cited data that indicate Blacks are equally internal to whites on the control ideology, but when a personal reference (personal control) was used, they were much more external. What this indicates is that Blacks may have adopted the general cultural beliefs about internal control but find that it cannot always be applied to their own life situations (because of racism and discrimination). It is interesting to note that whites endorse control ideology statements at the same rate as personal control ones. Thus the disparity between the two forms of control do not seem to be operative for white Americans. Another interesting finding was that personal control as opposed to the ideological one was more related to motivational and performance indicators. A student high on personal control (internality) had greater self-confidence, higher test scores, higher grades, and so on. Those subjects who were high on the ideological measure were not noticeably different from their externally oriented counterparts.

The I-E continuum is a useful one for counselors to use only if they make clear distinctions about the meaning of the external control dimension. High externality may be due to (*a*) chance-luck, (*b*) cultural dictates which are viewed as benevolent, and (*c*) a political force (racism or discrimination) that represents malevolent but realistic obstacles. In each case, it is a mistake to assume that the former is operative for a culturally different client. To do so would be to deny the potential influence of cultural values and the effects of prejudice and discrimination. The problem becomes even more complex when we realize that cultural and discriminatory forces may both be operative. That is, Native American cultural values that dictate an external orientation may be compounded by their historical experience of prejudice and discrimination in America. The same may be true for other ethnic groups as well.

Locus of Responsibility

Another important dimension in world outlooks was formulated from attribution theory (Jones et al., 1972) and can be legitimately referred to as "locus of responsibility." In essence, this dimension measures the degree of responsibility or blame placed on the individual or system. In the case of Blacks, their lower standard of living may be attributed to their personal inadequacies and shortcomings; or the responsibility for their plight may be attributed to racial discrimination and lack of opportunities. The former orientation blames the individual, while the latter explanation blames the system.

The degree of emphasis placed on the individual as opposed to the system in affecting a person's behavior is important in the formation of life orientations. Such terms as "person-centered" or "person-blame" indicate a focus on the individual. Those who hold a person-centered orientation (a) emphasize the understanding of a person's motivations, values, feelings, and goals, (b) believe that success or failure is attributable to the individual's skills or personal inadequacies, and (c) believe that there is a strong relationship between ability, effort, and success in society. In essence, these people adhere strongly to the Protestant ethic that idealizes "rugged individualism." On the other hand, "situation-centered" or "system-blame" people view the sociocultural environment as more potent than the individual. Social, economic, and political forces are powerful; success or failure is generally dependent on the socioeconomic system and not necessarily personal attributes.

Caplan & Nelson (1973) in discussing the causal attribution of social problems state that Western society tends to hold individuals responsible for their problems. Such an approach has the effect of labeling that segment of the population (racial and ethnic minorities) which differ in thought and behavior from the larger society as "deviant." Defining the problem as residing in the person enables society to ignore situationally relevant factors and to protect and preserve social institutions and belief systems. Caplan & Nelson (1973) go on to say:

What is done about a problem depends on how it is defined. The way a social problem is defined determined the attempts at remediation—problem definition determines the change strategy, the selection of a social action delivered system, and the criteria for evaluation. . . .

Problem definitions are based on assumptions about the causes of the problem and where they lie. If the causes of delinquency, for example, are defined in person-centered terms (e.g., inability to delay gratification, or incomplete sexual identity), then it would be logical to initiate person-change treatment techniques and intervention strategies to deal with the problem. Such treatment would take the form of counseling or other person-change efforts to "reach" the delinquent, thereby using his potential for self-control to make his behavior more conventional. . . .

If, on the other hand, explanations are situation centered, for example, if delinquency were interpreted as the substitution of extralegal paths for already preempted, conventionally approved pathways for achieving socially valued goals, then efforts toward corrective treatment would logically have a system-change orientation. Efforts would be launched to create suitable opportunities for success and achievement along conventional lines; thus, existing physical, social, or economic arrangements, not individual psyches, would be the targets for change. (pp. 200–201)

Avis & Stewart (1976) point out that a person-centered problem definition has characterized counseling. Definitions of mental health, the assumptions of vocational guidance, and most counseling theories stress the uniqueness and importance of the individual. As a result, the onus of responsibility for change in counseling tends to rest on the individual. It reinforces a social myth about a person's ability to control his/her own fate by rewarding the members of the middle class who "made it on their own" and increases complacency about those who have not "made it on their own."

Thus the individual system-blame continuum may need to be viewed differentially for minority groups. An internal response (acceptance of blame for one's failure) might be considered "normal" for the white middle-class, but, for minorities, it may be extreme and intrapunitive.

For example, a Black male client who has been unable to find a job because of prejudice and discrimination may blame himself ("What's wrong with me?" "Why can't I find a job?" "Am I that worthless?"). Thus an internal response becomes reinforced by counseling when, in actuality, an external response may be more realistic and appropriate ("Institutional racism prevented my getting the job.") Gurin et al. (1969) cite research findings which indicate that those Blacks who scored external (blame system) on this dimension (a) more often aspired to nontraditional occupations, (b) were more in favor of group rather than individual action for dealing with discrimination, (c) engaged in more civil rights activities, and (d) exhibited more innovative, coping behavior. It is important to note that the personal control dimension discussed in the previous section was correlated with traditional measures of motivation and achievement (grades), while individual system-blame was a better predictor of innovative social action behavior. This latter dimension has been the subject of speculation and studies about its relationship to militancy and racial identity (Gore & Rotter, 1963; Marx, 1976; Caplan & Paige, 1968; Forward & Williams, 1970; D. Sue, 1977).

FORMATION OF WORLD VIEWS

The two psychological orientations, locus of control (personal control) and locus of responsibility are independent of one another. As shown in Figure 4.1, both may be placed on a continuum in such a manner that they intersect forming four quadrants: internal locus of control-internal locus of responsibility (IC-IR), external locus of control-internal locus of responsibility (EC-IR), internal locus of control-external locus of responsibility (IC-ER), and external locus of control-external locus of responsibility (EC-ER). Each quadrant represents a different world view or orientation to life. Theoretically, then, if we know the individual's degree of internality or externality on the two loci, we could plot them on the figure. I would speculate that various ethnic and racial groups are not randomly distributed throughout the four quadrants. The previous discussion concerning cultural and societal influences on these two dimensions would seem to support this speculation. Because our discussion subsequently focuses on the political ramifications of the two dimensions, there is an evaluative "desirable-undesirable" quality to each world view.

Locus of control

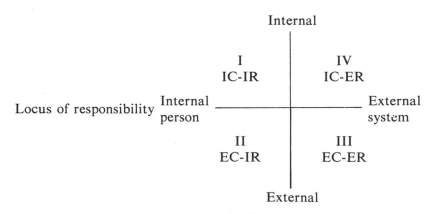

Figure 4.1   Graphic representation of world views.

From Sue, D. W. Eliminating cultural oppression in counseling: Toward a general theory. *Journal of Counseling Psychology*, 1978, **25**, 422.

Internal Locus of Control (IC)—Internal Locus of Responsibility (IR)

As mentioned previously, high internal personal control (IC) individuals believe that they are the masters of their fate and that their actions do affect the outcomes. Likewise, people high in internal locus of responsibility (IR) attribute their current status and life conditions to their own unique attributes; success is due to one's own efforts, and the lack of success is attributed to one's shortcomings or inadequacies. Perhaps the greatest exemplification of the IC-IR philosophy is U.S. society. (Gillin, 1955, describes American cultures as the epitome of the individual-centered approach that emphasizes uniqueness, independence, and self-reliance. A high value is placed on personal resources for solving all problems: self-reliance; pragmatism; individualism; status achievement through one's own effort; and power or control over others, things, animals, and forces of nature. Democratic ideals such as "equal access to opportunity," "liberty and justice for all," "God helps those who help themselves," and "fulfillment of personal destiny" all reflect this world view. The individual is held accountable for all that transpires. Constant and prolonged failure or the inability to attain goals lead to symptoms of self-blame (depression, guilt, and feelings of inadequacy). Most white middle-class members would fall within this quadrant.

Stewart, Danielian, & Festes (1969) and Stewart (1971) have described in detail five American patterns of cultural assumptions and values. These are the building blocks of the IC-IR world view and typically guide our thinking about mental health services in Western society. As we have seen in Chapter 2, these values are manifested in the generic characteristics of counseling. The five systems of assumptions may be described as follows:

1. **Definition of Activity:** Western culture stresses an activity modality of "doing," and the desirable pace of life is fast, busy, and driving. A "being" orientation that stresses a more passive, experiential, and contemplative role is in marked contrast to American values (external achievement, activity, goals, and solutions). Existence is action and not being. Activism is seen most clearly in the mode of problem solving and decision making. Learning is active and not passive. American emphasis is on planning behavior that anticipates consequences.

2. **Definition of Social Relations:** Americans value equality and informality in relating to others. Friendships tend to be many, of short commitment, nonbinding, and shared. In addition, the person's rights and duties in a group are influenced by one's own goals.

Obligation to groups is limited, and value is placed on one's ability to actively influence the group. In contrast, many cultures stress hierarchical rank, formality, and status in interpersonal relations. Friendships are intense, long term, and exclusive. Behavior in a group is dictated by acceptance of the constraints on the group and the authority of the leader.

3. **Motivation:** Achievement and competition are seen as motivationally healthy. The worth of an individual is measured by objective, visible, and materialistic possessions. Personal accomplishments are more important than place of birth, family background, heritage, or traditional status. Achieved status is valued over ascribed status.

4. **Perception of the World:** The world is viewed as distinctly separate from "humankind" and is physical, mechanical, and follows rational laws. Thus the world is viewed as an object to be exploited, controlled, and developed for the material benefit of people. It is assumed that control and exploitation are necessary for the progress of civilized nations.

5. **Perception of the Self and Individual:** The self is seen as separate from the physical world and others. Decision making and responsibility rest with the individual and not the group. Indeed, the group is not a unit but an aggregate of individuals. The importance of a person's identity is refinforced in socialization and education. Autonomy is encouraged, and emphasis is placed on solving one's own problems, acquiring one's own possessions, and standing up for one's own rights.

Counseling Implications   It becomes obvious that Western approaches to counseling occupy the quadrant represented by IC-IR characteristics. Most counselors are of the opinion that people must take major responsibility for their own actions and can improve their lot in life through their own efforts. The epitome of this line of thought is represented by the numerous self-help approaches currently in vogue in our field.

Clients who occupy this quadrant tend to be white middle-class counselees, and, for these counselees, such approaches might be entirely appropriate. In working with clients from different cultures, however, such an approach might be inappropriate. Diaz-Guerrero (1977) in his attempt to build a Mexican psychology presents much data on how Mexicans and U.S. Americans differ with respect to their "views of life." To be actively self-assertive is more characteristic of Anglo-Saxon sociocultural premises than of the Mexican. Indeed, to be actively self-assertive in Mexican socioculture, clinically, forecasts adjustment difficulties. Counselors with a quadrant I orientation are often so culturally encapsulated that they are unable to understand their minority client's (World View). Thus the damage of cultural oppression in counseling becomes an ever-present threat.

External Locus of Control (EC)—Internal Locus of Responsibility (IR)

Individuals who fall into this quadrant are most likely to accept the dominant culture's definition for self-responsibility but to have very little real control over how they are defined by others. The term "marginal man" (person) was first coined by Stonequist (1935) to describe a person who finds himself/herself living on the margins of two cultures and not fully accommodated to either. Although there is nothing inherently pathological about bicultural membership, Jones (1972) feels that Western society has practiced a form of cultural racism by imposing its standards, beliefs, and ways of behaving onto minority groups. Marginal individuals deny the existence of racism; believe that the plight of their own people is due to laziness, stupidity, and a clinging to outdated traditions; reject their own cultural heritage and believe that their ethnicity represents a handicap in Western society; evidence racial self-hatred, accept white social, cultural, and institutional standards; perceive physical features of white men and women as an exemplification of beauty; and are powerless to control their sense of self-worth because approval must come from an external source. As a result, they are high in person-focus and external control.

The key issue here is the dominant-subordinate relationship between two different cultures (Clark & Clark, 1947; Brody, 1963; Derbyshire & Brody, 1964; Freire, 1970; Jackson, 1975; D.W. Sue & D. Sue, 1977a). It is reasonable to believe that members of one cultural group tend to adjust themselves to the group possessing the greater prestige and power to avoid inferiority and feelings. Yet it is exactly this act that creates ambivalence in the minority individual. The pressures for assimilation and acculturation (melting pot theory) are strong, creating possible culture conflicts. Jones (1972) refers to such dynamics as cultural racism: (a) belief in the superiority of one group's cultural heritage—its language, traditions, arts-crafts, and ways of behaving (white) over all others; (b) belief in the inferiority of all other life-styles (nonwhite); and (c) the power to impose such standards onto the less powerful group.

The psychological costs of racism on minorities are immense. Constantly bombarded on all sides by reminders that whites and their way of life are superior and all other life-styles are inferior, many minorities begin to wonder whether they themselves are not somehow inadequate (Kardiner & Ovesey, 1962; Baldwin, 1963; Ellison, 1966; D.W. Sue, 1975), whether members of their own group are not to blame, and whether subordination and segregation are not justified. Clark & Clark (1947) first brought it to the attention of social scientists that racism may contribute to a sense of confused self-identity among Black children. In a study of racial awareness and preference among Black and white children, they found (a) Black children preferred playing with a white doll over a Black one, (b) the Black doll was perceived as being "bad," and (c) approximately one-third, when asked to pick the doll that looked like them, picked the white one.

It is unfortunate that the inferior status of minorities is constantly reinforced and perpetuated by the mass media through television, movies, newspapers, radio, books, and magazines. This contributes to widespread stereotypes that tend to trap minority individuals: Blacks are superstitious, childlike, ignorant, fun loving (Amos and Andy); Mexican Americans are dirty, sneaky, and criminals (Frito Bandido); Asian Americans are sneaky, sly, cunning, passive (Fu Manchu). Such portrayals cause widespread harm to the self-esteem of minorities who may incorporate them. That preconceived expectations can set up self-fulfilling prophesies has been demonstrated by Rosenthal and Jacobson (1968). The incorporation of the larger society's standards may lead minority group members to react negatively toward their own racial and cultural heritage. They may become ashamed of who they are, reject their own group identification, and attempt to identify with the desirable "good" white majority. In the *Autobiography of Malcolm X* (Haley, 1966), Malcolm X relates how he tried desperately to appear as white as possible. He went to painful lengths to straighten and dye his hair so that he would appear more like white males. It is evident that many minorities do come to accept white standards as a means of measuring physical attractiveness, attractiveness of personality, and social relationships. Such an orientation may lead to the phenomenon of racial self-hatred in which people dislike themselves for being Asian, Black, Chicano or Native American.

In the past, mental health professionals have assumed that marginality and self-hatred were internal conflicts of the person almost as if it arises from the individual. In challenging the traditional notion of marginality, Freire (1970) states:

. . . marginality is not by choice, marginal man has been expelled from and kept outside of the social system and is therefore the object of violence. In fact, however, the social structure as a whole does not 'expel,' nor is marginal man a "being outside of" . . .) [Marginal persons] are "beings for another." Therefore the solution to their problem is not to become "beings inside of," but men freeing themselves; for, in reality, they are not marginal to the structure, but oppressed men within it. (pp. 10–11)

It is quite clear that marginal persons are oppressed, have little choice, and are powerless in the face of the dominate-subordinate relationship between the middle-class WASP culture and their own minority culture. According to Freire (1970), if this dominant-subordinate relationship in society were eliminated the phenomenon of marginality would also disappear. For if two cultures exist on a basis of total equality (an ideal for biculturalism) the conflicts of marginality simply do not occur in the person.

Counseling Implications   The psychological dynamics for the EC-IR minority client are likely to reflect his/her marginal and self-hate status. For example, white counselors might be perceived as more competent and preferred than counselors of the client's own race. To EC-IR minority clients, focusing on feelings may be very threatening, since it ultimately may reveal the presence of self-hate and the realization that they cannot escape from their own racial and cultural heritage. A culturally encapsulated white counselor who does not understand the sociopolitical dynamics of the client's concerns may unwittingly perpetuate the conflict. For example, the client's preference for a white counselor, coupled with the counselor's implicit belief in the values of U.S. culture, becomes a barrier to successive and effective counseling. A culturally sensitive counselor needs to (*a*) help the client understand the particular dominant-subordinant political forces that have created this dilemma and (*b*) help the client to distinguish between positive attempts to acculturate and a negative rejection of one's own cultural values.

External Locus of Control (EC)—External Locus of Responsibility (ER)

The inequities and injustices of racism seen in the standard of living tend to be highly damaging to minorities. For example, the standard of living for Asian Americans, Blacks, Chicanos, Native Americans, and Puerto Ricans is much below that enjoyed by whites. Discrimination may be seen in the areas of housing, employment, income, and education. Taeuber (1965) found that in American cities, Black Americans were by far the most segregated of the minorities and that the inferior housing they are confined to is not the result of free choice or poverty but discrimination. This inequity in housing is also applicable to other minorities. D.W. Sue & D. Sue (1973) point out that contrary to popular belief, Chinatowns in San Francisco and New York City represent ghetto areas with high rates of unemployment, suicide, juvenile delinquency, poverty, and tuberculosis. Inferior jobs, high unemployment rates, and a much lower income than their white counterparts are also the plight suffered by other minorities. J. Jones (1972) in analyzing census figures concludes that the Black family's median income is 60% as large as that of the white family's and that a college-educated white person is worth $2668 more annually than a college-educated Black one! Thus lower income cannot be attributed primarily to less education. Haley (1966) concludes that Blacks also suffer from segregated and inferior education: class size, qualification of teachers, physical facilities, and extracurricular activities all place them at a disadvantage. Furthermore, extreme acts of racism can wipe out a minority group (Wrightsman, 1972). Native Americans have witnessed widespread massacres that destroyed their leadership and peoples. This group's population has dropped from 3,000,000 to 600,000, and the life expectancy is 44 years compared to 71 for white Americans. Wrightsman warns that the American Indian may soon disappear from the face of the earth.

A person high in system-blame and external control feels that there is very little one can do in the face of such severe external obstacles as prejudice and discrimination. In essence, the EC response might be a manifestation of (a) having "given up" or (b) an attempt to "placate" those in power. In the former, individuals internalize their impotence even though they are aware of the external basis of their plight. In its extreme form, oppression may result in a form of "learned helplessness" (Seligman, 1975). Seligman believes that humans exposed to helplessness (underemployment, unemployment, poor quality of education, poor housing) via prejudice and discrimination may exhibit passivity and apathy (poor motivation), may fail to learn that there are events which can be controlled (cognitive disruption), and may show anxiety and depression (emotional disturbance). When minorities learn that their responses have minimal effects from the environment, a phenomenon results that can best be described as an expectation of helplessness. People's susceptibility to helplessness depends on their experience with controlling the environment. In the face of continued racism, many may simply give up in their attempts to achieve personal goals. The basic assumption in the theory of learned helplessness is that organisms exposed to prolonged noncontrol in their lives develop expectations of helplessness in later situations. This expectation, unfortunately, occurs even in situations that are now controllable.

The dynamics of the placater, however, is not related to the giving-up response. Rather social forces in the form of prejudice and discrimination are seen as too powerful to combat at that particular time. The best one can hope to do is to suffer the inequities in silence for fear of retaliation. "Don't rock the boat," "keep a low profile," and "survival at all costs" are the phrases that describe this mode of adjustment. Life is viewed as relatively fixed, with nothing much the individual can do. Passivity in the face of oppression is the primary reaction of the placater.

Smith (1977) notes that slavery was one of the most important factors shaping the social-psychological functioning of Black Americans. Interpersonal relations between whites and Blacks were highly structured, placing Blacks in a subservient and inferior role. Those Blacks who broke the rules or did not show proper deferential behavior were severely punished. The spirits, however, of most Blacks were not broken. Conformance to white rules and regulations was dictated by the need to survive in an oppressive environment. Direct expressions of anger and resentment were dangerous; but indirect expressions were frequently seen.

Counseling Implications EC-ER Black clients are very likely to see the white counselor as symbolic of any other Black-white relations. They are likely to show "proper" deferential behavior and to not take seriously admonitions by the counselor that they are the masters of their own fate. As a result, an IC-IR counselor may perceive the culturally different client as lacking in courage and ego-strength and as being passive. A culturally effective counselor, however, would realize the bases of these adaptations. Unlike EC-IR clients, EC-ER individuals do understand the political forces that have subjugated their existence. The most helpful approach on the part of the counselor would be (*a*) to teach the clients new coping strategies, (*b*) to have them experience successes, and (*c*) to validate who and what they represent.

Internal Locus of Control (IC)—External Locus of Responsibility (ER)

Individuals who score high in internal control and system-focus believe in their ability to shape events in their own life if given a chance. They do not accept the fact that their present state is due to their own inherent weakness. However, they also realistically perceive that external barriers of discrimination, prejudice, and exploitation block their paths to the successful attainment of goals. There is a considerable body of evidence to support this contention. Recall that the IC dimension was correlated with greater feelings of personal efficacy, higher aspirations, et cetra, and that ER was related to collective action in the social arena area. If so, we would expect that IC-ER people would be more likely to participate in civil rights activities and to stress racial identity and militancy.

Racial Pride and Identity   Pride in one's racial and cultural identity is most likely to be accepted by an IC-ER person. The low self-esteem engendered by widespread prejudice and racism is actively challenged now by these people. There is an attempt to redefine a group's existence by stressing consciousness and pride in their own racial and cultural heritage. Such phrases as "Black is beautiful" represent a symbolic relabeling of identity from Negro and colored to Black or Afro American. To many Blacks, Negro and colored are white labels symbolic of a warped and degrading identity given them by a racist society. As a means of throwing off these burdensome shackles, the Black individual and Blacks as a group are redefined in a positive light. Many racial minorities have begun the process in some form and banded together into what is called the "Third World Movement" (Asian Americans, Blacks, Chicanos, Native Americans, and others). Since all minorities share the common experience of oppression, they have formed alliances to expose and alleviate the damage that racism has dealt. Problems like poverty, unemployment, housing, education, juvenile delinquency, and emotional problems are seen as arising from racism in society. Third World people have attempted to enhance feelings of group pride by emphasizing the positive aspects of their cultural heritage. That such an approach might be having great impact can be seen in a study by Hraba and Grant (1969). These two investigators replicated the 1947 doll study preference by Clark and Clark and found that Black children are no longer white oriented. Studies by others (Caplan & Paige, 1968; Caplan, 1970; Forward & Williams, 1970; Abeles, 1976; Turner & Wilson, 1976) also support the contention that racial solidarity among Blacks is increasing. This has led some to state that a "New Ghetto Man," committed to the removal of traditional racial restraints and who evidences racial consciousness, is on the rise.

Militancy   Another area seemingly in support of the IC-ER world view was intimately related to the concept of militancy and collective social action. Between 1964 and 1968 there were 239 violent riots, with racial overtones resulting in 8000 casualties, 191 dead, mostly Black (National Commission on the Causes and Prevention of Violence, 1969). These events occurred in epidemic proportions that left the American people dazed and puzzled. Rochester (1964), Chicago

(1965), Los Angeles (1965), Cleveland (1966), Detroit (1967), and Newark (1967), to name a few, were all struck by a seemingly senseless wave of collective violence in the Black ghettos. Confrontations between the police and Blacks, lootings, snipings, assaults, and burning of homes and property filled the television screens in every American home. In light of these frightened events, many people searched for explanations about what had happened. The basis of the riots did not make sense in terms of rising income, better housing, and better education for Blacks in America. After all, reasoned many, conditions have never been better for Black Americans. Why should they riot?

When the 1960s riots are studied, two dominant explanations seem to arise. The first called the "riffraff theory" (person-blame) explained the riots as the result of the sick, criminal elements of the society: the emotionally disturbed, deviants, communist agitators, criminals, or unassimilated migrants. These agitators were seen as peripheral to organized society and possessing no broad social or political concerns. The agitators' frustrations and militant confrontation were seen as part of their own *personal* failures and inadequacies.

A second explanation referred to as the "blocked-opportunity theory" (system-blame) views riot participants as those with high aspirations for their own lives and believe in their ability to achieve these goals. However, environmental forces rather than their own personal inadequacies prevent them from advancing to the society and bettering their condition. The theory holds that riots are the result of massive discrimination against Blacks that have frozen them out of the social, economic, and political life of America. Caplan & Paige (1968) found that more rioters than nonrioters reported experiencing job obstacles and discrimination which blocked their mobility. Further probing revealed that it was not lack of training or education that accounted for the results. Fogelson (1970) presents data in support of the thesis that the ghetto riots are manifestations of grievances within a racist society. In referring to the riots he states that the rioting "was triggered not only because the rioters issued the protest and faced the danger together but also because the rioting revealed the common fate of blacks in America. For most blacks, and particularly northern blacks, racial discrimination is a highly personal experience. They are denied jobs, refused apartments, stopped-and-searched, and declared ineducable—or so they are told—they are inexperienced, unreliable, suspicious, and culturally deprived—and not because they are black" (p. 145).

The recognition that ghetto existence is a result of racism and not to some inherent weakness, coupled with the rioters' belief in their ability to control events in their own lives, made a situation ripe for the venting of frustration and anger. Several studies support the contention that those who rioted have an increased sense of personal effectiveness and control (Gore & Rotter, 1963; Marx, 1967; Caplan & Paige, 1968; Caplan, 1970; Forward & Williams 1970; Abeles, 1976). Indeed, a series of studies concerning characteristics of the rioters and nonrioters failed to confirm the riffraff theory (Caplan & Paige, 1968; Caplan, 1970; Forward & Williams 1970; Turner & Wilson, 1976). In general, the following profile of those who engaged in rioting during the 1960s emerged: (*a*) rioters did not differ from nonrioters in income and rate of unemployment, so they appear to be no more poverty stricken, jobless, or lazy; (*b*) those who riot are generally better educated, so rioting cannot be attributed to the poorly educated; (*c*) rioters are better integrated than nonrioters in social and political workings of the community; thus the lack of integration into political and social institutions cannot be used as an explanation; (*d*) long-term residents were more likely to riot, so rioting cannot be blamed on outside agitators or recent immigrants; (*e*) rioters held more positive attitudes toward Black history and culture (feelings of racial pride) and thus are not alienated from themselves. Caplan (1970) concluded that militants are no more socially or personally deviant than their nonmilitant counterparts. Evidence tends to indicate that they are more "healthy" along several traditional criteria measuring mental health. Caplan also believes that attempts to use the riffraff theory to explain riots have an underlying motive. By attributing causes to individual deficiencies, the users of the riffraff theory relieve white institutions of the blame. Such a conceptualization means that psychotherapy, social work, mental hospitalization, or imprisonment should be directed toward the militants. Demands for systems-change are declared illegitimate because they are the products of "sick" or "confused" minds. Maintenance of the status quo rather than needed social change (social therapy) is reaffirmed.

Counseling Implications.   There is much evidence to indicate that minority groups are becoming increasingly conscious of their own racial and cultural identities as they relate to oppression in U.S. society (Fogelson, 1970; D.W. Sue, 1975; Turner & Wilson, 1976). If the evidence is correct it is also probable that more and more minorities are most likely to hold an IC-ER world view. Thus counselors who work with the culturally different will increasingly be exposed to clients with an IC-ER world view. And, in many respects, these clients pose the most difficult problems for the IC-IR white counselor. Challenges to the counselor's credibility and trustworthiness are likely to be raised by these clients. The counselor is likely to be seen as a part of the Establishment that has oppressed minorities. Self-disclosure on the part of the client is not likely to come quickly, and, more than any other world view, clients with an IC-ER orientation are likely to play a much more active part in the counseling process and to demand action from the counselor.

The theory being proposed here predicts several things about the differences between IC-IR and IC-ER world views in counseling. First, these two world views may dicate how a counselor and client define problems and how they use and are receptive to different styles of counseling. For example, IC-IR people will tend to see the problem as residing in the person, while IC-ER people will see the problem as being external to the individual. Furthermore, IC-ER counselors may use and are most receptive to counseling skills, styles, or approaches that are action oriented. This is in contrast to IC-IR counselors who may be more nondirective in their interaction with clients. Two particular studies seem to bear out these predictions.

Ivey (1977) cites the example of a study conducted by one of his doctoral students who compared Black and white counselor trainees viewing videovignettes of Black and white clients. The clients presented problems related to vocational choice. To a question of "What would you say next?" white males tended to ask questions, white females tended to reflect feelings and to paraphrase, and Blacks tended to give advice and directions. More important, Blacks identified the problem as being in society rather than in the individual, whereas whites tended to focus more on the individual. The assumption being made is that the Blacks in this study are most likely IC-ER counselor trainees. A similar study conducted by Atkinson, Marujama & Matsui (1978) with Asian Americans also revealed consistent findings. The more politically conscious Asian American (IC-ER) rated the counselor as more credible and approachable when using a directive (structure, advice, suggestions) rather than nondirective (reflection and paraphrase) approach.

CONCLUSIONS

The conceptual model presented in this chapter concerning world views and identity development among Third World groups is consistent with other formulations (Hall, Cross, & Freedle, 1972; Jackson, 1975; D.W. Sue, 1975). In all cases, these writers believe that cultural identity for minorities in America is intimately related to racism and oppression. Using this model in counseling culturally different clients has many practical and research implications.

1. It is obvious that counseling in the United States falls into the IC-IR quadrant. Clients are seen as able to intiate change and are held responsible for their current plight. A counselor operating from this frameowrk will most likely be person centered. While such a world view is not necessarily incorrect or bad, it may be inappropriately applied to clients who do not share this perception. When counselors are culturally/sociopolitically blind and impose their world views on clients without regard for the legitimacy of other views, they are engaging in a form of cultural oppression.

    Therefore, what is needed is for counselors to become culturally aware, to understand the basis of their world views, and to understand and accept the possible legitimacy of others. Only when counselor education programs begin to incorporate cross-cultural concepts in their training (not from a white perspective but from the perspective of each culture) will counseling possibly lose its oppressive orientation.

2. Another implication from this conceptual model is its use as an aid to understanding possible psychological dynamics of a culturally different client. For example, an EC-IR client who experiences self-hatred and marginalty may be a victim of the dominant-subordinant relationship fostered in American society. The problem is not inherent or internal, and counseling may be aimed at a reeducative process to get that client to become aware of the wider social-political forces at the basis of his or her plight.

    An EC-ER person, whether he or she has given up or is placating, must be taught new coping skills to deal with people and institutions. Experiences of success are critically important for clients in this quadrant.

    IC-ER clients are especially difficult for counselors to handle, because challenges to counseling as an act of oppression are most likely to arise. A counselor who is not in touch with these wider social-political issues will quickly lose credibility and effectiveness. In addition, IC-ER clients are externally oriented, and demands for the counselor to take external action on the part of the client will be strong (setting up a job interview, helping the client fill out forms, etc.). While most of us have been taught not to intervene externally on behalf of the client, all of us must look seriously at the value base of this dictate.

3. It is highly probable that problem definitions and specific counseling skills are differentially associated with a particular world view. One reason why Third World clients may prematurely terminate

counseling (D. Sue, 1977) is the fact that counselors not only differ in world views, but also use counseling skills inappropriate to their clients' life-styles. Our next step would be to research the following questions: "Are there specific counseling goals, techniques, and skills best suited for a particular world view?" If so, the implications for counselor training are important. First, this indicates an overwhelming need to teach trainees the importance of being able to understand and share the world views of their clients. Second, it is no longer enough to learn a limited number of counseling skills. Ivey (1977) makes a strong case for this position. The culturally effective counselor is one who is able to generate the widest repertoire of responses (verbal/nonverbal) consistent with the life-styles and values of the culturally different client. Particularly for minorities, the passive approaches of asking questions, reflecting feelings, and paraphrasing must be balanced with directive responses (giving advice and suggestions, disclosing feelings, etc.) on the part of the counselor.

4. The counselor needs to understand that each world view has much to offer that is positive. While these four psychological orientations have been described in a highly evaluative manner, positive aspects of each can be found. For example, the individual responsibility and achievement orientation of quadrant I, biculturalism and cultural flexibility of quadrant II, ability to compromise and adapt to life conditions of quadrant III, and collective action and social concern of quadrant IV need not be at odds with one another. The role of the counselor may be to help the client integrate aspects of each world view that will maximize his/her effectiveness and psychological well-being. Ivey (1977) calls this person the "culturally effective individual." He/she is a "functional integrator" who is able to combine and integrate aspects of each world view into a harmonious union. To accomplish this goal, however, means the counselor is also able to share the world view of his/her clients. In essence, the culturally skilled counselor is also one who is a functional integrator.

SOME CAUTIONS

In closing, there are some precautions that should be exercised in using this model. First, the validity of this model has not been directly established through research. While much empirical and clinical evidence are consistent with the model, many of the assertions in this chapter remain at the speculative level. Second, the behavior manifestations of each quadrant have not been specifically identified. Regardless of a person's psychological orientation, I would suspect that individuals can adapt and use behaviors associated with another world view. This, indeed, is the basis of training counselors to work with the culturally different. Third, each style represents conceptual categories. In reality, while people might tend to hold one world view in preference to another, it does not negate them from holding variations of others. Most Third World people represent mixes of each rather than a pure standard. Fourth, whether this conceptual model can be applied to groups other than minorities in America has yet to be established. Last, we must remember that it is very possible for individuals from different cultural groups to be more similar in world view than those from the same culture. While race and ethnicity may be correlated with one's outlook in life, the correspondence certainly is not one-to-one.

REFERENCES

Abeles, R.P. Relative deprivation, rising expectations and Black militancy. *Journal of Social Issues*, 1976, **32**, 119–137.

Atkinson, D.R., Marujama, M. & Matsui, S. The effects of counselor race and counseling approach on Asian Americans' perceptions of counselor credibility and utility. *Journal of Counseling Psychology*, 1978, **25**, 76–83.

Avis, J.P., & Stewart, L.H. College counseling: Intentions and change. *Counseling Psychologist*, 1976, **6**, 74–77.

Baldwin, J. *The Fire Next Time*. New York: Dial Press, 1963.

Battle, E., & Rotter, J. Children's feelings of personal control as related to social class and ethnic group. *Journal of Personality*, 1963, **31**, 482–490.

Brody, E.B. Color and identity conflict in young boys. *Psychiatry*, 1963, **26**, 188–201.

Bryde, J. F. *Indian Students and Guidance*. Boston: Houghton Mifflin, 1971.

Caplan, N. The new ghetto man: A review of recent empirical studies. *Journal of Social Issues*, 1970, **26**, 59–73.

Caplan, N., & Nelson, S. D. On being useful—the nature and consequences of psychological research on social problems. *American Psychologist*, 1973, **28**, 199–211.

Caplan, N., & Paige, J. M. A study of ghetto rioters. *Scientific American*, August 1968, **219**, 15–21.

Clark, K. B., & Clark, M. K. Racial identification and preference in Negro children. In T. M. Newcomb & E. L. Hartley (Eds.), *Readings in Social Psychology* New York: Holt, Reinhart & Winston, 1947.

Crandall, V., Katkovsky, W., & Crandall, V. Children's beliefs in their own control of reinforcements in intellectual achievement situations. *Child Development*, 1965, **36**, 91–109.

Derbyshire, R. L., & Brody, E. B. Marginality, identity and behavior in the Negro: A functional analysis. *International Journal of Social Psychiatry*, 1964, **10**, 7–13.

Diaz-Guerrero, R. A Mexican psychology. *American Psychologist*. 1977, **32**, 934–944.

Ellison, R. Harlem is nowhere. In *Shadow and Act*. New York: Random House, 1966.

Fogelson, R. M. Violence and grievances: Reflections on the 1960's riots. *Journal of Social Issues*, 1970, **26**, 141–163.

Forward, J. R., & Williams, J. R. International external control and Black militancy. *Journal of Social Issues*, 1970, **26**, 75–92.

Freire, P. *Cultural Action for Freedom*. Cambridge: Harvard Educational Review Press, 1970.

Garcia, C., & Levenson, H. Differences between black's and white's expectations of control by chance and powerful others. *Psychological Reports*, 1975, **37**, 563–566.

Gillin, J. National and regional cultural values in the United States. *Social Forces*, 1955, **34**, 107–113.

Gore, P. M., & Rotter, J. B. A personality correlate of social action. *Journal of Personality*, 1963, **31**, 58–64.

Gurin, P., Gurin, G., Lao, R., & Beattie, M. Internal-external control in the motivational dynamics of Negro youth. *Journal of Social Issues*, 1969, **25**, 29–54.

Haley, A. *The Autobiography of Malcom X*. New York: Grove Press, 1966.

Hall, W. S., Cross, W. E., & Freedle, R. Stages in the development of Black awareness: An exploratory investigation. In R. L. Jones (Ed.), *Black Psychology*. New York: Harper & Row, 1972.

Halleck, S. L. Therapy is the handmaiden of the status quo. *Psychology Today*, 1971, **4**, 30–34, 98–100.

Hersch, P., & Scheibe, K. Reliability and validity of internal-external control as a personality dimension. *Journal of Consulting Psychology*, 1967, **31**, 609–613.

Hraba, J., & Grant, G. Black is beautiful: A reexamination of racial preference and identification. *Journal of Personality and Social Psychology*, 1969, **16**, 398–402.

Hsieh, T., Shybut, J., & Lotsof, E. Internal versus external control and ethnic group membership: A cross-cultural comparison. *Journal of Consulting and Clinical Psychology*, 1969, **33**, 122–124.

Ivey, A. Toward a definition of the culturally effective counselor. *Personnel and Guidance Journal*, 1977, **55**, 296–302.

Jackson, B. Black identity development. *Journal of Education Diversity*, 1975, **2**, 19–25.

Jones, E. E., Kanouse, D., Kelley, H. H., Nisbett, R. E., Valins, S., & Weiner, B. (Eds.) *Attribution: Perceiving the Causes of Behavior*. Morristown, N.J.: General Learning Press 1972.

Jones, J. M. *Prejudice and Racism*. Reading, Mass.: Addison-Wesley, 1972.

Kardiner, A., & Ovesey, L. *The Mark of Oppression*. New York: Norton, 1962.

Lefcourt, H. Internal versus control of reinforcement: A review. *Psychological Bulletin*, 1966, **65**, 206–220.

Levenson, H. Activism and powerful others. *Journal of Personality Assessment*, 1974, **38**, 377–383.

Marx, G. T. *Protest and Prejudice: A Study of Belief in the Black Community*. New York: Harper & Row, 1967.

Mirels, H. Dimensions of internal versus external control. *Journal of Consulting and Clinical Psychology*, 1970, **34**, 226–228.

National Commission on the Causes and Prevention of Violence. *To Establish Justice, to Insure Domestic Tranqulity*. New York: Award Books, 1969.

Pine, G. J. Counseling minority groups: A review of the literature. *Counseling and Values*, 1972, **17**, 35–44.

Rotter, J. Some problems and misconceptions related to the construct of internal versus external control of reinforcement. *Journal of Consulting and Clinical Psychology*, 1975, **43**, 56–67.

Rotter, J. Generalized expectancies for internal versus external control of reinforcement. *Psychological Monographs*, 1966, **80**, 1–28.

Rosenthal, R. & Jacobsen, L. Self-fulfilling prophecies in the classroom. In M. Deutsch, K. Katz, & A. R. Jensen (Eds.), *Social Class, Race and Psychological Development*, 1968, **21**, 219–253.

Ruiz, R. A., & Padilla, A. M. Counseling Latinos. *Personnel and Guidance Journal*, 1977, **55**, 401–408.

Sanger, S. P., & Alker, H. A. Dimensions of internal-external locus of control and the women's liberation movement. *Journal of Social Issues*, 1972, **28**, 115–129.

Seligman, M. E. P. *Helplessness: On Depression, Development and Death*. San Francisco: Freeman, 1975.

Smith, E. J. Counseling Black individuals: Some sterotypes. *Personnel and Guidance Journal*, 1977, **55**, 390–396.

Stewart, E. C. *American Cultural Patterns: A Cross-Cultural Perspective*. Pittsburgh: Regional Council for International Understanding, 1971.

Stewart, E. C., Danielian, J., & Festes, R. J. *Stimulating intercultural communication through role playing* (Hum RRO Tech. Rep. 69–67). Alexandria, Va.: Human Resources Research Organization, May 1969.

Stonequist, E. The problem of the marginal man. *American Journal of Sociology*, 1935, **41**, 1–12.

Strickland, B. Aspiration responses among Negro and white adolescents. *Journal of Personality and Social Psychology*, 1971, **19**, 315–320.

Strickland, B. Delay of gratification and internal locus of control in children. *Journal of Consulting and Clinical Psychology*, 1973, **40**, 338.

Sue, D. Counseling the culturally different: A conceptual analysis. *Personnel and Guidance Journal*, 1977, **55**, 422–426.

Sue, D. W. Asian Americans: Social-psychological forces affecting their life styles. In S. Picou & R. Campbell (Eds.), *Career Behavior of Special Groups*. Columbus, O.: Charles E. Merrill, 1975.

Sue, D. W., & Sue, D. Barriers to effective cross-cultural counseling. *Journal of Counseling Psychology*, September 1977, **24**, 420–429.

Sue, D. W. & Sue, D. Understanding Asian Americans: The neglected minority. *Personnel and Guidance Journal*, 1973, **51**, 386–389.

Sue, D. W., & Sue, S. Ethnic minorities: Resistance to being researched. *Professional Psychology*, 1972, **2**, 11–17.

Szasz, T. S. The crime of commitment. *Readings in Clinical Psychology Today*. Del Mar, Calif.: CRM Books, 1970, 167–169.

Taeuber, K. E. Residential segregation. *Scientific American*, 1965, **213**, 12–19.

Trimble, J. E. Value differences among American Indians: Concerns for the concerned counselor. In P. Pedersen, W. J. Lonner, & J. G. Draguns (Eds.), *Counseling Across Cultures*. Honolulu: East-West Center, 1976, 65–81.

Tulkin, S. Race, class, family and school achievement. *Journal of Personality and Social Psychology*, 1968, **9**, 31–37.

Turner, C. B., & Wilson, W. J. Dimension of racial ideology: A study of urban Black attitudes. *Journal of Social Issues*, 1976, **32**, 193–252.

Wolfgang, A. Cross-cultural comparison of locus of control, optimism towards the future, and time horizon among Italian, Italo-Canadian, and new Canadian youth. Proceedings of the 81st Annual Convention of the American Psychological Association, 1973, **8**, 229–300.

Wrightsman, L. S. *Social Psychology in the Seventies*. Monterey, Calif.: Brooks Cole, 1972.

5
The Culturally
Skilled Counselor

We have come a long way in our discussion of counseling and the culturally different. It seems important, therefore, that we try to pull together earlier concepts into an integrated picture of relevant processes/goals in cross-cultural counseling and present some propositions which may (a) predict effective cross-cultural counseling and (b) describe characteristics of the culturally skilled counselor.

RELEVANT PROCESSES AND GOALS IN CROSS-CULTURAL

Thus far we have emphasized the necessity of the counselor working with a culturally different client to (a) be aware of the sociopolitical forces that have impacted the minority client; (b) understand that culture, class, and language factors can act as barriers to effective cross-cultural counseling; (c) point out how expertness, trustworthiness, and lack of similarity influences the minority client's receptivity to change/influence; and (d) emphasize the importance of world views/cultural identity in the counseling process. All these variables seem to imply one thing: counseling culturally different clients may require a different combination of skills (process) and goals. Yet the question still remains "How do we determine relevant processes and goals in cross-cultural counseling?" While a specific answer would not be possible, D.V. Sue (1977) has presented a conceptual model that may be of help in answering this question.

To be more responsive to the culturally different, we must begin the

Permission granted to reproduce any or all of the following article: D. W. Sue, Counseling the culturally different: A conceptual analysis. *Personnel and Guidance Journal*, 1977, **55**, 422, 424 much-needed task of systematically determining the appropriateness or inappropriateness of counseling approaches. Counselor education programs, mental health delivery systems, and counselors must take major responsibility to examine and evaluate the relevance of their particular theoretical framework with respect to the client's needs and values. This statement implies several things. First, there must be a knowledge of minority group cultures and experiences. The earlier chapters were attempts to provide insights into this area for mental health practitioners. Furthermore, each of the individual chapters on Native Americans, Asian Americans, Blacks, and Hispanics, in this book is designed to address this point.

Second, we must make clear and explicit the generic characteristics of counseling and the particular value assumptions inherent in the different schools of thought. Third, when these two aspects of our work are complete, we can compare and contrast them to see which approaches are (*a*) consistent, (*b*) conflicting, or (*c*) new to one another. Implicit in these statements is the assumption that different cultural and subcultural groups require different approaches. From there, a decision can be made about how to work with a culturally different individual.

Figure 5.1 reveals four conditions that may arise when counseling a person from a different culture. This schema is proposed as one approach to looking at counseling and the culturally different. As Ivey & Authier (1978) point out, the model can also be used for examining the appropriateness of alternative theoretical models of counseling for different individuals within a single culture.

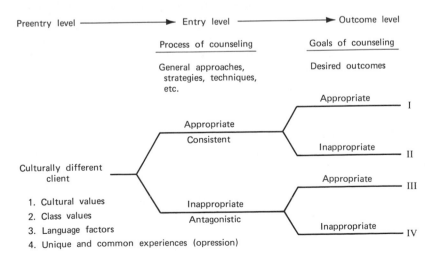

At the preentry level, culturally different clients inherit a whole constellation of cultural and class values, language factors, and life experiences. Further, the counselor is also a product of his or her culture, class, language, and experiences. This will influence the counseling activity as well as the particular school of counseling chosen by the counselor. On entering the "process of counseling," counselors choose a general approach, style, or strategy in working with clients. All theories of counseling rely heavily on some basic techniques (existentialists may disagree) in the therapeutic session. Closely linked to the actual process of counseling are certain implicit or explicit goals: insight, self-actualization, behavior change; or there may be more specific goals: studying better, dealing with aggression, or interviewing for jobs. As can be seen in Figure 5.1, a culturally different client may be exposed to one of four conditions: (I) appropriate process, appropriate goals; (II) appropriate process, inappropriate goals; (III) inappropriate process, appropriate goals; (IV) inappropriate process, inappropriate goals.

Condition I—Appropriate Process, Appropriate Goals

In condition I, the client is exposed to a counseling process that is consistent with his or her values and life experiences. A Black male student from the ghetto who is failing in school and getting into fights with other students can be treated by the counselor in a variety of ways. Sometimes, such a student lacks the academic skills necessary to get good grades. The constant fighting is a result of peers teasing him about his "stupidity." A counselor who is willing to teach the student study and test-taking skills as well as give advice and information may be using an appropriate process consistent with the expectations of the student. The appropriate goals defined between counselor and client, besides acquisition of specific skills, may be an elevation of grades. Notice that this particular activity of counseling (teaching, giving advice, etc.) is not traditionally seen as a legitimate part of it. Calia (1968) points out that in working with the culturally different, counselors must break away from their narrow definition of counseling activities. Lorion (1974) concludes that the expectations of the lower-class client are different from those of therapists. Lower-class clients are concerned more with survival and making it through on a day-to-day basis. They expect immediate, concrete suggestions and advice. Getting job interviews for clients, teaching specific educational skills, and helping clients to understand and fill out unemployment forms may be the desired and preferred help. Thus a counselor who uses counseling strategies that make sense to the client (consistent with his or her values) and defines suitable goals will be an effective and helpful one.

A study reported by Berman (1979) seems to lend credence to the fact that different groups and individuals need varying helping approaches and goals. Groups of white males, white females, and Third World people were shown videotapes of Black and white clients presenting job-related counseling problems. Observers were asked to write down what they would say at the end of the tape. It was found that white males ask more questions, white females use more reflection and paraphrasing, and Third World groups give more advice and make more interpretations. In addition, the locus of the problem was seen differentially by white and Black groups. White subjects tended to place greater emphasis on the individual, while Blacks more often stressed the cultural/societal dimensions. Atkinson, Maruyama, & Matsui (1978) also found evidence to support the fact that people of varying cultural backgrounds respond differently to the use of different counseling skills.

Condition II—Appropriate Process, Inappropriate Goals

Oftentimes, a counseling strategy may be chosen by the counselor that is compatible with the client's values, but the goals the strategy will help achieve are questionable. Let us again take the forementioned example of the Black ghetto student. Here the counselor may define the goal as the elimination of "fighting behavior." The technique chosen may be behavior modification. Since the approach stresses observable behaviors and provides a systematic, precise, and structured approach to the "problem," much of the nebulousness and mystique of counseling are reduced for the Black student. Rather than introspection and self-analysis that many Third World people find unappealing, the concrete tangible approach of behavioral counseling is extremely attractive. While the approach may be a positive experience for many minorities, there is danger here regarding control and behavioral objectives. If the Black student is being teased and forced to fight because he is a minority group member, then the goal of "stopping fighting behavior" may be inappropriate. The counselor in this situation may inadvertently be imposing his or her own standards and values on the client. The end goals place the problem in the hands of the individual rather than society, which produced the problem. Steiner (1975) and Bardo, Bryson, & Cody (1974) have termed these approaches "pacification programs."

To what extent does the client assume responsibility for deciding the direction of change? To what extent is the counselor forcing the client to adapt or adjust to a "sick" situation that ought to be changed? These are not easy questions to answer. They point out the complexity of certain social issues in counseling and the concern that many have of the "Clockwork Orange" type of society.

Condition III—Inappropriate Process, Appropriate Goals

More often than not, counselors tend to use inappropriate strategies in working with the culturally different. Early termination of counseling is most likely to occur when the process is antagonistic to the values of the client and forces him or her to violate some basic personal values. The counselor with the best of intentions and appropriate goals may fail because the process is incompatible with values of the client. For example, many Native Americans view the person as harmonious with nature. The world is accepted in its present form without undue attempts to change it (Trimble, 1976; Good Tracks, 1973). Unlike Native American society, Anglos are concerned with controlling and mastering the physical world. The more nature is controlled, the better. Native Americans who may operate under the principle of "noninterference" find coercion and the use of suggestions in counseling as rude, ill mannered, and hostile. Good Tracks (1973) states: "The Indian child is taught that complete noninterference in interaction with all people is the norm, and that he should react with amazement, irritation, mistrust, and anxiety to even the slightest indication of manipulation or coercion" (p. 31).

The counselor who leans heavily on some form of intervention like the behavioral techniques may be seen as coercive and manipulative. Native American clients exposed to counselors who stress individual responsibility for changing and mastering the environment are, in effect, asking their clients to violate a basic value. This may be one reason why Native Americans have such a high drop-out rate in our educational system.

Another example given by Ivey & Authier (1978) illustrates this condition with respect to client-centered counseling. The Rogerian conditions of respect for individuals, empathy, genuiness, and warmth may be very compatible with the values of many Third World people. However, the Rogerian process of paraphrasing, reflecting feelings, and summarizing can be incompatible with cultural patterns. Blacks, for example, may find the patient waiting and reflective type of a nondirective technique to be antagonistic to their values. Furthermore, empathy is difficult to establish when the counselor does not understand Black idioms, nonverbal modes of expression, and traditions and values of a Black life-style. In this case, other techniques to arrive at empathy may be called for. Harper (1973) contends that if a counselor is to be effective with Blacks, techniques that bring a client to a level of awareness and action would be best. Directive, confrontive, and persuasive approaches are more compatible.

There is some question about whether it is possible to use an inappropriate process to arrive at an appropriate goal. If a client, for whatever reason, stays in the counseling relationship, then does not his or her being exposed to a process that violates a basic value change the person? Can the client ever attain an appropriate goal? If we look only at the techniques and goals of different counseling theories, then the answer may appear to be yes. For example, Gestalt approaches emphasize the end goals of the "here and now" (present-time orientation) and getting in touch with bodily feelings. These goals may appear consistent with Native American values. Yet the body of techniques used in Gestalt counseling tends to be confrontive and controlling, actions that may prove embarrassing to Indian clients. The problem with looking solely at a particular theory is that doing such is "static." Counseling is a dynamic process, an activity that is ongoing. The relationships between process and goals are highly interrelated and complex. The question of whether condition III can ever exist cannot be easily answered. If the answer, however, is yes, then another issue presents itself: Do the ends justify the means?

Condition IV—Inappropriate Process, Inappropriate Goals

Approaches that are clearly inappropriate in terms of techniques and goals most generally lead to early termination of counseling. For example, Asian American clients who may value restraint of strong feelings and believe that intimate revelations are to be shared with only close friends may cause problems for the insight- or feeling-oriented counselor. Not only are the techniques inappropriate (reflecting feelings, asking questions of a deeply personal nature, making depth interpretations, and so on) and seen as lacking in respect for the client's integrity, but also the goal of insight into deep underlying processes may not be valued by the person. For example, Asian American clients who come for vocational information may be perceived by counselors as needing help in finding out what motivates their actions and decisions. Requests for advice or information from the client are seen as indicative of deeper more personal conflicts. Although this may be true in some cases, the blind application of techniques that clash with cultural values and the rigid adherence to a goal such as insight seriously places many Asian Americans at a disadvantage. This analysis indicates three important things. First, it is important for counselors to attend to group differences in working with racial or ethnic minorities. A culturally skilled counselor is one who is able to relate to minority group experiences and has knowledge of cultural and class factors. Second, counselors need to recognize that working with individuals from different cultures dictates not the same approach but a differential one consistent with life-styles. In counseling, equal treatment may be discriminatory. Third, it is important to systematically look at racial and ethnic differences as they relate to (*a*) the counselor's own approach and values and (*b*) the various schools of counseling. One way we can do this is to understand more clearly what we do in counseling (process) and what particular goals we hold for clients. It is hoped that a comparative analysis as proposed in Figure 5.1 will lead to a more realistic appraisal of the appropriateness of counseling approaches (psychoanalysis, Gestalt, behavior modification, client-centered approaches) in working with the culturally different.

CROSS-CULTURAL COUNSELING EFFECTIVENESS: SOME PROPOSITIONS

In this section, we put forth two propositions that seem to be important in determining cross-cultural counseling effectiveness. They are directly derived from the first four chapters. Our intent is to extract from these propositions, characteristics that describe the culturally skilled counselor.

Proposition I   *Cross-cultural counseling effectiveness is most likely to be enhanced when the counselor and client share the same world view. World views are frequently correlated with a person's cultural/racial heritage, ethnic identification, and experiences in society. As a result, the credibility and attractiveness of the counselor is likely to be high.*

Important in this proposition are several key elements. First, a counselor who shares the client's world view is most likely to use processes and to define goals in counseling consistent with the person's life-style. Thus counseling is likely to be seen as highly relevant and appropriate. Second, since similarity of world views is highly correlated with a person's cultural/racial heritage, ethnic identification, belief, and understanding are likely to be high. This facilitates the identification set and makes the counselor highly attractive and influential. Possible misunderstandings and fears of being misunderstood are minimized. Third, expertness and trustworthiness are more likely to be imputed to the counselor thus minimizing challenges and maximizing influence.

Proposition Ia   *All things being equal, attitudinal/belief similarity will tend to facilitate cross-cultural counseling because it enhances counselor credibility and attractiveness.*

Proposition Ib   *All things being equal, membership group similarity will tend to facilitate cross-cultural counseling because it enhances counselor credibility and attractiveness.*

Proposition Ic   *Whether membership group similarity is more important than attitudinal similarity in cross-cultural counseling depends on the client's minority identity development.*

Propositions Ia, Ib, and Ic recognize the importance of racial/cultural and belief similarity in cross-cultural counseling. The last proposition introduces the possibility that attitudinal similarity may be a more powerful determinant of counseling effectiveness than membership group similarity (under certain conditions). Chapters 3 and 4 discussed minority identity development in terms of stages involving self-rejection and racial self-hatred to conform with cultural differences. Obviously, clients who see their ethnicity and race as a handicap to be overcome and whose reference group is white Americans will respond more to belief similarity in the majority counselor. Also, clients who feel comfortable with being bicultural may also prefer a counselor who is similar to them in terms of beliefs.

Implications

These assumptions underscore the importance of the counselor understanding and being able to share the world view of his/her clients. This statement does not mean counselors have to *hold* these world views as their own. Rather it means that the counselor is able to see and accept, in a nonjudgmental manner, the legitimacy of alternative ways to view the world. This implies several things that make for a culturally skilled counselor.

1.   *The culturally skilled counselor is one who has moved from being culturally unaware to being aware and sensitive to his/her own cultural baggage.* Culturally skilled counselors have moved from

ethnocentrism to valuing and respecting differences. Other cultures are seen as being equally valuable as their own. A culturally unaware counselor is most likely to impose his/her values onto a minority client.

2. *A culturally skilled counselor is aware of his/her own values and biases and how they may affect minority clients.* He or she constantly attempts to avoid prejudice, unwarranted labeling, and stereotyping. He or she tries not to hold preconceived limitations/ notions about his or her minority clients. As a check on this process, culturally skilled counselors monitor their functioning via consultation, supervision, and continual education.

3. *The culturally skilled counselor will have a good understanding of the sociopolitical system's operation in the United States with respect to its treatment of minorities.* Understanding the impact and operation of oppression (racism, sexism, etc.), the politics of counseling, and the racist concepts that have permeated the mental health/helping professions are important. Especially valuable for the counselor is an understanding of the role cultural racism plays in the development of identity and world views among minority groups.

4. *A culturally skilled counselor is one who is comfortable with differences that exist between the counselor and client in terms of race and beliefs.* Differences are not seen as being deviant! The culturally skilled counselor does not profess "color blindness" or negate the existence of differences that exist in attitudes/beliefs. The basic concept underlying color blindness was the humanity of all people. Regardless of color or other physical differences, each individual is equally human. While its intent was to eliminate bias from counseling, color blindness has served to deny the existence of differences in clients' perceptions of society arising from membership in different racial groups. The message tends to be "I will like you only if you are the same" instead of "I like you because of your differences."

5. *The culturally skilled counselor is sensitive to circumstances (personal biases, stage of ethnic identity, sociopolitical influences, etc.; that may dictate referral of the minority client to a member of his/her own race/culture.* A culturally skilled counselor is aware of his/her limitations in cross-cultural counseling and is not threatened by the prospect of referring a client.

Proposition II *Cross-cultural counseling effectiveness is most likely to be enhanced when the counselor uses counseling modalities and* *defines goals consistent with the life experiences/cultural values of the client.*

This has been a basic premise that we have repeatedly emphasized throughout this chapter. Studies have consistently revealed that (*a*) economically and educationally disadvantaged clients may not be oriented toward "talk therapy"; (*b*) self-disclosure may be incompatible with cultural values of Asian Americans, Chicanos, and Native Americans; (*c*) the sociopolitical atmosphere may dictate against self-disclosure; (*d*) the ambiguous nature of counseling may be antagonistic to life values of the minority client; and (*e*) many minority clients prefer an active/directive approach to an inactive/nondirective one in counseling. Counseling has too long assumed that clients share a similar background and cultural heritage and that the same approaches with all clients are equally effective. This is an erroneous assumption that needs to be buried.

Because groups and individuals differ from one another, the blind application of techniques to *all* situations and *all* populations seems ludicrous. In the interpersonal transactions between the counselor and client what is needed are differential approaches consistent with the life experiences of the person. It is ironic that, in this particular case and as earlier mentioned *equal treatment in counseling may be discriminatory treatment!* Counselors need to understand this. In the past, Third World groups have pointed to studies revealing that minority clients are given less preferential forms of treatment (medication, electroconvulsive shock therapy, etc.) as a means of proving discriminatory mental health practices. Somewhere along the line a confusion occurred in which it came to be believed that to be treated differently was akin to discrimination. The confusion centered around the distinction between equal access and opportunities versus equal treatment. Third World groups may not be asking for equal treatment so much as they are for equal access and opportunities. This dictates a differential approach that is truly nondiscriminatory.

Implications

In the culturally skilled counselor, this proposition implies that the ability to determine appropriate processes and appropriate goals must be present. To do this, however, it appears that several conditions must be met.

6. *The culturally skilled counselor must possess specific knowledge and information about the particular group he/she is working* *with.* He/she must be aware of the history, experiences, cultural values, and life-styles of various racial/ethnic groups. The greater the depth of knowledge of a cultural group and the more knowledge he/she has of *many* groups, the more likely the counselor can be an effective helper. Thus the culturally skilled counselor is one who *continues* to explore and learn about issues related to various minority groups throughout their professional careers.

7. *The culturally skilled counselor must have a clear and explicit knowledge and understanding of the generic characteristics of counseling and therapy.* These characteristics encompass language factors and culture-bound and class-bound values. The counselor should clearly understand the value assumptions (normality and abnormality) inherent in the major schools of counseling and how they may interact with values of the culturally different.

8. At the skills level, *the culturally skilled counselor must be able to generate a wide variety of verbal and nonverbal responses.* Ivey & Authier (1978) state that the wider the repertoire of responses the counselor possesses, the better helper he/she is likely to be. We can no longer rely on a very narrow and limited number of skills in counseling. We need to practice and be comfortable with a multitude of response modalities. Counselor education training programs must make microskills training an intimate part of the curriculum.

9. *The culturally skilled counselor must be able to send and receive both verbal and nonverbal messages accurately and "appropriately."* The key words *send, receive, verbal, nonverbal, accurately,* and *appropriately* are important. These words recognize several things about cross-cultural counseling. First, communication is a two-way process. The culturally skilled counselor must not only be able to communicate (send) his/her thoughts and feelings to the client, but also be able to read (receive) messages from the client. Second, cross-cultural counseling effectiveness may be highly correlated with the counselor's ability to recognize and respond to not only verbal, but also nonverbal messages. Third, sending and receiving a message accurately means the ability to consider cultural cues operative in the setting. Fourth, accuracy of communication must be tempered by its appropriateness. This is a difficult concept for many to grasp. It deals with communication styles. A traditional Asian client for whom subtlety is a highly prized art may be offended by a confrontive counselor who sends a clear/accurate message but in a blunt manner. Ivey & Authier (1978) summarize characteristics 1 and 2 in Figure 5.2.

The individual with cultural expertise behaves appropriately to the culture and is able to generate an infinite array of verbal and nonverbal sentences to communicate with a maximum number of people. Few are competent in all skills with all members of their culture, and none is experienced with all cultural subgroups or with those of totally different cultural backgrounds. Each of the dimensions below is measurable.

1. The culturally experienced individual uses culturally appropriate basic skills: eye contact, body language, tone of voice, rate of speech and loudness, verbalization on acceptable topics. Style of usage of these skills varies with the cultural group.

2. The culturally experienced individual uses culturally appropriate communication skills to hear others and describe the self: attending skills of open and closed questions, minimal encourages, paraphrases, reflections of feeling, summarizations and influencing skills of directions, expressions of content, expressions of feeling (self-disclosure), influencing summarizations, and interpretations. These skills will be differentially appropriate in different cultures.

3. The culturally experienced individual uses culturally appropriate qualitative skills as an added dimension to communication: concreteness, respect and warmth, immediacy, confrontation, genuineness. Again, these skills vary as to use in different cultures.

4. The culturally experienced individual can focus skillfully on a variety of culturally appropriate subjects: self, other individuals, topics, group, cultural-environmental-contextual issues.

Figure 5.2 The culturally experienced individual

CONCLUSIONS

We have pointed out previously that cross-cultural counseling implies major differences between the counselor and client. Not only are there major cultural differences, but also those associated with minority status in the United States. As a result, the counselor is most likely to be constantly tested in the sessions. These tests will challenge the counselor's competencies ("What makes you think you can work with me effectively?" "What is the nature of your training?"), trustworthiness

Taken from Ivey, A. E. & Authier, J. *Microcounseling*. Springfield, Ill.: Charles C. Thomas, 1978, 229.

("Prove to me you can be trusted." "How do I know you won't hurt me?" "What makes you any different from all other whities?"), and lack of similarity ("Can you really understand my concerns?" "Wouldn't it be better if I saw a counselor of my own race?"). In cross-cultural counseling, issues of expertness, trustworthiness, and similarity are likely to be extremely important considerations. Counselors who possess those attributes listed in this chapter will be most likely to meet and resolve these challenges. Such individuals are what we call "culturally skilled counselors."

REFERENCES

Atkinson, D. Maruyama, M., (& Matsui, S. Effects of counselor race and counseling approach on Asian Americans' perceptions of counselor credibility and utility. *Journal of Counseling Psychology* 1978, **25**, 76–83.

Bardo, H., Bryson, S. L., & Cody, J. J. Black concerns with behavior modification. *Personnel and Guidance Journal*, 1974, **53**, 334–341.

Berman, J. Counseling skills used by Black and white male and female counselors. *Journal of Counseling Psychology*, 1979, **26**, 81–84.

Calia, V. F. The Culturally deprived client: A reformulation of the counselor's role. *Journal of Counseling Psychology*, 1968, **13**, 100–105.

Good Tracks, J. G. Native American noninterference. *Social Work*, **18**, 1973, 30–34.

Harper, R. What counselors must know about the social sciences of Black Americans. *Journal of Negro Education*, 1973, **3**, 16–19.

Ivey, A., & Authier, J. *Microcounseling*. Springfield, Ill.: Charles C. Thomas, 1978.

Lorion, R. P. Patient and therapist variables in the treatment of low-income patients. *Psychological Bulletin*, 1974, **81**, 344–354.

Steiner, C. (Ed.) *Readings in Radical Psychiatry*. New York: Grove, 1975.

Sue, D. W. Counseling the culturally different: A conceptual analysis. *Personnel and Guidance Journal*, 1977, **55**, 422–424.

Trimble, J. Value differences among American Indians: Concerns for the concerned counselor. In P. Pedersen, W. Lonner, & J. Draguns (Eds.), *Counseling Across Cultures*. Honolulu: University of Hawaii Press, 1976.

II
Counseling Specific Populations

In Part I we were concerned with providing a broad conceptual and theoretical base from which to analyze counseling and its relationship to the culturally different. While differences among minority groups have been mentioned, we have dealt mainly with concepts that seem equally applicable to minority experiences in the United States. This has been necessary to supply us with an analytical framework from which to view cross-cultural counseling. Yet it is equally important for us to recognize that while commonalities exist among varying cultural groups, differences are also present. These differences seem intimately correlated with (a) cultural values unique to an ethnic group, (b) historical experiences in the United States, and (c) U.S. treatment and stereotyping of the minority group.

Four different ethnic groups are presented: Chapter 6—Asian Americans, Chapter 7—Blacks, Chapter 8—Hispanics, and Chapter 9—American Indians. In reading each of these chapters, we suggest that you apply concepts learned from Part I. Ask yourself these questions:

1. What are the cultural values of the group?
2. What has been the historical experience of this group in the United States?
3. How may cultural values/historical experiences affect behavior, motivation, and the minorities' perception of counseling?
4. Can you apply the concepts of world views and cultural identity to each of the groups? What factors were important for consideration? Why?

5. In reviewing the generic characteristics of counseling, which seem to be potential barriers to cross-cultural counseling? Why?

6. What approaches were suggested by the author in counseling the culturally different client? In what way was it appropriate/relevant to the group?

6
Cultural and Historical Perspectives in Counseling Asian Americans

According to the 1970 census (Urban Associates, 1974) there are a total of 1,539,412 Asian Americans (Japanese, Chinese, Philippinos*, Koreans, and Hawaiians) residing in the United States. This figure constitutes less than 1% of the population of the United States. Although this group's numbers are seemingly few in proportion to the general population, the lessons that we can learn from the experience of Asian Americans are important. First, the counseling profession, in studying Asian Americans, can learn much about how traditional counseling approaches can be modified to fit the life experiences of Asian clients. This is especially important for counselors residing on the West Coast and in Hawaii or New York, where large concentrations of Asians live. Second, the understanding of how counseling relates to Asian Americans has implications beyond this particular group. Issues of racism, cultural identity development, and the appropriateness or inappropriateness of traditional counseling approaches may be generalized and useful beyond the specific case. Third, the unique aspects of Asian Americans will, it is hoped alert counselors not only to similarities

---

*Just as ethnically conscious Asians find a perjorative association to the word *Oriental* so they find *Phillipinos* or *Filippinos* (white definitions). The preferred reference is now *Pilipinos*.

Permission granted to reproduce any or all of the following articles: D. W. Sue, Asian Americans: Social psychological forces affecting their life styles. In Picou, S., & Campbell, R. (Eds.), *Career Behavior of Special Groups*. Columbus, OH: Charles E. Merrill, 1975. And S. Sue, D. W. Sue, & D. Sue, Asian Americans as a minority group. *American Psychologist*, 1975, **31,** 906–910.

but also to differences existing among this minority group and other minority groups as well.

ASIAN AMERICANS: A SUCCESS STORY?

In contrast to many Third World groups, the contemporary image of Asian Americans is that of a highly successful minority who have "made it" in society. For example, the belief that Asian Americans represent a "model" minority has been played up by the popular press in such headlines as "Success Story: Outwhiting the Whites," and "Success Story of One Minority Group in the U.S." (*U.S. News & World Report,* 1966 *Newsweek,* 1971). Indeed, a close analysis of the 1970 census (S. Sue, D. W. Sue, & D. Sue, 1975) seems to support this contention. The Chinese and Japanese in this country have exceeded the national median income, and even Pilipinos, who in 1968 were far below the nation's median income level, have now attained parity. The same holds true for educational attainment, where Asian Americans complete a higher medium number of grades than all other groups.

Even more striking evidence of "success" is the apparent reduction of social distance between Asians and whites. Bogardus (1925) developed a Social Distance Scale that is presumably a measure of prejudice and/or discrimination against minority groups. If a minority group is allowed to marry and form intimate relationships with the dominant group, then a reduction in social distance is said to have occurred. The incidence of interracial marriages for Japanese Americans (mainly Japanese-white) in 1970 for areas like Los Angeles, San Francisco, and Fresno, California, has approached 50% (Kikumura & Kitano, 1973; Tinker, 1973). The rates are astoundingly high among Japanese and Pilipino youths. This is in marked contrast to Black-white marriages for all married Blacks in 1970 that was well under 2% (Urban Associates, 1974).

Besides these economic and social indicators of success, other mental health statistics reinforce the belief that Asians in America are relatively well adjusted, functioning effectively in society, and experience few difficulties. Studies consistently reveal that Asian Americans have low official rates of juvenile delinquency (Kitano, 1967; K. Abbott & E. Abbott, 1968), low rates of psychiatric contact and hospitalization (Kimmich, 1960; Yamamoto, James, & Palley, 1969; Kitano, 1969a; Sue & Sue, 1974; Sue & Kirk, 1974; Sue & McKinney, 1975), and low rates of divorce (S. Sue & Kitano, 1973). Indeed, there seems to be a prevalent belief that Asian Americans are somehow immune to the forces of prejudice and discrimination.

These facts seem ironic in light of the massive discrimination that has historically been directed at Asians. Denied the rights of citizenship, denied ownership of land, assaulted, murdered, and placed in concentration camps during World War II, Asians in America have at one time or another been subjected to the most appalling forms of discrimination ever perpetrated against any immigrant group (DeVos & K. Abbott, 1966; Sung, 1967; Kitano, 1969a; Daniels, 1971; D. W. Sue & Frank, 1973).

A closer analysis of the status of Asian Americans does not support their success story. First, reference to the higher median income of Asian Americans does not take into account (*a*) the higher percentage of more than one wage earner in Asian than white families, (*b*) an equal incidence of poverty despite the higher median income, (*c*) lower poverty assistance and welfare than the general population, and (*d*) a discrepancy between education and income; while Asian wage earners may have higher levels of education, their wages are not commensurate with their training (Urban Associates, 1974).

Second, in the area of education, Asian Americans show a disparate picture of extraordinary high educational attainment and a large undereducated mass. This bimodal distribution when averaged out indicates how misleading statistics can be (Urban Associates, 1974). Furthermore, there is evidence that Asian Americans do experience educational difficulties. In a study conducted by the Asian Studies Division at the University of California, Berkeley (Watanabe, 1973), it was found that over 50% of entering Asian students failed a "bonehead" English examination and were required to makeup their language deficits in remedial noncredit courses. Asian American students are twice as likely to fail the English examination when compared to their Caucasian counterparts. Furthermore, the assumption that the direct teaching of language skills will correct this deficiency indicates a failure to understand the Asian's difficulty with the English language and has made existing remedial programs generally ineffective (Watanabe, 1973). While a bilingual background is a major contributor to their difficulty with the English language, the Asians' strong cultural injunctions against assertiveness, the shame and disgrace felt by the students at having to take such courses, and the isolation imposed on this group by a racist society are equally strong forces in their performance.

Third, there is now widespread recognition that, apart from being tourist attractions, Chinatowns, Manilatowns, and Japantowns in San

Francisco and New York represent ghetto areas with prevalent unemployment, poverty, health problems, and juvenile delinquency. People outside these communities seldom see the deplorable social conditions that exist behind the bright neon lights, restaurants, and quaint shops. Statistics support the fact that San Francisco's Chinatown has the second greatest population density for its size in the country, second only to Harlem (Charnofsky, 1971). The Chinese community has an extremely high tuberculosis rate and a suicide rate three times that of the national average (Jacobs, Landau, & Pell, 1971). Continuing and recent mass murders committed over the years have been traced to Chinese juvenile gangs operating in Chinatown, and recent news reports show this trend to be on the increase.

Fourth, whether underutilization of mental health facilities is due to low rates of socioemotional adjustment difficulties, discriminatory mental health practices, and/or cultural values inhibiting self-referral is not known. D. W. Sue & Kirk (1972, 1973) found that Asian American students in one university campus expressed greater feelings of loneliness, isolation, and anxiety than the general student population. This finding is inconsistent with the explanation of lower incidence of mental health problems among Asians. Some investigators (Kimmich, 1960; Kitano, 1969; S. Sue & D. W. Sue, 1971b, 1972; Brown et al., 1973; D. W. Sue & Kirk, 1975; S. Sue & McKinney, 1975) suggest that much of the mental illness, adjustment problems, and juvenile delinquency among Asians are hidden. The discrepancy between official and real rates may be due to such cultural factors as the shame and disgrace associated with admitting to emotional problems, the handling of problems within the family rather than relying on outside resources, and the manner of symptom formation, such as low acting-out disorders.

One revealing study conducted by D. W. Sue & Kirk (1975) compared the use of counseling and psychiatric services on a large university campus over a four-year period for Asian American and non-Asian students. These two investiagors found that Chinese and Japanese American students, in keeping with previous studies, underutilize the campus psychiatric service. However, a significantly greater percentage of Asian Americans were seen at the counseling center when compared with the non-Asian counterparts. In one particular group (Chinese American females), the rate approached 50%! These investigators concluded that (a) the need for counseling services among Asian Americans is no lower than that of the general population, (b) Asian Americans may have greater need for academic, career, and vocational counseling than other groups, and (c) the increased contact at the Counseling Center of Asian students represents a "runoff" of those who would ordinarily be seen at a psychiatric service.

The myths and stereotypes about Asians in America—such as the popular belief that they represent model minorities and that they experience no great difficulties in society—must be dispelled. Asian Americans view these stereotypes as having functional value for those who hold power in society. First, these stereotypes reassert the erroneous belief that any minority can succeed in a democratic society if the minority group members work hard enough. Second, the Asian American success story is seen as a divisive concept used by the Establishment to pit one minority group against another by holding one group up as an example to others. Third, the success myth has shortchanged many Asian American communities from receiving the necessary moral and financial commitment due them as a struggling minority with unique concerns. It is especially important for counselors, pupil personnel workers, and educators who work with Asian Americans to look behind the success myth and to understand the Asian experience in America. The matter is even more pressing for counselors when we realize that Asian Americans are more likely to seek help at a counseling service rather than a psychiatric service.

The approach of this chapter is threefold. First, it attempts to investigate how certain forces (the experience of Asians in America, Asian cultural values, Western influences, etc.) have served to shape and define the life-style of Asian Americans. Second, the systematic effects of these forces on academic abilities, personality adjustment, and vocational interests is discussed. Third, this chapter explores how an understanding of the Asian American experience suggests major modifications in counseling and psychotherapeutic practices to fit the needs of Asians in America.

FORCES SHAPING THE IDENTITY OF ASIAN AMERICANS

It is widely accepted that sociocultural forces have a strong impact on the behavioral expression of different racial/ethnic groups. While many investigators believe that Asian Americans possess distinct subcultural systems (DeVos & Abbott, 1966; Kitano, 1969b; Abbott, 1970; D. W. Sue, 1973; Cordova, 1973), little is known about how these values have interacted with Western values and how they have influenced Asians in America. Although most social scientists continue to pay lip service to the fact that psychological development is not an isolated phenomenon

apart from sociocultural forces, most theories of human behavior tend
to be culturally exclusive. It seems important, therefore, that to understand the Asian American experience, it is necessary to discuss the
wider social milieu in which behavior and identity originate.

Historical Experience in America

Unknown to the American public, Asians in America have suffered
from some of the most inhumane treatment ever accorded any immigrant group. Beginning in the 1840s, the Chinese were the first Asian
group to arrive in large numbers. Because of the high demand for cheap
labor (the discovery of gold in Sacramento Valley and building of the
transcontinental railroad), coupled with political unrest and overpopu-
lation in certain provinces of China, a large steady stream of Chinese
male peasants began to immigrate to the United States (DeVos & K.
Abbott, 1966; Daniels, 1971). By about the 1860s nearly all the Chinese
lived and settled on the West Coast, with the heaviest concentrations in
California. Because their presence in the labor force served to fill a void
in the labor market, these early Chinese peasants were not particularly
mistreated.

However, a series of business recessions, coupled with the comple-
tion of the Union-Central Pacific Railroad in 1869, made competition
for jobs fierce. Because the Chinese constituted a large fraction of the
California population and labor force, white working men saw them as
an economic threat. The Chinese were especially vulnerable as scape-
goats because of their "strange" customs and appearance; that is, they
wore their hair in queues (pigtails), spoke in a strange tongue, and ate
"unhealthy" food. As a result, labor began to agitate against the
Chinese with rallying cries such as "The Chinese Must Go." Although
based originally on economics, Daniels (1971) feels that "the movement
soon developed an ideology of white supremacy/Oriental inferiority
that was wholly compatible with the mainstream of American racism"
(p. 3).

The systematic harassment of the Chinese resulted in legal discrimination that denied them the rights of citizenship; Chinese testimony in
court was ruled inadmissible as evidence. Indeed, the Chinese were seen
as heathens and subhuman aliens who were detrimental to the well-
being of America. Exclusionist legislation was passed at all levels of
government and culminated in the passing of a racist immigration law,
the Chinese Exclusion Act of 1882, which was not repealed until 1943.
Kagiwada & Fujimoto (1953) point out that the phrase "not a China-

man's chance" alludes to these conditions. They point out further that these actions did not seem to satisfy the racist elements of society. Individual and mob violence such as mass murder, physical attacks, and having homes and property destroyed were common occurrences. Large-scale massacres of the Chinese in Los Angeles in 1851 and Rock Springs, Wyoming, in 1885 are examples of such abuse (Kitano, 1969b; Daniels, 1951). In many cases, the treatment of the Chinese was no better than that of African slaves.

The next Asian group to immigrate in large numbers to the United States were the Japanese. By the time the Japanese came in numbers to the United States beginning in the 1890s, the "Chinese problem" had been relatively solved. Most of the early Japanese immigrants found employment on railroads, canneries, mining, and so on. Since many of the Japanese had previously come from a farming class, their gravitation toward farming and gardening could be predicted (Kitano, 1969b). The Japanese's knowledge of agriculture and perserverance made them highly successful in these fields, where they subsequently became economic competitors. The now-familiar pattern of violence and harassment previously directed at the Chinese was now channeled toward the Japanese. This pervasive anti-Oriental feeling became labeled as "the Yellow Peril."

Because Japan was a rising international power, the anti-Japanese feeling did not manifest itself in direct governmental legislation to restrict immigration but led to a "gentlemen's agreement" to seal the flow of Asians to the United States. To further harass the Japanese, California passed the Alien Land Law in 1913 that forbade aliens to own land. The discrimination and prejudice toward the Japanese were most blatantly evident in the World War II incarceration of 110,000 Japanese Americans into concentration camps. The effects of this atrocity, perpetrated against the Japanese, and its humiliating effects are still very much evident today in the suspiciousness that many Asians have for the American mainstream. Indeed, nothing in the Constitution forbids such an action from being taken again. Chin (1971) quotes a statement made by former FBI Director J. Edgar Hoover in 1969 (and since deceased): "We are being confronted with a growing amount of work in being alert for the Chinese Americans and others in this country who would assist Red China in supplying needed material or promoting Red Chinese propaganda. For one thing, Red China has been flooding the country with its propaganda and there are over 300,000 Chinese in the United States, some of whom could be susceptible to ties of hostage situations because of relatives in Communist China" (p. 5). This statement is irresponsible and only serves to inflame the suspicions and fears of the Asian and white communities. Worst, the statement represents a continuing white antagonism toward Asians today.

Likewise, the historical treatment of Pilipinos and Koreans fared no better than their Chinese and Japanese counterparts. The Chinese Exclusion Act of 1882 and Gentlemen's Agreement eventually created another imbalance in the labor situation (Rabaya, 1971; Shin, 1971). The Hawaiian sugar plantation owners (mainly white) and the mainland businesses were forced to find another cheap source of labor. The two potential reservoirs of labor were Puerto Rico and the Phillipines. The Pilipino immigrants who came to the United States also encountered much prejudice and discrimination. Labor unions led by the American Federation of Labor condemned the Pilipinos as "cheap labor" lowering the standard of living for other white workers. The blame, however, was misdirected, since it was white employers who set up the system in order to increase profits.

Thus it would appear that the treatment of Asians was highly correlated with the needs of the United States. Asians were used by white profiteers and subsequently blamed for economic downturns and a host of other events. That the treatment is not unique to Asians can be seen in the history of Black slavery and the bitter treatment of Mexican workers. In any case, the Asian experience of racism and its continuing manifestation in our society has had a tremendous impact on Asians in America.

Cultural Influences

Asian immigrants who came to the United States carried with them many ancient traditions and customs that still are in evidence today. Finding a hostile and threatening environment, the early immigrants were both externally and voluntarily isolated from their wider society. They clung tenaciously to their old ways and formed segregated communities that served as buffers for their survival. As a result, an already-complex and well-ingrained culture was reinforced by a racist society (Watanabe, 1973).

Since cultural values have such an impact upon the behavior of Asian Americans, it is necessary that we describe them in detail. For purposes of brevity and since the cultural values of the Chinese and Japanese have been described similarly (Kimmich, 1960; DeVos & Abbott, 1966; Kitano, 1969a, 1969b; Abbott, 1970; S. Sue & D. W. Sue, 1971a), Chinese and Japanese patterns of interactions and their cultural values are described as an entity. Space limitations do not allow us to focus on the Pilipinos and Koreans. We regret that the following sections must be limited to only the Chinese and Japanese.

In the traditional family, age, sex, and generational status are primary determinants of role behavior. Ancestors and elders are viewed with great reverence and respect. Being patriarchical, the father is traditionally the head of the household, and his authority is unquestioned. The primary duty of the son is to be a good son, and his obligations to be a good husband or father come second to his duty as a son. In other words, the son's primary allegiance is to the family into which he is born. The role of females in the family was that of subservience to males and performance of domestic duties. Women were expected to marry, become obedient helpers of their mother-in-law, and bear children, especially male ones.

The dominant orientation of Asian families has always been conservative and resistant to change. The roles of family members are rigidly defined, allowing for few significant deviations. Conflicts within the family are minimized, because the structure is so arranged that roles do not interfere with others. Built into the family relationships are strong values stressing the need to approach problems subtly and indirectly rather than openly. Much effort is expended to avoid offending others. Furthermore, if family members have feelings that might disrupt family harmony, they are expected to restrain them (Wright, 1964; Kitano, 1969a; Abbott, 1970). In fact, restraint of possibly disruptive emotions is strongly emphasized in the development of the Chinese character, and this has led many Westerners to observe that Asians are "inscrutable." Because family members are expected to submerge aggressive tendencies and inclinations to act independently, dependency and conformity are prolonged within the family.

The welfare and integrity of the family is of great importance. Members of the family are expected to submerge behaviors and feelings to further the welfare of the family and its reputation (D. W. Sue & S. Sue, 1972). The behavior of individual members of a family is expected to reflect credit on the entire family. If a member of a family behaves in such a manner as to embarrass or shame himself or herself, the entire family shares in the shame and "loses face." So important is the stress on reputation and face that "bad behaviors" (exhibiting disrespect for parents, juvenile delinquency, failure in school, psychopathology, etc.) are handled as much as possible within the family, and public admission of problems is suppressed (Kimmich, 1960; Sommers, 1960; Kitano, 1969a, 1969b; D. W. Sue & S. Sue, 1972).

The primary means used within the family to keep members in line and to suppress deviations from family norms are the inculcation of

guilt and shame and appeals to obligation. Parents constantly emphasize their sons' and daughters' obligations to the family. If children
attempt to act independently, contrary to the wishes of the parents, they
are told that they are selfish and inconsiderate and not showing grati-
tude for all their parents have done for them.

Western Influence and Culture-Conflict

As Asians become progressively exposed to the standards, norms, and
values of the wider society, increasing assimilation and acculturation
are frequently the result (Arkoff, 1959; Fong, 1965; Kitano, 1962,
1967, 1969b). Bombarded on all sides by peers, schools, and the mass
media upholding Western standards as better than their own, Asian
Americans are frequently placed in situations of extreme culture-
conflict that may lead to much pain and agony. For example, restraint
of strong feelings is highly valued in Asian culture. However, Westerners see an individual exhibiting this trait as passive and inhibited. As a
result of attaching negative connotations to such values, many Asian
Americans become confused about how they should behave.

Unfortunately, it is extremely difficult for one to reconcile loyalties
to two different cultural traditions, especially if one's parents are
strongly in favor of retaining ethnic values. S. Sue & D. W. Sue (1971a)
recently proposed a conceptual scheme of three different ways used by
Asian Americans to adjust to these conflicting demands.

First, individuals may remain "loyal" to their own ethnic group by
retaining traditional values and living up to the expectations of the
family. The "traditionalist" adheres closely to the norms, standards,
and values of the traditional Asian family.

Second, the individuals who are caught up in a culture-conflict may
oftentimes attempt to become overwesternized by rejecting traditional
Asian values. Their pride and self-worth are defined by the ability to
acculturate into white society. In their attempts to assimilate and
acculturate into white society, they are often forced to reject the Asian
side of themselves and thus feel ashamed of anything that reminds them
of being Chinese or Japanese. They come to view their ethnicity as a
handicap that may lead to various forms of racial self-hatred. This type
of adjustment leads to an identity crisis, because the minority individuals cannot completely rid themselves of certain traditional ways and
may lead a marginal existence, that is, they exist between the margin of
two different cultural traditions. The "marginal person" can become
quite contemptuous of Asian customs, values, behaviors, and even
physical appearances. The male may sarcastically describe Asian

females as "flat chested" and "short-legged" when compared to Caucasian females. An anthropologicl field study conducted by Weiss (1970) found that many Chinese American females viewed their male counterparts as inhibited, passive, and lacking in sexual attractiveness. He states that "perhaps the most damaging indictment of Chinese-American male 'dating ineptness' comes from the dating age Chinese-American female. Girls who regularly date Caucasians can be quite vehement in their denunciation and disapproval of Chinese-American males as dating partners. But even the foreign born Chinese girls—who do not usually inter-date—also support a demeaning courtship image of the Chinese-American male. Moreover, 'Chinese inadequacies' and 'failures' are contrasted with Caucasian 'confidence' and 'success' in similar situations" (p. 275).

Third, a more recent development is the Asian American movement sometimes referred to as the "Yellow Power Movement." Like the marginal person, the Asian American is rebelling against parental authority, as he or she attempts to develop a new identity that will enable him or her to reconcile viable aspects of his/her heritage with the present situation. The roots of the Asian American movement spring from two main sources. The first lies in the need to attain self pride in one's racial and cultural identity by reversing the trend of negativity instilled in them by white society. Second, the Asian American movement has strong political connotations in that the problems of minorities are seen to reside in society. The Asian American may become extremely militant in his/her concern with racism and civil rights. He/she appears to be much more sensitive to the forces in society that have served to shape and define his/her limited identity. Problems such as poverty, unemployment, and juvenile delinquency and individual, institutional, and cultural racism of Asians must be exposed and changed.

SOCIOCULTURAL EFFECTS ON ACADEMIC ABILITIES, PERSONALITY, AND VOCATIONAL INTERESTS

There have been few systematic attempts to provide a comprehensive and global picture of the psychological functioning of Asians in America (D. W. Sue & Kirk, 1972, 1973). Most studies tend to limit themselves to a narrow area of functioning such as personality (Fenz & Arkoff, 1962; Abbott, 1970), acculturation (Kitano, 1962; Fong, 1965; Weiss, 1970; Matsumoto, Meredith, & Masuda, 1970), behavior disorders (Kimmich, 1960; Kitano, 1970; Marsella, Kinzie, & Gordon, 1971), child-rearing practices (Kitano, 1964; DeVos & Abbott, 1966), and use of English (Smith, 1975; Smith & Kasdon, 1961). Furthermore, explanations of human behavior are frequently seriously lacking in considering the multitude of forces that serve to shape and define a person's life-style (D. W. Sue, 1973; D. W. Sue & Frank, 1973). As shown in the following section, the sociocultural milieu exerts a strong influence on the Asian Americans' development of abilities, personality, and vocational interests.

Academic Abilities

In a series of studies conducted at the University of California, Berkeley, Sue & Kirk (1972, 1973) investigated the academic abilities of both Chinese and Japanese American college students using the School and College Ability Test. Japanese and Chinese Americans of both sexes were found to score significantly lower on the verbal section of the test than their Caucasian counterparts. Although the Japanese American group did not differ significantly on the quantitative section from the Caucasian group, the Chinese Americans did score significantly higher.

Even though the prospect of inherited racial characteristics cannot be eliminated, an exploration of the Asian American experience seems to suggest several answers. First, Asian Americans often come from a bilingual background in which Chinese or Japanese is spoken in the home. Studies conducted in Hawaii (Smith, 1957; Smith & Kasdon, 1961) indicate that English usage is noticeably affected by this factor even though Asian Americans may be unable to speak their own native tongue. Second, cultural modes of behavior in Asian families frequently tend to restrict and hinder verbal communication. Clearly defined roles of dominance and deference minimize argumentation and debate (Watanabe, 1973). Communication generally flows one way; from parent to child. The limited communication patterns in the home and the high value placed on restraining strong feelings does not provide opportunity for free and open verbal communication. Third, Asian American reaction to white society and white society's treatment of them also serves to greatly affect self-expression. The isolation imposed by a racist society on Asians is well documented. Denied the rights of citizenship, forbidden to own land, massacred, maligned, and otherwise mistreated, Asians in America were forced to live in segregated communities. Having already to contend with strong cultural injunctions that discouraged self-expression, Asians found white society forcing them into a state of structural isolation which minimized the need to interact with Westerners. Watanabe (1973) believes that Asians thus learned the value of silence and inconspicuousness in a society that punished out-spokenness in minorities.

In addition, the lower verbal performance and expression of Asian Americans tend to be maintained and perpetuated by stereotypes. For example, the picture of the clumsy, inarticulate Asian who is good with numbers but poor with words is held by many educators. These stereotypes, although largely based on facts, tend to perpetuate discrepancies by setting up rigid expectations. This is accomplished directly by having well-meaning educators channel Asian American students into courses or fields that minimize English and maximize mathematical skills. Furthermore, many students of Asian descent begin to believe these stereotypes about themselves and behave accordingly. Rosenthal & Jacobson (1968) found that it was possible to affect the IQ scores of grade school children at random by setting up false expectations in teachers about the children's intellectual potentials. Thus these self-fulfilling prophecies greatly restricted the Asian Americans' academic capabilities.

Personality Adjustment

The personality adjustment of both Chinese and Japanese Americans also seemed influenced by their historical experience in America and by their cultural heritage. Studies tend to show that Asian Americans possess a more practical and applied approach to life and problems than their Caucasian counterparts (D. W. Sue & Kirk, 1972, 1973). Ideas are evaluated more on the basis of their immediate practical applications. In addition, concrete, well-structured, and predictable situations are preferred over ambiguous ones. An explanation of these differences can be found in the highly structured role expectations of the traditional families in which each member knows precisely what is expected of him or her. Furthermore, early immigrants may have strongly emphasized the necessity of being practical in order to survive in a seemingly strange and hostile environment. Specific concrete skills were stressed to insure economic and social mobility.

Asian Americans also appear less autonomous, more dependent, conforming, and obedient to authority (Meredith, 1966; D. W. Sue & Kirk, 1972, 1973). Other investigators also describe Asian Americans as inhibited, less ready to express impulses, law abiding, less assertive, and more reserved (Fenz & Arkoff, 1962; Meredith, 1966; Abbott, 1970; D. W. Sue & Kirk, 1972, 1973). The cultural emphasis on restraint of strong feelings, unquestioning obedience to family authority, and submergence of individuality to the welfare of the family is certainly consistent with these traits. In addition, Asian Americans may also have learned that outspokenness on the part of minorities only invited harsher retaliation from the host society (Watanabe, 1973).

With respect to their socioemotional adjustment characteristics, Asian Americans tend to withdraw from social contacts and responsibilities. They are less extroverted and seem to be experiencing more psychological distress than their Caucasian counterparts. They tend to exhibit attitudes and behaviors that characterize socially alienated individuals (D. W. Sue & Kirk, 1972, 1973), and express feelings of suspiciousness, rejection (Meredith, 1966), isolation, anxiety, self-blame, and guilt (Arkoff, 1959; Fenz & Arkoff, 1962).

Asian cultural emphasis on formality in interpersonal relations versus the much more informal and spontaneous nature of Westerners can often make Asian Americans uncomfortable about relating to others outside their ethnic group. Furthermore, since Asian culture is family centered Asian Americans tend to view outsiders with a great degree of suspicion. The mistrust of the host society is also reinforced by the historical and continuing racism directed against Asians in America. A large part of the Asian Americans' alienation, anxiety, and guilt stems from their role as a minority group in America and the severe cultural conflicts they often experience. In addition, Asian culture tends to be a "shame" culture in that failures that may have nothing to do with the individual's efforts tend to be internalized.

Care must be exercised in using these findings to indicate that Asian Americans are "inherently" maladjusted, since ethnic minorities are extremely sensitive to such unfair portrayals (D. W. Sue & S. Sue, 1972). Results indicating psychological "maladjustment" may represent more of a damaging indictment of American society that has too long been intolerant of different life-styles (D. W. Sue, 1973; D. W. Sue & Frank, 1973). The minority status of Asians in America and the historical documentation of prejudice and discrimination definitely contribute to these findings.

Vocational Interests

The state of the literature on career behavior for Asian Americans tends to be deficient, thus presenting only limited available information. Because of its relatively unexplored nature, a comprehensive discussion of vocational interests will have to wait until further studies are conducted. Thus reliance on studies conducted at Berkeley (D. W. Sue & Kirk, 1972, 1973; D. W. Sue & Frank, 1973), along with clinical impressions, will have to suffice for the time being. However, it is my contention that career behavior is a resultant of many social-psychological forces, and understanding the impact of these variables will shed much light on the vocational choices of Asian Americans.

Many educators have frequently commented on the number of Asian Americans who seem to enter the physical sciences and to avoid vocations requiring forceful self-expression. In extensive studies conducted at the University of California, Berkeley, D. W. Sue & Kirk (1972, 1973) investigated the vocational interests of the entire entering freshman class in 1966. All students were asked to participate in a testing program that included the Strong Vocational Interest Blank. The following is a simplified summary of these investigators' findings.

As a group, Chinese Americans showed significantly greater interests in the physical sciences (mathematician, engineer, physicist, and chemist), skilled technical trades (farmer, carpenter, vocational-agricultural teacher, forest service man, etc.), and business detail professions (certified public accountants, office worker, purchasing agent, banker, etc.) and less interests in the social sciences, sales, and verbal-linguistic fields (advertising man, lawyer, author-journalist, etc.) than all other students. In addition, Chinese American females scored significantly higher on those occupations traditionally associated with a domestic orientation (housewife, elementary teacher, office worker, stenographer-secretary) than their control counterparts. That these expressed interests manifest themselves in the students' choice of majors is clearly evident in a wide-ranging study by D. W. Sue & Frank (1973). These investigators found that many Chinese Americans choose majors in the engineering and physical science fields and were underrepresented in majors such as sales, social science, and the verbal-linguistic areas.

Several factors seem to be affecting the career behavior of Chinese Americans. Although we cannot directly infer cause-effect relationships, the culture, history, and psychological attributes of the Chinese American seem logically consistent with this group's movement into certain occupations. The physical sciences, skilled technical trades, and business detail fields represent the more concrete, structured, impersonal, and practical occupations more so than the other general groupings. In addition, these fields minimize contact with people and require less verbal skills, with a maximal emphasis on other forms of communication such as mathematics. The social sciences, sales (business contact), and the verbal-linguistic occupations stress persuasive verbal skills and a high emphasis on social interactions. Furthermore, these occupations tend to be somewhat more ambiguous in that problems and answers are not as clear as in the physical sciences.

An additional consideration is the actual or perceived restriction of vocational choices that Chinese Americans may feel affect them. Early immigrants probably strongly encouraged sons and daughters to select occupations that would give them the greatest survival value in white society. In addition to cultural barriers to the people-contact professions, these occupations might be perceived as being fraught with the hazards of discrimination. The physical sciences and the skilled technical trades represent job opportunities that require concrete, specific skills which have greater functional value in American society. As a result, the Chinese Americans' gravitation toward and avoidance of certain occupations is understandable. The finding that Chinese American females express more interest in the domestic fields is also consistent with Chinese values.

When we begin to talk about vocational interests for Asian Americans, differences begin to appear between the Chinese and Japanese groups that indicate that the earlier discussion of culture and history for both groups may be more complex than previously realized. For purposes of brevity, we have been discussing the Chinese and Japanese as a single group. However, this has necessarily simplified the analysis and perhaps made us guilty of overgeneralizations. Although Japanese Americans did have many similarities to their Chinese counterparts, there were several major differences. Earlier it was noted that Japanese Americans did not differ from control students in the mathematics section of the ability test. This fact seems reflected in their choice of occupations. Japanese American students did not differ from all other students in the physical or social sciences. Furthermore, Japanese American females did not appear more domestically oriented than the control females, as in the case of the Chinese Americans. Like the Chinese Americans, the Japanese Americans' expressed interests are also manifested in their choice of majors (D. W. Sue & Frank, 1973).

Some social scientists (Lyman, 1970; Kitano, 1969b; D. W. Sue, 1973) believe that the Japanese in America have acculturated at a much more rapid rate than the Chinese. In psychological studies of Chinese and Japanese Americans (D. W. Sue & Kirk, 1973; D. W. Sue & Frank, 1973), it was found that the Japanese group consistently occupied an intermediate position between the Chinese and Caucasian groups. This implies one of two things. First, Japanese cultural values are closer to Western ones than are Chinese values. Another variation of this theme may be that Japanese cultural values, in comparison with those of the Chinese, possess characteristics that predispose them to adopt more readily Western ways. A second explanation is that in some way, because of historical or political circumstances, the Japanese have acculturated much more rapidly than their Chinese counterparts. Several explanations of this latter point of view have been offered by various investigators (Lyman, 1970; Kitano, 1969b; D. W. Sue, 1973; D. W. Sue & Frank, 1973; D. W. Sue & Kirk, 1973).

Prior to the bombing of Pearl Harbor, many Japanese Americans had noticed the increasing antagonism between the United States and Japan. Fearful that war would break out between the two nations, many Japanese American citizens strongly proclaimed their loyalty to the United States and encouraged their children to acculturate. These steps were seen as a necessity to dispel the potential hostility and mistrust that Americans had of Japanese in America. When war finally broke out between the two nations, hysteria swept the West Coast. Rumors of Japanese spies and the inherent hostility toward nonwhite groups surfaced in the belief that Japanese Americans were a risk to the nation, and, as a result, 110,000 Japanese Americans were placed in relocation camps. This event did much to foster acculturation among the Japanese. First, it broke up the Japanese communities by uprooting residents and confiscating homes and property. Thus symbols of ethnic identity were destroyed (note the lack of comparability between Chinatowns and Japantowns). Second, in a traditionally patriarchical family, the traditional lines of authority became disrupted. Elderly males no longer possessed a functional value as household heads. In the concentration camps women and children gained a degree of freedom never before obtained. Control and clear lines of authority became noticeably weakened. The strong family system of passing on customs and traditions became diluted. Third, many Japanese Americans chose to immigrate to the Midwest or East rather than suffer the humiliation of internment, thereby dispersing themselves and encouraging acculturation. The increased contact with members of the host society no doubt aided this latter process.

IMPLICATIONS FOR COUNSELING ASIAN AMERICANS

We have just seen how important it is for us to understand the culture and history of an ethnic minority in order to explain that minority's life-style. Educators, counselors, and pupil personnel workers often do not have enough knowledge of the Asian American experience to make enlightened decisions. These professionals' ignorance of minority experiences has greatly shortchanged Asians from obtaining needed help in the areas of mental health. The following discussion dwells on three aspects of Asian American mental health. First, it explores the popular

assumption that Asians experience few adjustment difficulties in society. Second, it attempts to reveal to counselors some typical adjustment
problems often encountered by Asian Americans. Third, specific suggestions are given about how to make counseling and psychotherapy
more consistent with the experiences of Asian Americans.

Utilization of Psychiatric Resources

It was mentioned earlier that studies revealing low official rates of
psychiatric hospitalization and low rates of juvenile delinquency have
been used to support an Asian American success myth. However, it is
unclear whether underutilization of mental health facilities is due to low
rates of psychopathology or cultural values inhibiting self-referral for
therapy. Studies by D. W. Sue & Kirk (1972, 1973) tend to reveal that
Asians in America are experiencing greater psychological discomfort
than their Caucasian counterparts. If this is true, then lower utilization
of psychiatric resources does not seem to be due to lower rates of
adjustment difficulties. Three alternative explanations seem to account
for this discrepancy.

First, both Chinese (DeVos & K. A. Abbott, 1966) and Japanese
(Kitano, 1969a) families stress the importance of obedience and conformity to elders, high achievement, and behaviors that bring honor to the
family name. Since the family name is so strongly implicated by a
member's behavior, public admission of personal problems is suppressed. Second, Asian emphasis on restraint of strong feelings and the
shame and disgrace associated with psychological problems might make
many Asian Americans who do experience difficulties express them via
physical complaints. Physical complaints represent a more acceptable
way of expressing emotional problems for which family upbringing
cannot be easily blamed. Support for these hypotheses comes from two
studies. Marsella, Kinzie, & Gordon (1971) did find that the Chinese
tend to somaticize their depressive reactions. S. Sue & D. W. Sue
(1971b) also found that in a psychiatric population Chinese and Japanese students exhibited more somatic complaints than their control
counterparts. In addition, Asian American students were found to
possess a greater severity of disorders than their controls (white students who used services). This finding was interpreted to indicate that
only the most severely disturbed Asians seek help, while less disturbed
ones avoid the clinic services.

Third, studies (Hollingshead & Redlick, 1958; Yamamoto, James,
& Palley, 1969) seem to indicate that minorities and disadvantaged
groups who do seek treatment receive less lengthy and intensive help

than their Caucasian counterparts. These findings suggest that perhaps the orientation of the white therapist may cause them to be less accepting of minorities or the minority patient may feel that the white therapist, as an agent of society, is attempting to adjust them to a "sick" society (D. W. Sue & S. Sue, 1972). This may partially account for the low utilization of mental health facilities among Asians, Blacks, and Chicanos (Karno & Edgarton, 1969; Yamamoto, James, & Palley, 1969; S. Sue & D. W. Sue, 1971b).

Thus it seems imperative that attention be focused on minority group experiences and how to institute therapeutic intervention within their cultural experiences. Using psychiatric contact as indicators of mental health may be an inappropriate means of assessing adjustment among minorities.

Asian Americans and Adjustment Difficulties

Not only is personality characteristics influenced by culture and its interaction with the host society, but the manifestation of behavioral problems among Asian Americans seem intimately linked to these forces. Counselors who work with Asian Americans need to be aware of these conflicts. These problems can best be understood if we briefly return to our earlier discussion of culture-conflict and the three reactions that many Asians have exhibited in their attempts to cope with society. The following three case descriptions are typical of the kinds of problems that have been observed in the traditionalist, marginal person, and Asian American.

THE CASE OF JOHN C.

John C. is a 20-year-old junior student, majoring in electrical engineering. He is the oldest of five children, born and raised in San Francisco. The father is 58 years old and has been a grocer for the past twenty years; and the mother is a housewife. The parents have always had high expectations for their eldest son and constantly transmitted these feelings to him. Ever since he could remember, John's parents had decided that he would go to college and become an engineer—a job they held in high esteem.

Throughout his early school years, John was an outstanding student and was constantly praised by his teachers. He was hardworking, obedient and never gave his teachers any trouble. However, his parents seemed to take John's school successes for granted. In fact, they would always make statements such as, "You can do better still."

John first came to the counseling center during the latter part of his junior year because of severe headaches and a vague assortment of bodily complaints. A medical checkup failed to reveal any organic malfunctioning, which led the psychologist to suspect a psychophysiological reaction.

John exhibited a great deal of anxiety throughout the interviews. He seemed suspicious of the psychologist and found it difficult to talk about himself in a personal way. As the sessions progressed, it became evident that John felt a great deal of shame about having come to a therapist. John was concerned that his family not be told since they would be disgraced.

Throughout the interviews, John appeared excessively concerned with failing his parents' expectations. Further exploration revealed significant sources of conflict. First, his grades were beginning to decline and he felt that he was letting his parents down. Second, he had always harbored wishes about becoming an architect, but felt this to be an unacceptable profession to his parents. Third, increasing familial demands were being placed on him to quickly graduate and obtain a job in order to help the family's financial situation. The parents frequently made statements such as, "Once you are out of school and making good money, it would be nice if you could help your brothers and sisters through college." John's resentment of these imposed responsibilities was originally denied and repressed. When he was able to see clearly his anger and hostility towards his parents, much of his physical complaints vanished. However, with the recognition of his true feelings, he became extremely depressed and guilty. John could not see why he should be angry at his parents after all they had done for him (S. Sue & D. W. Sue, 1971a, p. 39).

The counselor who works with John C. is most likely working with an individual with a strong traditional orientation. As such, John C.'s problems tend to be somewhat different from the other two types, that is, the marginal person and Asian American. First, the counselor must be aware that when the traditionalist seeks counseling or therapy, as in the case of John C., this person is most likely to experience intense feelings of shame and guilt at admitting that problems exist. Issues of confidentiality are important to deal with. The counselor who is not sensitive to such feelings can greatly increase John's discomfort and cause an early termination of counseling. Second, the traditionalist may find it difficult to directly admit to problems and will present them in an indirect manner, that is, psychophysiological reactions, declining grades, vocational indecisions, and so on. It may be wise for the counselor to initially respond to these superficial problems, since they are less threatening to the traditionalist, until a degree of rapport and trust can be formed. Third, it is imperative that the counselor recognize that vocational indecision, often presented by Asian Americans, may mask deeper conflicts. In the case of John C. it tends to be a conflict between his own desires for independence and the extremely strong obligations he feels toward his parents. Last, counselors working with a person of traditional background must be willing to alter their usual style of counseling and therapy. The actual practice of counseling and psychotherapy may be inherently discriminating to the ethnic minorities. Since the counseling-therapy situation is essentially a white middle-class activity that values verbal expressiveness, openness, and a certain degree of psychological mindedness, these values may cause problems between the counselor and minority client (Vontress, 1971; S. Sue & D. W. Sue, 1971a; D. W. Sue & S. Sue, 1972; Kaneshige, 1973). For example, the traditionalist may find it difficult to talk about feelings and may find counseling so ambiguous that the counselor must take a much more active approach in structuring the interview sessions. A recent study by Atkinson, Maruyama, & Matsui (1978) provides empirical support for this contention. These investigators found Asian Americans to prefer a logical, rational, structured counseling approach over an affective, reflective, ambiguous one. Since Asians respond more to structured situations and direct suggestions, the counselor must make modifications to his or her counseling style to incorporate such in order to be therapeutically effective.

THE CASE OF JANET T.

Janet T. is a 21-year-old senior, majoring in sociology. She was born and raised in Portland, Oregon, where she had limited contact with members of her own race. Her father, a second-generation Chinese American is a 53 year old doctor. Her mother, age 44, is a housewife. Janet is the second oldest of three children and has an older brother (currently in medical school) and a younger brother, age 17.

Janet came for therapy suffering from a severe depressive reaction manifested by feelings of worthlessness, by suicidal ideation, and by an inability to concentrate. She was unable to recognize the cause of her depression throughout the initial interviews. However, much light was shed on the problem when the therapist noticed an inordinate amount of hostility directed towards him. When inquiries were made about the hostility, it became apparent that Janet greatly resented being seen by a Chinese psychologist. Janet suspected that she had been assigned a Chinese therapist because of her own race. When confronted with this fact, Janet openly expressed scorn for "anything which reminds me of Chinese." Apparently, she felt very hostile towards Chinese customs and especially the Chinese male, whom she described as introverted, passive, and sexually unattractive.

Further exploration revealed a long-standing history of attempts to deny her Chinese ancestry by associating only with Caucasians. When in high school, Janet would frequently bring home white boyfriends which greatly upset her parents. It was as though she blamed her parents for being born a Chinese, and she used this method to hurt them.

During her college career, Janet became involved in two love affairs with Caucasians, both ending unsatisfactorily and abruptly. The last breakup occurred four months ago when the boy's parents threatened to cut off financial support for their son unless he ended the relationship. Apparently, objections arose because of Janet's race.

Although not completely conscious, Janet was having increasing difficulty with denying her racial heritage. The breakup of her last torrid love affair made her realize that she was Chinese and not fully accepted by all segments of society. At first she vehemently and bitterly denounced the Chinese for her present dilemma. Later, much of her hostility was turned inward against herself. Feeling alienated from her own subculture and not fully accepted by American society, she experienced an identity crisis. This resulted in feelings of worthlessness and depression. It was at this point that Janet came for therapy (S. Sue & D. W. Sue, 1971a, p. 41).

This particular case represents some of the conflicts encountered by the marginal person. The phenomenon of racial self-hatred is clearly evident. In their perception that traditional Asian ways serve as a hindrance to their own development and growth, many Asians attempt to become overwesternized by adopting white standards and customs. They become ashamed of Chinese or Japanese ways and rebel strongly against them. Counselors need to have a wider perspective of what culture-conflicts really mean. Although there is nothing inherently wrong in acculturation, Western society has frequently been so intolerant of other life-styles that deviations from Western norms are seen as abnormal. No wonder many Asian Americans begin to accept these comparisons and feel ashamed of their own racial and cultural identity. Viewed in this light, cultural conflicts may be manifestations of cultural racism.

In working with the marginal person, the counselor has an obligation to help the counselee sort out his/her identity conflicts by some form of reeducation. That is, somewhere in the process of counseling, the counselor must deal with the issue of cultural racism and its potential effects on individuals of minority backgrounds. Only in this manner can the counselor clear up the two sources of confusion that the marginal person apparently experiences. Specifically, the marginal person must be helped to distinguish between positive attempts to acculturate and a negative rejection of his or her own cultural values. Also, many Asians who desire independence from parental control are confusing independence for rejection of parental control. Such was the case of Janet T. In her attempts to show her independence, Janet had equated in her mind rebellion with independence. For the counselor to work effectively with such an individual, he or she must be conversant with the culture, history, and experiences of Asians in America. If not, this minority group is obligated to seek consultation from others more experienced in these matters or who refer their clients to appropriate resources.

THE CASE OF GALE K.

Gale K. is a 22-year-old first-year graduate student in biochemistry. His father, once employed in an engineering firm died recently from cancer. His 52-year-old mother is currently employed at the San Francisco Airport as a receptionist. Gale was born and raised in Oakland, California. He has three sisters, all of whom are married.

Much of Gale's early life was filled with conflict and antagonism between him and his parents. Like Janet T., Gale did not confine his social life exclusively to other Chinese Americans. Being the only son, his parents were fearful that they would lose their son should he marry a Caucasian. Five years earlier, their eldest daughter had married a Caucasian which caused great turmoil in the family and the subsequent disowning of the daughter.

Througout much of his life, Gale attempted to deny his racial identity because he felt shameful about being Chinese. However, within the last four years, a phenomenal change occurred in Gale. He actively participated in the Third World Strike at the University and became involved in a number of community change committees. Gale recalls with great fondness the "esprit de corps" and contagion he experienced with other concerned Asians. His parents had been delighted about his reorientation towards certain Chinese values. They were especially happy to see him dating other Asian girls and volunteering his time to tutor educationally deprived children in Chinatown. However, they did not understand his activist thinking and outspoken behavior towards authority figures.

Gale came for therapy because he had not fully resolved guilt feelings concerning the recent death of his father. Several weeks prior to his father's death, Gale had a violent argument with him over his recent participation in a demonstration. When his father passed away, Gale felt a great deal of remorse. He had often wished that his father would have understood the Asian American movement.

Throughout our sessions, Gale exhibited an understanding and awareness of economic, political, and social forces beyond that of the average student. He attributed the plight of Asian Americans to the shortcomings of society. He was openly suspicious of therapy and confronted the therapist on two different issues. The first objection dealt with the use of tests in therapy. Gale felt them to be culturally biased and somewhat inapplicable to ethnic minorities. The second issue concerned the relationship of therapy to the status quo. Since therapy had traditionally been concerned with the adjustment of individuals to society, Gale questioned the validity of this concept. "Do you adjust people to a sick society?" Only after dealing with these issues was it possible for Gale and the therapist to focus on his feelings regarding the death of his father (S. Sue & D. W. Sue, 1971a, pp. 43–44).

Unlike the traditionalist who defines self-worth by one's ability to bring honor to the family name and unlike the marginal person who defines self-worth via his or her ability to acculturate and be accepted by white society, the Asian American attempts to throw off the shackles of society by defining for himself/herself a new identity. All remnants of this person's old identity such as the term "Oriental" are replaced by such terms as "Asian American." This may be seen as a symbolic redefinition of this group's entire existence. The Asian American is much more aware than the other two groups of the political, social, and economic forces that have shaped his or her identity. The Asian American's greater social awareness makes him/her somewhat more sensitive to the effects of racism and often react with overt anger and militancy.

The emphasis on the inequities of society and the feeling that change must be instituted in racist institutions make many Asian Americans suspicious of counseling services. Many feel that counseling services are agents of the Establishment and that their primary goal is to adjust clients to society. This can cause difficulties both for the client whose political beliefs may mask his/her problems and for the counselor who must deal appropriately with certain challenges before counseling can proceed effectively. In the former, growing pride in self-identity frequently makes it difficult for many Asian students to accept their difficulties as personal rather than external. The client must be made to realize that although many problems of minorities are rooted in the shortcomings of society there is no inherent contradiction in viewing society as racist and having personal problems. On the other hand, the counselor must be sensitive enough to know that many problems encountered by his or her clients are caused by society and that he or she must act accordingly. Militance and emphasis on group pride are not signs of maladjustment as many individuals would have us believe. It is imperative, however, that counselors be able to distinguish between the two types of confusion.

CONCLUSIONS

Hopefully, the foregoing discussion has given you the readers an idea of the complexity of human behavior and how futile it is to attempt an understanding of ethnic minorities without an adequate exploration of their historical background, subcultural values, and unique conflicts. In the case of Asian Americans, these influences affect academic abilities, personality, vocational interests, and the manifestation of behavioral disorders. The lack of such knowledge and the insensitivity of Western society to the plight of minorities have done much harm to Asian Americans. Educators and social scientists have a moral obligation to enlighten themselves and others to the life experiences of disadvantaged groups. Only in an atmosphere of trust and understanding can different groups live together in health and harmony.

REFERENCES

Abbott, K., & Abbott, E. Juvenile delinquency in San Francisco's Chinese-American Community. *Journal of Sociology*, 1968, **4**, 45–56.

Abbott, K. *Harmony and Individualism*. Taipei: Orient Cultural Press, 1970.

Arkoff, A. Need patterns of two generations of Japanese-Americans in Hawaii. *Journal of Social Psychology*, 1959, **50**, 75–79.

Atkinson, D. R., Maruyama, M., & Matsui, S. The effects of counselor race and counseling approach on Asian Americans' perceptions of counselor credibility and utility. *Journal of Counseling Psychology*, 1978.

Bogardus, E. Measuring social distance. *Journal of Applied Sociology*, 1925, **9**, 229–308.

Boxley, R., & Wagner, N. N. Clinical psychology training programs and minority groups: A survey. *Professional Psychology*, 1971, **2**, 75–81.

Brown, T. R., Stein, K. M., Huang, K., & Harris, D. E. Mental illness and the role of mental health facilities in Chinatown. In S. Sue & N. N. Wagner (Eds.), *Asian Americans: Psychological Perspectives*. Palo Alto: Science & Behavior Books, 1973.

Charnofsky, S. Counseling for power. *Personnel and Guidance Journal*, 1971, **49**, 351–357.

Chin, R. New York Chinatown today: Community in crisis. *Amerasia Journal*, 1971, **1**, 1–24.

Chinatown gangs. *San Francisco Chronicle*, July 5, 1972.

Cordova, F. The Filipino-American, there's always an identity crisis. In S. Sue & N. N. Wagner (Eds.), *Asian Americans: Psychological Perspectives*. Palo Alto: Science & Behavior, 1973.

Daniels, R. *Concentration camps USA: Japanese Americans and World War II*. New York: Holt, Rinehart & Winston, 1971.

DeVos, G., & Abbott, K. *The Chinese family in San Francisco*. MSW dissertation, University of California, Berkeley, 1966.

Fenz, W., & Arkoff, A. Comparative need patterns of five ancestry groups in Hawaii. *Journal of Social Psychology*, 1962, **58**, 67–89.

Fong, S. L. M. Assimilation of Chinese in America. Changes in orientation and social perception. *American Journal of Sociology*, 1965, **71**, 265–273.

Hollingshead, A., & Redlich, F. *Social Class and Mental Illness*. New York: Wiley, 1958.

Jacobs, P., Landau, S., & Pell, E. *To Serve the Devil. Vol. 2 Colonials and Sojourners*. New York: Vintage Books, 1971.

Kagiwada, G., & Fujimoto, I. Asian-American studies: Implications for education. *Personnel and Guidance Journal*, 1973, **51**, 400–405.

Kane, M. B. *Minorities in textbooks: A study of their treatment in social studies texts*. Chicago: Quadrangle, 1970.

Kaneshige, E. Cultural factors in group counseling and interaction. *Personnel and Guidance Journal*, 1973, **51** 407–412.

Karno, M., & Edgarton, R. B. Perception of mental illness in a Mexican-American community. *Archives of General Psychiatry*, 1969, **20** 233–238.

Kikumura, A., & Kitano, H. H. Interracial marriage: A picture of the Japanese Americans. *Journal of Social Issues*, 1973, **29**, 67–81.

Kimmich, R. A. Ethnic aspects of schizophrenia in Hawaii. *Psychiatry*, 1960, **23**, 97–102.

Kitano, H. H. L. Changing achievement patterns of the Japanese in the United States. *Journal of Social Psychology*, 1962, **58**, 257–264.

Kitano, H. H. L Inter- and intragenerational differences in maternal attitudes toward child rearing. *Journal of Social Psychology*, 1964, **63**, 215–220.

Kitano, H. H. L. Japanese-American crime and delinquency. *Journal of Psychology*, 1967, **66**, 253–263.

Kitano, H. H. L. Japanese-American mental illness. In S. C. Plog & R. B. Edgarton (Eds.), *Changing Perspectives in Mental Illness*. New York: Holt, Rinehart & Winston, 1969a.

Kitano, H. H. L. *Japanese-Americans: The Evolution of a Subculture*. Englewood Cliffs, N. J.: Prentice-Hall, 1969b.

Kitano, H. H. L. Mental illness in four cultures. *Journal of Social Psychology*, 1970, **80**, 121–134.

Lyman, S. M. *The Asian in the West*. Reno, Nev.: University of Nevada Press, 1970.

Marsella, A. J., Kinzie, D., & Gordon, P. Depression patterns among American college students of Caucasian, Chinese, and Japanese ancestry. Paper presented at the Conference on Culture and Mental Health in Asia and the Pacific. Honolulu, March 1971.

Matsumoto, G. M., Meredith, G., & Masuda, M. Ethnic identification: Honolulu and Seattle Japanese-Americans. *Journal of Cross-Cultural Psychology*, 1970, **1**, 63–76.

Meredith, G. M. Amae and acculturation among Japanese-American college students in Hawaii. *Journal of Social Psychology*, 1966, **70**, 171–180.

Rabaya, V. Filipino immigration: The creation of a new social order. In A. Tachiki, E. Wong, F. Odo, & B. Wong (Eds.), *Roots: An Asian American Reader*. Los Angeles: UCLA, 1971.

Rosenthal, R., & Jacobson, L. *Pygmalion in the Classroom*. New York: Holt, Rinehart & Winston, 1968.

Shin, L. Koreans in America, 1903–1945. In A. Tachiki, E. Wong, F. Odo, & B. Wong (Eds.), *Roots: An Asian American Reader*. Los Angeles, UCLA, 1971.

Smith, M. E. Progress in the use of English after twenty-two years by children of Chinese ancestry in Honolulu. *Journal of Genetic Psychology*, 1957, **90**, 255–258.

Smith, M. E., & Kasdon, L. M. Progress in the use of English after twenty years by children of Filipino and Japanese ancestry in Hawaii. *Journal of Genetic Psychology*, 1961, **99**, 129–138.

Sommers, V. S. Identity conflict and acculturation problems in Oriental-Americans. *American Journal of Orthopsychiatry*, 1960, **30**, 637–644.

Success story of one minority group in the U. S. *U. S. News & World Report*, December 1966.

Success story: Outwhiting the whites. *Newsweek*, June 1971.

Sue, D. W. Ethnic identity: The impact of two cultures on the psychological development of Asians in America. S. Sue & N. Wagner (Eds.), *Asian Americans: Psychological Perspectives*, Palo Alto, Calif.: Science and Behavior Books, 1973.

Sue, D. W., & Frank, A. C. A typological approach to the study of Chinese- and Japanese-American college males. *Journal of Social Issues*, 1973, **29**, 129–148.

Sue, D. W., & Kirk, B. A. Asian Americans: Use of counseling and psychiatric services on a college campus. *Journal of Counseling Psychology*, 1975, **22**, 84–86.

Sue, D. W., & Kirk, B. A. Differential characteristics of Japanese-American and Chinese-American college students. *Journal of Counseling Psychology*, 1973, **20**, 142–148.

Sue, D. W., & Kirk, B. A. Psychological characteristics of Chinese-American college students. *Journal of Counseling Psychology*, 1972, **6**, 471–478.

Sue, D. W., & Sue, S. Ethnic minorities: Resistance to being researched. *Professional Psychology*, 1972, **2**, 11–17.

Sue, S., & Kitano, H. H. L. Stereotypes as a measure of success. *Journal of Social Issues*, 1973, **29**, 83–98.

Sue, S., & McKinney, H. Asian Americans in the community mental health care system. *American Journal of Orthopsychiatry*, 1975, **45**, 111–118.

Sue, S., & Sue, D. W. Chinese-American personality and mental health. *Amerasia Journal*, 1971a, **1**, 36–49.

Sue, S., & Sue, D. W. MMPI comparison between Asian-American and non-Asian students utilizing a student health psychiatric clinic. *Journal of Counseling Psychology*, 1974, **21**, 423–427.

Sue, S., & Sue, D. W. The reflection of culture conflict in the psychological problems of Chinese and Japanese students. Paper presented at the American Psychological Association Convention, 1971b, Honolulu.

Sue, S., Sue, D. W., & Sue, D. Asian Americans as a minority group. *American Psychologist*, 1975, **31**, 906–910.

Sung, B. L. *Mountains of Gold*. New York: Macmillan, 1967.

Takayama, G. Analysis of data on Asian students at U. C. Berkeley, 1971. Project Report, AS 150, Asian Studies Division, University of California, Berkeley, Winter, 1971.

Tinker, J. N. Intermarriage and ethnic boundaries: The Japanese American case. *Journal of Social Issues*, 1973, **29**, 49–66.

Urban Associates. A study of selected socioeconomic characteristics based on the 1970 census. *Asian Americans*, vol. 2. Washington, D.C.: U.S. Government Printing Office, 1974.

Vontress, C. E. Racial differences: Impediments to rapport. *Journal of Counseling Psychology*, 1971, **18**, 7–13.

Watanabe, C. Self-expression and the Asian-American experience. *Personnel and Guidance Journal*, 1973, **51**, 390–396.

Weiss, M. S. Selective acculturation and the dating process: The patterning of Chinese-Caucasian interracial dating. *Journal of Marriage and the Family*, 1970, **32**, 273–282.

Wright, B. R. Social aspects of change in the Chinese family pattern in Hong Kong. *Journal of Social Psychology*, 1964, **63**, 31–39.

Yamamoto, J., James, J. C., & Palley, N. Cultural problems in psychiatric therapy. *Archives of General Psychiatry*, 1969, **19**, 45–49.

STUDY QUESTIONS

1. Statistics seem to support the myth that Asians in America are a successful minority with no great counseling needs. What factors may be creating this illusion?

2. How may the historical experiences of Asians in America affect their world views?

3. What cultural values of traditional Asians negate the effectiveness of Western counseling approaches?

4. What sociocultural forces were considered important in affecting academic abilities, personality, and vocational interests? In what ways are the academic abilities and personality adjustments of Asian Americans consistent with their vocational interests?

5. How has cultural racism (culture-conflict) affected the identity development of Asians in America?

6. What counseling approaches were suggested by the author in working with Asian Americans? How may the use of the approaches depend on the cultural identity of the student?

7

Cultural and Historical Perspectives in Counseling Blacks

ELSIE J. SMITH

It has become increasingly clear that the crises observed between Blacks and whites and between the haves and the have-nots in the broad American society are reenacted daily in the counseling interview. The forces that have historically estranged Blacks and whites; that is, the lack of trust, the prejudices surrounding cultural differences, the subtle and the not-so-subtle forms of racial discrimination have infiltrated the counseling relationship (Gardner, 1971; Sattler, 1970; Lerner, 1972). In America, prejudice runs deep and dies hard. It is nurtured by generations of "hand-me-down" hatreds.

Despite the counseling profession's firm public avowal of the dignity and worth of all human beings, the profession has taken a backseat in the cause of human dignity and good mental health for minorities. As Martin Luther King (1968) stated, social scientists have played little or no role in disclosing the truth about the plight of minorities in the United States. Instead, "it was the Negro who educated the nation [to the brutal facts of segregation] by dramatizing the evils through nonviolent protest" (King, 1968, p. 180).

The liberal facade of counseling has only camouflaged its internal difficulties regarding the treatment of minorities. All too often counselors have entered the counseling relationship unmindful of the intrusion of their excess, white middle-class cultural baggage. They have tried to make their values, their clients' values; their racial and cultural perspectives, those of their clients. The net result has been that the counseling profession has demanded a type of racial and cultural conformity in client behavior that has been demeaning and that has denied different ethnic and racial minorities the right of their cultural heritage in counseling.

Clearly, there is a crisis in counseling Black people, one that must be analyzed from the perspectives of race, cultural background, and socioeconomic class. The following discussion attempts to integrate the research and to analyze the various findings regarding the use of counseling and psychotherapy with Black Americans. Attention is directed toward examining how historical factors and cultural perspectives have helped to shape the psychological, educational, and vocational development of members of this racial group.

THE BLACK EXPERIENCE IN AMERICA

The history of Black Americans is the struggle of a people to survive against great odds and injustices. It is a record of people's inhumanity to people. As such, it is something that many white Americans want to forget, to put behind them as if it never happened. This feeling was typified by one literary critic's review of *Roots*, the recent best-seller about a Black man's search for his past. The critic's review went something like this: "At least this book does not try to make us [white people] feel guilty. This, in itself, is a pleasant relief. We've already heard too much about slavery, about the white man's injustices to Blacks. . . . Except for the blood curdling section about the treatment of slaves on the ships, *Roots* does not try to gain our sympathy. . . . It lets us draw our own conclusions" (Simon, 1977, p. 25).

As I finished reading the review, I wondered if the critic would have been so cavalier in dismissing his own history—the roots of his particular ethnic and racial group. Would he say, for instance: "We've already heard too much about white history—about the American Revolution, the Bicentennial, and the like? I think not, for those events are a part of his life, perhaps a part of his parents' life and that of his grandparents. These events are, in short, moments he would like to remember because they symbolize his sense of peoplehood, while the history of Blacks—slavery, the Constitution's three-fifth's man, lynchings, and the institutionalization of injustice are moments he would like to forget and dismiss under the banner that they are "sympathy-getters." There are no trees without roots, and people seek their ancestry no matter how bitter and gnarled such roots may be.

Black history should not be taken for granted or ignored in counseling minority clients. Nor should it be viewed as a "sympathy arouser," for understanding and sympathy—although two fruits—do not grow from the same tree. As counselors, we can learn a great deal from looking at Black history. We can see some of the roots of our present-day difficulties in counseling members of this racial group.

The history of Black people is both the bond that welds them together and sets them apart from other Americans. Black Americans, if one can speak of them as a homogeneous group, have experienced a cultural press different from that experienced by many minority groups in America. Few ethnic or racial minorities in American society have been so thoroughly blocked from having a constructive identity group formation, have been pressed to trust whites more so than themselves, have had a value system imposed on them that so totally and forcefully undermined their self-esteem and their very existence. As W. E. B. DuBois (1947) has noted: "Prolonged policies of segregation and discrimination have involuntarily welded the mass almost into a nation within a nation with its own schools, churches, hospitals, newspapers, and many business enterprises" (p. 263). The common bond, then, that unites Black people is not the color of their skins (for their colors vary) but rather the experiences they have collectively and individually been forced to endure because of their skin color.

Slavery

Slavery was one of the most important factors that shaped the social, psychological, economic, educational, and political development of Black people. From slavery came a host of structured interpersonal dynamics between Blacks and whites and among Blacks themselves. False belief systems regarding Black people's "genetic inferiority" and their childlike nature and the white man's burden and natural superiority were used to rationalize the existence of slavery in the so-called free democracy. Slavery in America was complete and, according to Elkins (1959), it was one of the most destructive forms of slavery on record. The Black family, the basic unit of Black society, was systematically destroyed for more than two centuries. Only after the Civil War was it to be born again.

Black reactions to slavery were varied—ranging from numerous revolts aboard ship to suicide, mass suicide, work slowdowns, and running away in America (Wilkinson, 1970). Perhaps more important, however, were the psychological and sociological adjustments Black people made under varying conditions of slavery. For example, a great deal of African culture was expunged, with only those nonthreatening elements—like music and dance—remaining. Identification with the master/aggressor and self-debasement were two coping strategies Black people used to survive. Other responses included imitation and emulation of the slave master's values and life-style and dependency behaviors.

It is no small secret, for instance, that Blacks themselves often-times made the same insidious color distinctions as did whites. Those with straight hair were known as those who had "good hair," and light-complexioned Blacks often refused to associate with those who had darker skins. Even the cultural sayings such as "If you're white, you're all right. If you're brown, stick around, and if you're Black, get back" attempted to reveal comically the state of affairs. But there was no real comedy in this saying—only a mirror of stark reality. Beauty was then (as it often is now) defined by white people, and the closer one came to looking like whites, the more Black people considered that person attractive.

These attitudes were reinforced by slave masters. Frequently, it was the light-skinned Black who was taken as a house servant and who was given less arduous physical work; hence the present-day expression "house nigger" is used by Blacks to describe one who receives preferential treatment by whites and one who may even collude with whites to bring about Black destruction.

According to Howard (1972), identification and emulation of the aggressor is not indigenous to Black people. These acts reflect the condition of any people who suffer from a colonial mentality. Comparing the actions of Blacks and Asians, Howard states: "But when the wife of General Nguyen Cao Ky has plastic surgery done on her eyes to make them less slanted, as some 200,000 Asian women do annually, it is scarcely noticed in the black community. Both of these attempts to become more 'beautiful' are of the same order of phenomena, for they are both attempts to become more European looking. Both are manifestations of what my colleagues and I call the 'colonized mentality' " (p. 327). One could also report similar findings for other racial minorities.

Moreover, present-day research has attempted to revive the colonial mentality—not just for Blacks—but for whites as well. According to Shockley (1971) lighter-skinned Blacks are more intelligent than dark-skinned ones, for they have more "white blood" in them. Eysenck (1972) has also taken the same position regarding "white blood" and the IQ's of Blacks.

Just as slavery was devastating for Black people, it provided a psychological boom for whites. Nowhere, as in the United States (with the exception of some parts of Africa, i.e., South Africa, Rhodesia), have white people been so elevated for the simple factor of the color of their skins (Herkovits, 1958; Myrdal, 1944; Delaney, 1968). To be white in America meant more than just being a member of a privileged economic class. It meant that one had massive governmental support for white people's assumed superiority that one could obtain a sense of person adequacy and control, regardless of one's socioeconomic status. To achieve this end, all one had to do was to compare oneself with the Black slave. As J. D. B. DeBow (1963) wrote in his pre-Civil War periodical in the South: "No white man in the South serves another as a body servant, to clean his boots, wait on his table, and perform the menial services of his household" (p. 174).

The U. S. Constitution's notion of the three-fifth's Black man was but one more clear instance of the psychological and political benefit of being white in America. The three-fifth's Black man provision was written into the Constitution by the Founding Fathers to keep the loyalty of the slaveholders and slave traders in the North and South. The provision stated that since slaveholders were to be taxed for their slaves as property, slaveholders were to be allowed three votes for every five slaves owned.

The Mental Health Profession

During slavery, the mental health field only mirrored the racism of white American society; it did not seek to cure it. Like every other aspect of American life, it sought ways to justify the white treatment of Black people. For example, the establishment of mental hospitals in the late eighteenth and early nineteenth centuries in the United States provided for separate quarters for Blacks and whites. Grob (1966) has reported that the Worchester State Hospital in Massachusetts, a landmark state institution established in 1833 by leading reformers in the field, remodeled a brick shop to provide separate facilities for the Black mentally ill.

Prior to the Civil War, members of the mental health field used several arguments and lines of reasoning to demonstrate that slavery was actually beneficial for Black people (A. Deutsch, 1944). It was reported that Blacks and Indians suffered from lower levels of mental illness, presumably because these were the less civilized races, according to Darwinian-like conceptualization of the evolution of different races. Mental illness, in the opinion of researchers at that period, was the price one paid for advanced civilization and progress. Low levels of mental illness among slaves was, then, further proof of the slaves' retarded, childlike development.

Second, the figures cited from the 1840 census regarding insanity in the United States were used to buttress the argument that slavery was good for Black people (A. Deutsch, 1944). Through specious reporting of statistics, it was concluded that free Blacks living in the North were more prone to insanity than were slaves living in the South. According to proponents who held this point of view, the free Black person in the North found it difficult to cope with the absence of a master. This line of reasoning was used even after evidence was given to demonstrate that the census figures were erroneous.

Third, studies on the alleged small craniums of Black people were used to demonstrate that Blacks were psychologically and intellectually inferior. This position became known as the "inferior brain thesis" and was only later resoundly demolished in centuries to come (Tobias, 1970). However, the vestiges of this theory continue to reappear in different forms in modern-day America—notably in the works of Jensen (1969) and Shockley (1971).

In short, the concept of genetic inferiority was the prevailing theme of mental health workers during slavery. This concept, as well as other ideas already noted, laid the foundation for the later treatment of Black people in the mental health field. Although slavery as an institution became a thing of the past with the end of the Civil War, the myths, stereotypes, and issues that accompanied this period remained basically intact.

The Reconstruction period (1865–1877) and the years that followed marked the beginning of an uphill battle for the former slaves to gain access to equal opportunity. During the 1800s (1870 to 1890), white mental health professionals argued that the emancipation of Blacks had increased their rates of insanity from 35 to 285% (Babcock, 1895). Psychological breakdown was said to occur because Black people did not know how to deal appropriately with their new freedom. Little, if any, research was done to see if the abolition of slavery had any positive effects on the mental or physical health of Blacks.

During the early 1900s, statistics on the mental health of whites and Blacks were also distributed. It was reported that Blacks suffered from a high rate of schizophrenia, a claim that is still made today because of this group's precarious racial position in the United States. As late as 1930, however, it was believed that Black people could not be psychoanalyzed. Concern was expressed over freeing the Black person's libido.

During the 1950s, there was a notable shift in the helping professionals' conceptualization of the mental health problems of Black people. The genetic inferiority theory was replaced with the theory of social pathology. Black people were believed to be inferior and beyond counseling redemption because of the social pathology within their own communities.

One of the more important developments for minorities in the field of health was the introduction of counseling into the schools on a widespread basis (Miller, 1961). Armed with their psychological tests and notions of what was good for minorities, counselors helped to place a significant number of minority students into vocational curricula that led to dead-end streets (Cicourel & Kituse, 1963; Sexton, 1971) and unemployment.

In the 1960s, researchers embellished the "tangle of pathology" theme, put forth by Kardiner and Ovesey (1951), with the concept of cultural deprivation. Here Riessman's book, *The Culturally Deprived Child* (1962), was to be a major influence in analyzing Black clients' behavior.

It was not until the Civil Rights movement of the 1960s and the subsequent Black power movement that Blacks themselves began to refute on a large-group basis many of the research statements regarding them and their behavior. The popular song "Say it Loud; I'm Black and Proud" became the battle cry of many young Black people. At this time, Black Americans also began to confront themselves with the cultural meanings of Blackness, and a resurgence of interest in Black culture took place. Some members of the helping professions picked up on this theme and outlined the ramifications of the Black pride movement for the counseling relationship (Kincaid, 1969; & Pinderhughes, 1969). Thus both of these movements served as massive dosages of "sociotherapy" for Black people. Yet the increase in Black pride had a side effect: it was met with white rage, white fear, and, in some instances, white assistance and respect.

In the 1970s, increased numbers of investigators began to speak out against person-blame research (Ryan, 1971; Caplan & Nelson, 1974; Herzog, 1971; Smith, 1977). Such investigators argued that too much attention had been concentrated on analyzing social problems in such a manner that the causations of these problems were found to lie in the victims themselves rather than in the racist institutions of the United States.

Some researchers have also stressed the need for a Black psychology (Pugh, 1972), and new models of Black mental health must do more than merely emphasize the psychology of adjustment or the traditional coping mechanisms members of this racial group have used to survive. As Simpkins, Williams, & Gunnings (1971) have stressed: Blacks have almost always used coping mechanisms that have resulted in adjustments on their part and not on the part of whites. To be successful, counseling for minorities must be a combination of both "survival" and "change" mechanisms. Such counseling for minorities must involve a poignant sense of minorities' history, the present, and the future of the members of various groups (Howard, 1972).

The 1970s marked a curious blend of backward and forward movement in terms of the conceptualizations of the problems of Black mental health. Summarizing the plight of Blacks and the mental health movement, Kramer (1973, p. 3) has stated:

In the United States the mental health movement has had White middle-class Americans as its historic core of concern. While exceptions and changing trends are discernible, it is nonetheless a fact that race and class have decisively determined the character of the mental health movement.

Education and Career Development

The history of Blacks' education and career development shares many points in common with what took place in the field of mental health. Despite the existence of slavery and laws that prohibited Black people from obtaining an education, a small minority managed to acquire an elementary and, in some few instances, a secondary education (Woodson, 1919). These early accomplishments can be attibuted to (1) Christian missionary efforts; (2) philanthropic actions; (3) Black people's determination to obtain an education, even under adverse conditions; and (4) the activities of abolitionists (West, 1972).

Slavery had several important effects on Black education. First, it left over 90% of Black people illiterate at the end of the Civil War. Second, it set the trend for the low educational achievement of this group. Third, it set the precedent for legal segregation in schools. Fourth, it established the belief that Blacks needed a special kind of education. The primary issue here was whether Blacks should receive a classical/academic or industrial/vocational education. Even minorities did not agree on this latter point, as evidenced by the different positions taken later by Booker T. Washington (industrial) and W. E. B. DuBois (classical).

Hopes awakened by the end of the Civil War resulted in intense activity in education for this minority group. Education became a symbol of the ex-slaves' "badge of freedom." During Reconstruction, northern liberals and teachers traveled to the South to establish schools for Blacks. The efforts of these groups contributed much to the educational development of minorities. For example, in 1870 only 3% of the Black population of the southern states was enrolled in schools. By 1898, the number had increased to 18% (Woodson, 1919).

The movement of Blacks away from southern agriculture and into the cities of the North and the South had a significant impact on their educational and career development (Briggs, 1975). By 1930, for example; 20% of all Blacks lived in the North. For the most part, those who migrated during this time did so with few skills and poor education. The movement to the North increased family disorganization, and those who migrated met with hostility from both members of their race and whites. Hence, the displaced family often moved into an environment that was unaccepting.

During the 1930s, concern was expressed regarding the educational and personality development of Black children. Several studies were conducted to ascertain the effects of minority group status on the personality development of Black youth (Davis & Dollard, 1964; Frazier, 1940; Warner, Junker & Adams, 1969). These studies found that the environment in which Black youth lived not only adversely affected their personality development and self-concepts, but also their educational achievements.

These core studies led to increased research on the self-concepts of Black youth, culminating in the historic report of Kenneth Clark (1952) on the effects of discrimination on Black children and the 1954 Supreme Court decision outlawing de jure (legislated) school desegregation.

Since Clark's early findings regarding the negative effects of school segregation on Black children's self-concepts, several investigators have given conflicting findings in this area (Douglas, 1971; Moses, Zirkel & Green, 1973; Bartee, 1967; Soares & Soares, 1969; Gibby & Gabler, 1967; Powell, 1973; Arnez, 1972). Obviously, racial discrimination has had a negative effect on the self-concepts and educational achievement of Blacks. Given the developments and accomplishments of Blacks over the past 28 years, it would appear that the belief in the widespread negative self-concepts of Blacks may be an overgeneralization.

The problem is not so much one of negative concepts on the part of Black people as it is one of socioeconomic and political injustice. Theories regarding the negative self-concepts of Blacks, the "tangle of pathology" of the Black family, and the "cultural deprivation" of Blacks have been used by social scientists to avoid dealing with the real and significant issues that affect negatively the education progress of Black people—issues such as racism in the schools, inferior schools, unemployment, and underemployment of Black parents.

Evidence to support, for example the theory of the negative influences of Black culture and family is missing or at best conflicting. Although M. Deutsch & Brown (1964) reported that Black children from broken homes had lower IQ scores than those from intact families, a follow-up study by Whiteman & M. Deutsch (1968) found no such relationship. Moreover, both the Coleman et al. (1966) study and Wilson's California study (1967) have indicated that the presence or absence of a father in the home was not a significant factor in the achievement of lower socioeconomic Black and white students.

Beliefs concerning the Black culture's low evaluation of education have likewise been challenged. In an extensive review of the literature on Black culture and education, Proshansky & Newton (1968) concluded that the real difference between Blacks and whites lies not so much in their goals or values but rather in the expectations each racial group has regarding the achievement of their goals. Whereas lower socioeconomic Black youth expressed few expectations of achieving their educational aspirations, middle-class Black youths' expectations of accomplishing their educational goals were high and comparable to those of their white counterparts. Support for this theory is partially reflected in Black students' attempt to obtain college educations.

Several features have been noted about the Black college student. First, the Black college student's persistence rate compared favorably with that of non-Black students of similar academic ability (Astin & Panos, 1969). Second, more Black students than non-Black said they wanted to obtain a graduate degree (Bayer & Boruch, 1969; Astin, 1970). However, Astin & Bisconti's study of the career plans of minority graduates of 1965 and 1970 indicated that most chose to go into business and teaching, while few gave plans to enter engineering and the sciences. To compete successfully in the decades to come, more Blacks will have to major in the sciences and technological areas as well as the professional fields of medicine, dentistry, and law.

BLACK CULTURE

Black American culture has been analyzed from several perspectives: (1) the cultural deficit approach, (2) the cultural difference model and (3) the high- and low-context conceptual framework. Each of these theoretical formulations has implications for counseling minority youth.

The Cultural Deficit Approach

Since the cultural deficit approach has been alluded to in earlier sections, it is only briefly described here. Basically, the cultural deficit approach has asserted that Blacks are lacking in their educational and career achievements because of problems that exist within their culture and not within the broad American treatment of them.

There are two primary variations on the cultural deficit model of Black life. The first variation has emphasized that for Blacks to achieve they must first undergo cultural enrichment. For example, M. Deutsch & Brown (1964) have argued that cultural enrichment and compensatory education can reverse the spiral of cognitive and learning deficits. In the guidance and counseling sector, this position has been translated to mean that Black youth need more positive adult role models.

The opportunity deprivation theme has been a second variation of the deficit model. Advocaters of this approach to Black culture have maintained that Blacks are not so much culturally deprived as they are opportunity deprived. Guidance/counseling and educational policies associated with this version of the deficit model have concentrated on developing intervention strategies that would increase the opportunities for Blacks in work, education, and positive psychological health (Lieberson & Fugitt, 1967).

The Cultural Difference Model

The cultural difference model has stressed that differences in Black culture are not deficits or signs of racial inferiority; rather they are "manifestations of visible and well-delineated" culture (Simpkins, Williams & Gunnings, 1971). Counseling literature espousing this point of view has proposed that programs should be designed to take into account variations among the cultures of minority groups in American society.

According to Valentine (1971), however, the cultural difference approach has little significant explanatory validity and may be harmful if used to establish educational policies and programs. In place of the cultural difference theory, Valentine has suggested the concept of biculturation to describe Black life. As Valentine (1971) has stated:

The collective behavior and social life of the Black community is bicultural in the sense that each Afro-American group ethnic segment draws upon both a distinctive repertoire of standardized Afro-American group behavior and simultaneously, patterns derived from the mainstream cultural system of Euro-American derivation. (p. 143)

Valentine maintains that reeducating white professionals to accept the cultural differences will only result in failure and possibly even hostility. He states:

Certainly nothing will be accomplished by trying to teach professionals respect for sub-cultural systems when all their other training and experience has already taught them to regard these same cultures as impersonally pathogenic and personally threatening. (1971, p. 156)

In a rejoinder to Valentine, Simpkins, Williams, & Gunnings (1971) have asserted that the bicultural model (1) equates the exposure of Blacks to white culture with acculturation into it; (2) gives lip service to the existence of a Black culture, while elevating that of whites; and (3) biculturation is a one-way street for Blacks to experience; the case for the reverse situation to occur is dismissed by Valentine.

The High- and Low-Context Model

Hall (1976a) has suggested that most cultures can be categorized as either high- or low-context cultures. Low-context cultures place a greater reliance on the verbal part of the message than on the non-verbal aspect of communication. Low-context cultures are also more opportunistic, more individually than group oriented, more prone to emphasizing rules of procedures and laws for governing a person's interpersonal behavior rather than on moral commitment. The opposite is true of high-context cultures, wherein the emphasis is on group identification and the nonverbal aspects of communication. According to Hall (1976a), American culture is more oriented toward a low- rather than a high-context culture.

Hall (1976, 1976b) has maintained that the grass roots of ethnic Black culture (as opposed to that of the Black middle class) is "considerably higher in context than the white culture" (p. 54). Such differences in the type of cultural context of Blacks and whites have led to misunderstandings between members of these two groups. For example, Hall relates the story of how a Black draftsman was almost fired from his job because of his employer's perception that the draftsman was not listening to him.

Entering into the white listening system has traditionally been a problem for Blacks. To show that they are listening, some Blacks have adopted an exaggerated version of what they thought whites expected. As Hall (1976a) has stated:

Old-time Pullman porters used to do a lot of head-bobbing and foot-shuffling and yessing, which was a response to their being hassled by whites. In those days, not knowing the nature of the white listening system, they didn't want to take chances and so they produced an exaggerated version of what whites expected, to show their customers they were paying attention. (pp. 74, 97)

No one model can entirely explain Black culture. As with other minority groups, it is easier to be a part of Black culture than to describe it. Yet, throughout the centuries, Black people have developed certain cultural perspectives or outlooks on life that have helped to shape their identity.

Cultural Diversity

However, it is a misnomer to speak of Black culture as a monolithic experience. Within this culture, there are broad ranges of behavior as well as important class and geographic distinctions that may be observed among members of this cultural/racial group. Along such lines, Gordon (1964) has made a useful distinction regarding the cultural perspectives of Black people. According to him, there are two types of identities Black people share: the historical and the participational. The historical definition refers to Black people's development as a race and their sense of peoplehood. The participational definition centers around the behavior similarities they may share. As Gordon (1964) has stated:

Within a person of the same class but of a different ethnic group, one shares a sense of peoplehood. With those of the same ethnic but different social class one shares the sense of peoplehood but not behavioral similarities. The only criterion which meets both these criterion are people of the same ethnic and social class. (p. 53)

Hence it is with these limitations in mind—the sharing of peoplehood and the sharing of behavior—that we must examine the cultural perspectives of Blacks.

The Oral Tradition

Such perspectives have included a strong oral tradition of storytelling as a means of preserving and expressing the philosophy of their philosophy of their people. The "Uncle Remus" tales and the adventures of Br'er Rabbit, who always managed to get the best of the bigger animals that seemingly had control, are examples of this tradition. The folk sermons of James Weldon Johnson's "God's Trombones"; the poetry of Paul Lawrence Dunbar and Langston Hughes; and the novels of Richard Wright, Ralph Ellison, James Baldwin, and countless others also bear witness to this admixture of oral and written tradition. Through their stories, Black people have been able to compress years of their history into a few statements. They have been able to pass on to their children and their children's children the philosophy of their race.

Black humor has been an important part of the oral tradition. Consciously or unconsciously, it has invariably taken a stand against racial injustice and brought insights to Black life. Bogle (1975), for example, reports the conversation of two slaves who, exhausted from a hard day's work, sat in their cabins and said: "You hear tell a white hen done laid a Black egg." "Yeah," the other answered, "They sho gonna hang her tonight."

More recently, Richard Pryor's comedy has brought Black comedy and the oral tradition full circle. In explaining the stereotypes whites have of Blacks and the debilitating aspects of trying to cope in a white world, Pryor relates the poignant and touching conversation between a wino and a junkie. "Look at that nigger," the wino said. . . . "Nigger used to be a genius. . . . Booked the numbers, didn't need paper or pencil. Now that nigger can't remember who he is." In the case of Richard Pryor, Black humor and the oral tradition were used to explain Blacks without trying to demean their experiences. White counselors and educators are not just beginning to decipher (although they laughed) the political and social meanings of Richard Pryor's humor.

Moreover, an appreciation of music and dance has also been a part of Black people's culture—far beyond what some white Americans could ever imagine. The spirituals, the blues, jazz, and soul music in general, have all been forms of expression for Black people's feelings. People like Bessie Smith, Ma Rainey, Billie Holiday, Charlie Parker, and Alvin Ailey have captured, in many respects, the essence of Black people. It is through these measures that minorities have manifested their personality and their emotional state.

Cultural Connotations of Blackness and Whiteness

For some minorities, there have come to be certain cultural connotations of being Black. Being Black has come to symbolize honesty, the capability of bearing great pain and sorrow, and strength and truth in the face of great adversity (Toldson & Pasteur, 1976). The term "soul" embodies many of these sentiments and the cultural ramifications in interpersonal encounters. When one Black person talks privately with another, he or she might say: "Look, we don't have to jive each other or be like white folks; let's be honest with one another." These statements reflect the familiar Black saying that "talk is cheap," that actions speak louder than words, and that whites beguile each other with words.

In contrast, the white mind symbolizes to many Black people deceit, verbal chicanery, and sterile intellectivity. For example, after a long discourse with a white person, a Black individual might say: "I've heard what you've said, but what do you really mean?" Eldridge Cleaver (1970) made reference to this type of polarizing of cultural opposites between the two races when he said that in the slave-master relationship, the Black person was a "soul on ice." Whereas white people had lost touch with the spiritual and physical (and were desperately trying to regain these missing links in such activities as encounter groups, transcendental meditation, and Yoga), Black individuals had been denied the full development of their intellectual strengths.

Communication Styles

Black people place a great deal of importance on the nonverbal behavior of individuals in their cultural connotations. They are apt to spend much time observing people to see "where they are coming from." Much of this observance takes place so unobtrusively that the observed person is usually unaware that he or she is being watched carefully. According to Hall (1976b), the keen ability of minorities to read nonverbal cues has facilitated their survival in white American society.

There are also other kinds of cultural differences in Black and white individuals' styles of communication. It is not necessary, for example, for minorities to look one another in the eye at all times in order for them to communicate. In fact, some Blacks may be actively involved in a conversation with another person while continuing to do other things. When white counselors observe this style of communication, they are likely to interpret it as sullenness, lack of interest, or fear.

For instance, one Black female student was sent to the office by her gymnasium teacher because the student was said to display insolent behavior. When the student was asked to give her version of the incident, she replied: "Mrs. X asked all of us to come over to the side of the pool so that she could show us how to do the backstroke. I went over with the rest of the girls. Then Mrs. X started yelling at me because she said that I wasn't paying attention to her because I wasn't looking directly at her. I told her I was paying attention to her (throughout this conversation, the student kept her head down, averting the principal's eyes) and then she said that she wanted me to face her and look her squarely in the eye like the rest of the girls (who were all white). So I did. The next thing I knew she was telling me to get out of the pool—that she didn't like the way I was looking at her. So that's why I'm here."

The principal told the student that she was going to let her off easy this time, that she had had a good record in the past, but the next time there was any trouble between her and Mrs. X, he was going to call in her mother. The student returned to class angry with Mrs. X but glad that her mother was not being contacted about the incident.

As Hall (1976a) has observed, lower-socioeconomic Blacks do not nod their heads or make little noises to show that they are listening to a person the manner in which whites do. From a counseling perspective, one might say that Blacks do not feel obligated to give the traditional "un-hum" that is often expected in some counseling relationships.

There may also exist differences in the types of verbal messages that Blacks and whites give to each other. Sometimes middle-class whites' and Blacks' use of say certain phrases much in the same manner as the perfunctory greetings: "Hello," "How are you doing"? or "Why don't you stop by some time?" The truth of the matter is that many middle-class whites and Blacks say these phrases with little forethought. They would probably be quite surprised if an individual "just dropped in some time."

Emphasis on Humanism

Black culture is a people- rather than a thing-oriented culture. It places an important emphasis on humanism. This situation occurs despite the typical Saturday night rows that claim Black lives or the infiltration of drugs into Black communities. Such occurrences have distressed more Blacks than whites, because these factors indicate the destruction of minorities' lives and their communities. They also indicate remnants of the slave culture, wherein Blacks were consistently told by whites that their lives meant very little.

To support the thesis on humanism, Foster (1971) has stressed that service to the family and to the community is viewed as a natural consequence rather than as a burden. In a study of Black and white Princeton students, Foster found that whereas white students conceptualized humanity in terms of abstract concepts of the individual and tolerance, minority students conceived of humanism as an affirmation of life. They emphasized the beauty of diversity.

The humanism of minorities is also evidenced in the family situation. It has been reported that despite the negative white association with children out of wedlock, few Black women give their children up for adoption (Staples, 1970). Instead, within the minority community, children are treated usually with little distinction regarding the legitimacy or illegitmacy of their birth, even though out of wedlock pregnancies are not condoned.

The humanistic orientation of minorities has been supported by studies of their vocational interests and choices. In an early study of the interests of Black and white youth, Witty, Garfield, & Brink (1941) found that the vocational interests of members of these two racial groups seemed to be between the extremes of "thing" versus the "people" dimension. Whereas whites appeared to prefer occupations that were primarily "thing-oriented," Blacks tended to prefer occupations that were "people-oriented." The authors conjectured that this polarity in interests and choices suggested that racial backgrounds and cultural values may have been in operation.

Similar findings have likewise been reported by Chansky (1965) in his study of the vocational interests of Black and white ninth graders. Chansky found that while minority youth were interested in interpersonal, business, verbal, and long-term training occupations, white youth manifested more of an interest in occupations that had high presitge rather than ones that related to their own true interests. Likewise, Bayer & Boruch (1969) found that minority people were more likely to choose social occupations than were whites. This situation occurred even in the face of increasing occupational opportunity. Blacks preferred occupations where they would be allowed to work with people as ends in themselves. Black males also manifested more interest in social service occupations on the Strong Vocational Interest Blank than did whites (Hager & Elton, 1971). Similar results were given by Kimball, Sedlacek, & Brooks (1973) for Blacks on Holland's Self-Directed Search (1971).

There are, of course, other explanations for the occupational interests and choices of Blacks. Historically, many minorities have entered the social sciences because they were the major fields open for them. For example, in a study of the process of vocational choice of Black college students, Brazziel (1961) found that several students chose teaching as a career. When questioned about their choice, more than half of the total group said that teaching was their second choice, and slightly less than half revealed that they planned to use it as a stepping-stone to another occupation. From Brazziel's research, it would appear that minority students were both aware of race and the restrictions it placed on their occupational choices. This was most readily seen in their adoption of "second best" but realizable goals.

It would seem that one of the needs in counseling is to help minority students find outlets for their humanistic orientation in a variety of occupational areas, including the technical as well as the social science fields.

The Black Family

Typically, the Black family has been described as the core of this racial group's problems (Moynihan, 1965). However, recent research has seriously challenged this point of view. Billingsley (1969) and Herzog's (1968) studies have shown that the Black family has remained basically intact, despite the existence of negative forces surrounding it.

Other investigators have questioned the use of the term "matriarchy" to describe minority families. According to Comer (1972), a true matriarchy exists when women control the property, economics, government, and culture and enact specific roles for men to follow. Such has not been the case with Black Americans. For example, TenHouten (1970) found that lower-socioeconomic Black and white husbands exercised the same degree of family decision-making power. Likewise, Mack (1971) has also found that Black and white families do not differ significantly in their perceptions and uses of power in the marital relationship. Social class rather than race was a more important determining factor of the power structure within such families.

Many researchers have confused the strong assistance of Black women toward their husbands and families with the existence of a matriarchal family system. They have seen large numbers of Black women working outside the home, in sometimes more prestigeful positions than their husbands, and have concluded that Black women are the heads of the household or that they have more power than their men. Such a conclusion ignores certain everyday survival behavior of members of this racial group. Throughout history, Black women have always played an important role. From Harriet Tubman to Sojourner Truth, from Mary McLeod Bethune to Coretta King, Black women have stood by their men and their families. At best, then, the matriarchy theory only holds true for families that are bereft of husbands and fathers—the types of families for whom Frazier (1948) had in mind when he used this system of family classification for Black people.

Despite this observation, one of the problems in Black families has been the differential gap between the educational and the occupational achievements of men and women. Traditionally, it has been the female who has been encouraged to obtain an education. This situation has occurred primarily because of the precarious situations minority females have been placed in while working in white people's homes. The goal of protection of females has led, in some instances, to educational, occupational, and income disparities among men and women of this racial group. Hence, in some families, one may find schoolteachers married to bus drivers and janitors. As a result of these types of incongruities in achievement, some Black men have proposed that their women must take a backseat in the 1970s and focus primarily on uplifting the male situation (Wallace, 1979). Such a request has been met with mixed responses. While most females strongly support increased educational and occupational sacrifices for their men, they also assert that now is the time that both sexes must move forward together. Having women take a backseat will only hurt the Black family more (Hare & Hare, 1970).

One of the important cultural heritages of the Black family has been its customary deemphasis on rigid, sex-linked roles (Billingsley, 1970). Both men and women may share in household responsibilities, the caring of children, and work outside the home. Recent studies have indicated, for example, that minority men are less inclined to insist that their wives adhere to strict sex-linked roles. Along such lines, Axelson's (1970) findings have indicated that although both Black and white men feel that women should discontinue their career efforts if they conflicted with their husband's, more Black men (86.7%) agreed that a wife should work according to her own needs and desires than did white men (48.1%)This finding appears to be in keeping with the traditional Black male and female tendency not to hold each other rigidly to certain stereotypic roles. It also reflects the economic realism of minority men. In most cases, family survival is dependent on the income of husband and wife.

Another cultural heritage of the Black family has been the extended family kinship system and the use of this system as a supportive and therapeutic base. For instance, in an exploratory study of the extended kinship relations in Black and white families, Hays & Mendel (1973) found that Black families (1) interacted with relatives more often and perceived them as more significant (2) considered a broader range of their kin as important, and (3) were given more assistance in child care. This situation existed even when such variables as socioeconomic status, geographic mobility, marital status, and family size were controlled. Hays & Mendel concluded that "Black families have apparently developed a more pervasive and encompassing structure which meets more needs with more intensity than was found among white families" (1973, p. 56).

Childbearing patterns in Black families have been one of the most widely written about but least understood aspects of Black culture. Generally, it has been stated that lower-class minorities establish strict standards of behavior that are physically enforced, whereas middle-class families tend to rely on threats of withdrawal of love as a form of punishment. For the most part, this is true. The average lower-class Black family would consider the withdrawl of love (or the threat of it) a most inhumane and senseless activity. It is believed that punishment must be related to the misdeed that was done and not to the existence or the nonexistence of parental love.

Gilbert's (1973) description of a group counseling session with minority elementary children provides a case in point. During the group session, a child described how her mother had taken a strap to her because the girl had torn her dress while playing. The child had been told by her mother that she must always take off her school clothes before going outside to play. The counselor was horrified by the child's description of what had happened and considered reporting the girl's mother to the Society for the Prevention of Cruelty to Children. The counselor noticed, however, that none of the children in the group were disturbed by the incident. There was general agreement among the children that the girl had been wrong in not changing her dress and that her actions would probably cost her mother money for a new dress.

Hence most Black youngsters understand and accept their parents' behavior. Children are taught at a very early age that no child is an adult and that they must be able to differentiate adult verbal roles from those appropriate for children. Hence the discussion of family matters with outsiders is considered to be a violation of family ethics. Counselors who attempt to get Black youngsters to open up and to discuss their relationships with their parents or their family life should take into consideration that they are likely to run into cultural resistance.

The family system is used for working out personal problems that individuals may have. Here, the mother may assume a prominent role, for frequently she is viewed as being not only as warm and accepting, but also self-sacrificing. Because of this ascribed position (both strong and loving), the mother occupies a favorite position within the family. The cultural reverence for the mother has pervaded all of Black life. One of the worst things that a person can do to infuriate another is to mention his or her mother's name in an indecent way. Typically, channels of communication also start first with her; she, in turn, goes to the father for a final decision.

Furthermore, in many Black families, there is a strong emphasis on education, even though the parents themselves may not have many skills. Parents are inclined to tell their children: "I don't want you to grow up the way I did. I want you to have an education, to have more than I had." Despite this emphasis, few lower-socioeconomic parents have the knowledge or the skills needed to assist their children's educational careers. This situation exists because the parents themselves have usually had limited work experiences. They cannot teach their children what they do not know. The problem, then, is not necessarily one of parental neglect or indifference, as some individuals would have the public to believe. Indeed, neglect may, in some cases, be present. But I believe the majority of Black parents would assist their children in their educational/career development, if they only knew how.

Traditionally, religion has also constituted a part of Black family life. Parents have tended to teach their children that a strong faith in God will see them through their difficult moments. Thus it is in the church and not in counseling that one should explore his or her deepest thoughts and psychological stresses. Moreover, minorities have tended to believe in fatalism—that eventually everything will be worked out for the better. This sentiment is expressed in the phrase "what goes around comes around." In other words, what you put out eventually comes back to you. It is believed that God will eventually punish white people for their misdeeds to Blacks.

The counselor working with the Black family, particularly one from the lower-socioeconomic level, must be slow to prejudge that family's cultural differences. The role of the counselor should be to work closely with minority families so that they will be better informed to help their children in their educational and vocational endeavors.

Part of the problem in counseling people of different cultural backgrounds is that the obvious oftentimes has to be explained. To understand Blacks, one must know their history and their culture. One must understand the inconsistencies in Blacks' lives, their cruelty as well as their deep sense of humanity toward one another. In short, one must understand what pushes Blacks forward and what pulls them back. One must become familiar with Blacks' humor and the paradoxes within it and with their literature and music, for these mediums have expressed Black's desires in life.

ISSUES IN COUNSELING BLACKS

Throughout the Black experience in America, there have been some white counselors who have tried to understand Black clients and to learn the implications of both cultures on the counseling relationship. These accomplishments have occurred against great odds and should be lauded.

The Myth of Sameness

Yet despite the successes of these counselors, the truth remains that there are still far too many of their peers who not only do not understand Blacks, but also refuse to take the necessary steps to gain understanding and rapport with these clients. Such counselors have buried their heads in the sand and have used such phrases as "I never notice the color of my clients' skin" or "What really counts in counseling is empathy and not the cultural backgrounds of my clients" to avoid dealing with sensitive racial and cultural issues. Although individual empathy is important to the counseling relationship, it is not sufficient by itself. To work effectively with minority clients, counselors must have insight to their own attitudes regarding their clients' racial and cultural backgrounds.

As Pettigrew (1973) has pointed out, approximately three-fifths of white Americans may be classified as conforming bigots—as those who follow the path of least social resistance and as those who are quietly anti-Black because they fear rejection from members of their racial group. The attitudes and behaviors of this group, as well as those who seek to bury their heads in the sand, have led to the current crisis in counseling.

Hence, many of the issues in counseling minorities are related to cultural differences and the extent to which these differences affect the counseling interview. Cultural considerations have, in large measure, determined how counselors define a client's needs, how they function in the therapeutic situation, how they determine treatment, cure, and even reality itself. Culture has been, then, the silent intruder in the counseling relationship, and, because of its very silence, it has often gone unrecognized.

Much of the counseling literature has tended to support this idea (Vontress, 1970; Golightly, 1971). Whenever we have talked about the existence of differential client-counselor expectations or the difficulties in counseling minorities, we were alluding essentially to the issue of culture and how it affects the helping relationship. Counseling is culture bound, and this fact becomes even clearer when the counselor and client are also members of different racial and socioeconomic groups.

But it is in the area of cultural expectations that we get into the most difficulty with each other. When white majority Americans expect minorities (and vice versa) to think the way they do, to act the way they act, and talk the way they talk, we set the stage for conflict instead of understanding. As one Black client put it: "Let white people tell it, we [meaning Blacks] don't do anything right. We don't talk right; we're supposed to be lazy. Sometimes I just laugh to myself. If Black people did as many things wrong as white folks say we do, we wouldn't have been able to survive."

Hence simply talking about cultural differences and how we must respect them has become a hollow cliché in the counseling profession. Most of us have heard, for example, these phrases: "We're all alike under our skins"; "They're just like us"; or "I treat everyone the same—be they Black, blue, or green." Such statements are at best self-delusionary and at worst, simplistic in thinking. To treat everyone the same is to deny their humanness, their individuality, and their sense of cultural heritage.

As Hall (1976b) has stated, any time we hear someone say that

Blacks or other ethnic groups are no different from us, then we also know that that person is living in a single-context world and is as incapable of describing his or her world as he or she is of describing that of Blacks. We are not the same under our skins. Our culture and our individual interpretations of it are more than skin deep.

The failure to recognize true differences in thought among groups of people leads us to a well-meaning but false sense of humanism and brotherhood. We cannot make all people the same simply by stating so or by treating them alike. This is what is called reducing all people to a common denominator—the double-edged sword that has the potentiality for both dehumanizing and humanizing them.

Discrimination in Counseling

The crisis in counseling has also been affected by discrimation. During its first year of a three-year proposed study, the Joint Commission on Mental Health of Children (1968) stated: "Racism is the number one public health problem facing America today. The conscious and unconscious attitudes of superiority which permit and demand that a majority oppress a minority are a clear and present danger to the mental health of all children and their parents" (p. 29).

The Commission used the following criteria to define a public health problem: (1) a difficulty that menaces a large number of people; (2) a problem that requires large sums of money to correct; (3) a problem that is almost impossible to treat or cure on an individual and private basis; and (4) a problem that could lead to chronic economic, social, or psychological disability of a large number of people. According to the Commission, each of these conditions are present in the case of Blacks and other minorities.

Black Culture and Views on Mental Health

Clients and counselors of the same cultural background share a common view of the world and have basically similar thoughts on causation and a common method of classifying mental health and illness. Such similarity in thought is known as "cognitive" and "cultural" congruence (Torrey, 1972) and generally tends to facilitate the helping relationship. Conversely, lack of cognitive and cultural congruence may lead to problems in the counseling relationship. For example, a counselor trying to work with a client who does not believe in Oedipal conflicts and a witch doctor trying to work with a client who does not believe in spirit possession are likely to be equally ineffective unless they can persuade the client to accept their theory of causation (Torrey, 1972). The crucial factor lies in both the counselors' and the clients' beliefs regarding causation of behavior.

Much of white majority culture emphasizes the importance of childhood experiences as the cause of behavior. People are made ill by what their parents did to them when they were infants. Both the couch and talk are used by therapists to help their clients regress to earlier stages in order to unravel the negative experiences that occurred in these times. Even though counselors do not usually use the "couch," they often conceptualize their clients' problems in terms of childhood adjustment experiences.

On the other hand, Blacks are less inclined to focus on childhood experiences within the family as a major cause of poor mental health. They look at the system surrounding the family. From the perspective of Blacks, the psychoanalytic-type theory of cause and effect presupposes that a child is a kind of "tabula rasa," a blank mind on which primarily parents create almost indelible personality characteristics for the first five years of the child's life. Many Black parents believe, and there appears to be some support for this belief (Skolnick, 1978; DeVore, 1977), that children may inherit certain personality traits and that parents are limited in affecting their child's development. Hence Black parents are less prone than whites to punish themselves when their children go astray from their teachings. In such circumstances, Black parents are likely to say: "I've done all I can. All I can do now is pray and hope that he will see the light. He'll have to do the rest for himself."

Thus minorities are inclined to perceive mental health as situationally or environmentally determined. Whites are inclined to view mental health as a quality that exists independent of the situation in which one is involved. This difference in views accounts partly for some minorities' rejection of the intrapsychic model of counseling, which assumes that talk and resolution of childhood conflicts provide, in part, the answer to individuals' problems.

For example, a former male addict reported the following encounter with his counselor. "It was about our third session and up to this point, things had gone pretty well. Then the counselor started asking me about my family. I had told him all the information before. Yea, I said, my parents are divorced, but that don't mean they're the cause of my problem. Then he started asking me questions about my mother—if I ever felt neglected by her because she worked when I was growing up. I told him no, because I knew that she had to work, that part of our survival depended on it. . . . But he just kept on probing until I blew up. I told him, look, man, I've told you just about everything about me, and you still keep on asking me about my mother and my stepfather. I know what you're trying to do. You're trying to blame them for my being in here. . . . I'm in here because of me, do you hear, because of me and this damn system. . . . You can take all of your intellectual crap and shove it. I know what it's like being out there."

Both the counselor and the client were obviously shaken by this incident. From the counselor's perspective, the client's behavior was only further proof of the addict's resistance to counseling and his attempt to protect his parents. In contrast, the client saw the situation as another attempt of white people to shift the blame from society's treatment of Blacks to his parents.

Counseling for Minorities: Part of the Problem or Solution?

Black people tend to view the role of the counselor as quite alien. As noted previously, the family and the church are often used as places to deal with the inner self and to search for understanding. When minority clients seek counseling, they frequently go with the belief that they will be able to obtain advice about a specific matter. This view of the counselor's role may cause conflict in the counseling setting.

For some Black people, however, counseling has become "part of the problem" rather than "part of the solution" to their difficulties. According to Russell (1970), Black students view counselors as instruments of oppression and as stumbling blocks around which they must somehow maneuver if their ambitions and aspirations do not coincide with those their counselors consider appropriate for them. Payne's (1971) findings have indicated that Black students feel counselors give different academic counseling to them than they do to their white counterparts—that counselors guide Black students into less difficult curricula.

Some of the Black counselees' attitudes toward counselors have not been without foundation. Counselors have functioned as important allocaters of the educational environment. The research of Cicourel & Kituse (1963) has revealed that Black students who had manifested average to high academic performance were actively discouraged by their counselors from attending college, while white, upper-class students who had demonstrated marginal and even low academic performance were consistently encouraged to attend college.

More recently, Erickson (1975) found that students' race and communication style influenced the quality of the counseling services they received. In some cases, counselors' evaluations of students were based on such variables as their interpretation of what was "best" for students, the congruency of the students' value system with theirs, and the students' physical appearance.

Similarly, Tucker & Gunnings (1974) have asserted that the majority of Black youth see the function of counselors as irrelevant and, in some instances, counterproductive to the development of survival skills necessary for life in a hostile environment. In these author's opinions, middle-class counselors' predominantly individualistic and intrapsychic orientation has tended to minimize the significance of the social and cultural forces that affect many Black clients' lives.

Moreover, the findings of Clark (1965), Thomas & Sillen (1972), and Lorion (1973) have shown the gross inequities in the delivery of mental health services to Black people from lower-socioeconomic levels. Rosenthal & Frank (1958) found, for instance, that Black clients tended to be less frequently chosen for individual therapy than whites and that those who were selected for this treatment modality were seen fewer times than their white counterparts. There seemed to be an important relationship between clients' adoption of their counselors' value system and their improvement in therapy. Clients who were likely to improve from counseling services tended to revise or to reconstruct their values so that they more closely resembled those of their counselors.

Reporting their experiences as Black psychiatrists in residency, B. Jones et al. (1970) have likewise pointed out the importance of race in the selection of clients for individual therapy. Based on their observance of residency programs in the East and Midwest, the authors concluded that there appeared to be a preselection process in operation that limited, either by design or by default, the number of Black individuals initially seen and ultimately treated. Of prime importance in the preselection process was the attitude of the referring person or agency toward the clients. Individuals who were described as good treatment cases were usually young, introspective clients—students, suburban housewives, or upwardly mobile junior executives.

Summarizing some of the issues in counseling minorities, Sue et al. (1974) have stated that (1) discriminatory institutional policies and the cost of treatment services have been major factors in the denial of psychotherapy to Black people; (2) Black individuals receive inferior forms of therapeutic treatment; and (3) traditional forms of counseling and psychotherapy may not take into consideration the cultural background of such clients.

Hence regardless of whether investigators have examined who is most likely to be considered a desirable candidate for counseling, who is most probably to remain in counseling, or who has the best chances of being evaluated as having benefited from counseling, the conclusions have been basically the same. Blacks, other ethnic and racial groups, and the poor come out with the short end of the stick (Lerner, 1972; E. Jones, 1975).

Black Clients: The Other Side of the Coin

The problem, however, has not been all one-sided. In some instances, Blacks have been just as rejecting of their counselors as their counselors have been of them. In a study of Black and white students' attitudes toward white counselors, Burrell & Rayder (1971) found that although neither Black nor white students reflected an overwhelmingly favorable attitude toward counselors, Black students expressed significantly less positive dispositions toward their counselors than did white students.

Moreover, some Black clients may conceal basic personality difficulties by overstressing the importance of their Blackness in the interracial counseling situation (Sommers, 1953; Grier & Cobbs, 1968); in order to avoid personal involvement in the therapeutic interview Black people may substitute social problems for personal ones, and some clients may attempt to "act white" in order to please their counselors (Calnek, 1970). Moreover, English (1957) has posited that Black people experience the pain of their minority and second-class citizenship so deeply that they are hesitant to share such feelings with each other, let alone with counselors of different racial groups.

Underutilization of counseling services by Black students on predominantly white college campuses has likewise been cited as a problem (Mitchell, 1970). It has been suggested that Black students resist using the conventional college and university services because they perceive such services to be oriented toward mainly white, middle-class students. They also fear being used as "guinea pigs."

In short, both Black clients and counselors are "part of the solution" as well as "part of the problem" of counseling members of this racial group. Some Blacks must realize that not all problems can be resolved within the family network and that the family may constitute the major source of a person's difficulty. Not all problems are externally caused. Sometimes the problem lies within the manner in which one responds to a situation. Instead of giving in to the deleterious effects of racism, more minorities must learn how to transcend the restrictions placed on them, to label appropriately the source of their difficulties, and to take and follow through with the necessary actions, based on their analysis of the problem.

Transference and Countertransference with Black Clients

The cultural connotations of Black and white are directly related to the issues of transference and countertransference in the counseling interview. For some white counselors, Black clients stir up unconscious negative racial attitudes. One counselor who worked in a recently desegrated city school complained of headaches and nightmares so frequently that she finally sought therapy for herself. During the process of counseling, the counselor uncovered the sources of the teacher's problems. The desegregation of the teacher's school had placed her in direct contact with teenage Black males, and part of her upbringing had stressed that she should be careful of Black men. Working in close contact with Black youth had rekindled her early teachings about Black men, hence the headaches and the nightmares she was experiencing.

When counselors experience unconscious negative racial feelings about their clients, they may be inclined to use such defensive behaviors as projection, denial, flight, and avoidance (Gardner, 1971). For example, the counselor might attempt to avoid the racial/cultural issue by referring the client to another counselor or by using more impersonal treatment approaches, such as drug therapy. Counselors' guilt feelings may also lead them to attribute all the clients' problems to cultural and racial conflict, thereby ignoring or overlooking the clients' personal difficulties.

Conversely, minorities who have historically and culturally been taught to fear or distrust whites may consciously or unconsciously subject white counselors to a series of tests to find out if they are prejudiced against minorities. As one white counselor working in a federally funded program said: "I'm tired of having to prove myself to every new Black I come in contact with. It's a drag, a kind of endless nightmare of paying for someone else's mistakes."

On other occasions, clients who have not dealt adequately with their own racial and cultural identity may attempt to deny and to repress any memory of having suffered from racial discrimination and to go out of their way to avoid any behavior that might support the negative stereotypes about members of their race. Moreover, Black clients who incorporate the racist ideas of whites have also been known to reject members of their own race. For example, when one Black woman was assigned to a Black counselor, she felt insulted and accused the clinic of trying "to railroad all Blacks together." Another minority client told her counselor: "There's not one thing a Black person can do for me. My lawyer is white; my doctor is white; and I want my counselor to be white also."

Calnek (1970) has suggested that some Black counselors overidentify with their clients and encourage them to focus primarily on racial rather than personal problems. There is also the other extreme. Imbued with their own professional success and stature, some Black counselors may attempt to imitate the white middle class and to put as much psychological distance as possible between themselves and the lower-class minority client. S. Jones (1970) has, however, attributed some of the Black counselors' difficulties with clients of their own race to the type of training counselors receive, that is the white mental health cultural perspective.

Language Differences

Language differences may also influence the counseling relationship. It has been found, for example, that Blacks tend to have greater language elaboration in the presence of members of their racial group than in the presence of whites (Harrison, 1975). However, it has not been clearly demonstrated that language differences affect the outcome of the counseling relationship (Grantham, 1970). While Black counselees may prefer counselors of the same race, counselors' ability to communicate is considered to be more important than similarity in the counselors' and clients' racial membership group.

Yet the problems with many of these studies is that they have tended to emphasize primarily two ideas: (1) the client's attitude toward the counselor's use or nonuse of the Black vernacular or (2) the effect of the counselor's knowledge of Black slang on the counseling relationship. More studies are needed to test the counselor's attitudes toward language usage in the therapeutic encounter.

Furthermore, some minority clients resent white counselors' attempts to use Black slang in order to show that they understand them. As one client put it: "I knew that I didn't ever want to see that counselor again when he started talking about 'I hope you don't think I'm trying to rip you off.' He was just trying too hard, and I didn't trust him. Anyone who tries too hard to show you that he understands Blacks doesn't understand them at all."

Likewise, counselors who are unfamiliar with the directness of some Black Americans may find their style of communication offensive and interpret directness as hostility. Conversely, some minority clients, particularly males, may use the "playing-it-cool syndrome." Basically, the playing-it-cool syndrome means acting worldly, unconcerned, and "together." It is usually a strong defense mechanism that allows the minority client to limit his ostensible amount of personal involvement, to test the counselor, or to save face in case he cannot receive the counseling aid he is seeking.

Then, too, some minority clients hesitate to talk with counselors because they feel the latter will evaluate their speech negatively. On such occasions, clients may give only brief responses to the counselor's inquiries. This behavior has often led counselors to conclude erroneously that minority clients are uncooperative and sullen. To work effectively with such clients, counselors must understand their different styles of communication as well as their attitudes toward counselors. Do counselors react negatively, for instance, on the basis of minorities' language usage?

Differences in Black Family Life

Differences in the structural organization of Black family life has also affected the counseling relationship. In an effort to bring about closer relationships between the school and the community, the guidance department of some school systems have initiated home visitations on a selective basis. Both families of honor students and those who were doing poorly academically were visited. After one such visitation, one counselor indicated that she no longer wanted to participate in the outreach program. She had gone to a home with the intention of talking with the mother about the progress of her son, an honor student at the school. "There just seemed to be too many people in that house," the counselor said. "There was the grandmother; then a couple of cousins stopped by. It was just ridiculous. I felt as if we had no privacy to talk. It's amazing that Eric is doing so well in school." What the counselor had observed was one lower-socioeconomic family's version of the extended kinship system. Under this system, family members are welcomed into each other's home and stop by to visit whenever they can. Lack of knowledge of this family arrangement and the reasons for it had caused the counselor to evaluate negatively Eric's home life.

Some Counseling Needs

Several points are essential in the counseling of Blacks. First, Black people need to affirm the essence of their Blackness and to use their Blackness as a means of examining their mental health. What I am talking about here is the necessity of "self-identity." Through understanding who they are, Black people can go forward. Along such lines, group therapy may be more harmonious to the cultural and psychological needs of members of this racial group. Group interaction compels individuals to examine their own behavior patterns and offers the potentiality of raising a person's level of self-worth more quickly than the individual format.

Second, counselors must focus on "sociotherapy." The sociotherapeutic approach requires that counselors use multiple, comprehensive interventions that will help individuals realize their potentialities in the social, educational, and career spheres. A balance has to be reached between service to individuals and social change. Counselors must support those forces that improve the development of individual and group potential. The provision of services to minorities should be a means to change for the positive growth of individuals and groups.

Third, counselors must be able to help minority clients develop "good survival behavior" without necessarily having them to compromise themselves. For example, one counselor used small group discussions to help students learn how to negotiate their college environment. The groups discussed such issues as how to maintain their identity in the presence of the displacement of reference groups, racial hostility, and the development of new goals. Participants also gave each other feedback concerning how they were presenting themselves to each other as well as to majority white individuals.

Learning good survival skills is also important to adults. For example, some Black professionals run into difficulty and frustration when they expect their work environments to provide the same nurturance as that given to their fellow white workers, for example, feelings of colleagueship and being able to let down one's hair. On such occasions, Blacks may be prone either to blame themselves for not being able to secure the kinds of work-related nurturance they seek or to siphon important energy into nonproductive conflict situations.

The case of Bill Moore, a bright young college professor, provides an illustration in point. When Bill first came to the predominantly white private college, college officials laid out the red carpet for him. Within less than a year, Bill found himself in difficulty on his job. According to him, the white professors were receiving better treatment than he was. They often shared informal conversations with each other. They visited each other in their offices and generally gave each other moral, professional, and ego support. When Bill attempted to engage in the same behavior, he was treated as an outsider, and it became clear to him that the buddy system was not available to him in the department.

Gradually, Bill began to get into more conflict situations with his work colleagues, even though his intent was just the opposite. He sought their support by serving on committees no one else wanted to serve on and by establishing a national reputation for himself. Bill's goal was to become liked, to obtain the same nurturance as his white work associates. By the end of the academic year, Bill was expressing negative feelings about himself, despite his numerous academic achievements.

After going through several bouts of severe depression, Bill sought counseling. Where he had once published prolifically, he was now unable to complete one page of writing.

Bill was fortunate in that the counselor, who happened to be a Black male, understood his predicament. The counselor suggested that Bill actively seek nurturance from other sources—involvement in the Black community, professional discussion groups with other members of his race. Eventually, Bill established a minority faculty and staff association on campus. His energies now being channeled constructively, Bill no longer bemoaned the fact that his white colleagues rejected him. The irony of the entire situation was that his white peers began to pay him more attention, for they wanted to know what he was doing and why he no longer sought their support.

Another survival dilemma facing upwardly mobile Blacks is their "displacement of reference groups" as they climb the career ladder. As in the case of Bill Moore, upwardly mobile Blacks tend to experience feelings of isolation, stress, and marginality. Frequently, they are rejected by both the group to which they anticipate becoming a member of and the group they left behind. The new won status of these Blacks may also leave them too economically and psychologically vulnerable to be of much assistance to the less fortunate members of their race. Hence individuals who face the displacement of reference groups may need two kinds of counseling services: (1) a type of supportive therapy that helps make them less vulnerable and (2) a mechanism or network of communication that will bridge the gap between them and the other members of their race. The latter approach relies on using the version of the social systems model of counseling. Such an approach would not only identify, but also put into operation "stress resistant" factors within the Black community. Counselors must be able to recognize and deal effectively with the sources of stress their clients face.

For instance, Ruiz & Padilla (1977) have maintained that minority clients suffer from intra- and extra-psychic sources of stress. "Intra-psychic sources of stress" refer to those problems that are of a personal or individual nature; they are independent of one'e ethnic minority group membership. Conversely, "extrapsychic sources of stress" originate outside the person and are generally considered more environmentally based than personally anchored. To counsel Blacks, counselors need to learn how to distinguish between these two sources as well as understand the effects of combining the two. We need to identity "stress resistant" factors both within the Black community and in the broader American culture that will promote effective behavior on the part of Black people.

The Stress-Resistant Delivery Model of Counseling

In keeping with the rest of this chapter, it is important that we recognize that there is no one monolithic model for counseling all Blacks. There is just too much diversity among Blacks to engage in any such theoretical folly. The similarity of historical and cultural experiences Blacks tend to have suggest, however, a set of core counseling ingredients that might prove helpful to clients of this racial group. These core ingredients are incorporated in the Stress-Resistant Delivery Model (SRD) of counseling. The SRD model of counseling emphasizes basically three areas: (1) identifying the source of stress a client encounters, (2) outlining and implementing stress resistant forces within Black culture and the broader American society, and (3) deciding on a method of delivering services to the client.

Under the SRD model of counseling, the first task of the counselor is to identify the sources of stress that the client faces. For instance, having to make a decision is a problem that all people face at one point or another in their lives. It may or may not, according to Ruiz & Padilla (1977) be related to a person's ethnic membership group. Therefore, this source of stress may be labeled as "intrapsychic." Having to come to grips with one's inner self is another example of a problem that is intrapsychic in nature.

As noted previously, extrapsychic sources of stress originate outside the individual and are usually more societal or environmentally based than personal in nature. For example, an individual's race may be a significant factor in determining the type of opportunities he/she has in the work world or the kind of health and living conditions he/she has to encounter. In the case of Blacks, extrapsychic sources of stress often lead to intrapsychic maladaptive behavior, that is, poor self-concept, feelings of hopelessness, and rage.

Once the predominant source of stress has been identified, the second step of the SRD model of counseling is to outline stress resistant factors that will help the client with his/her problem. The extended family kinship system may provide stress resistance to members who are having problems. Other stress resistant factors might include the church, social and political groups within the Black community, music, and so on. Once the counselor has labeled or isolated several stress resistant factors that have the potentiality of helping the individual with his/her problem, the counselor then enters the third stage, the delivery of counseling services.

In working with clients, counselors may select one or a combination of service delivery systems. For instance, if the counselor believes that the client's problems are mainly intrapsychic in nature, the counselor might focus on individual counseling and techniques designed to help the client explore intensively himself or herself. If the client's problems are primarily extrapsychic in nature, the counselor must take into account such factors as the client's degree of acculturation into the white majority cultural system and the client's socioeconomic status. Some questions the counselor might try to determine are these: To what extent is the client's predominant style of communication? Are paraprofessionals needed to facilitate the delivery system?

As much as possible, the counselor should select a service delivery system that stresses a self-help approach. Less emphasis should be placed on seeing the individual as a client or patient, and more emphasis should be placed on highlighting potential areas of competence. The self-help model requires that the counselor be aware of the Black experience and the sources of strength within that experience.

When race seems to be a factor in the counseling relationship, the counselor should deal with this topic forthrightly instead of trying to avoid it. This procedure is particularly important if the counselor is white and the client Black. The counselor's ability to approach rather than avoid racial factors that enter into the counseling relationship lets the client know that (1) the counselor is aware of the difference in their ethnic backgrounds and that he/she is not afraid or hesitant to talk about the client's feelings concerning race—even if such feelings are hostile (Heacock, 1976).

The primary benefit of the SRD model of counseling is that it provides an easy conceptual framework for counseling individuals. Moreover, counselors of varying theoretical orientations may find that the framework can be used without it necessarily conflicting with their chosen theoretical orientation. The model also suggests that the counselor will use nontraditional counseling techniques and become more involved with his/her clients.

THE CASE OF LARRY JONES

The case of Larry Jones, a Black sophomore student who entered one of the local state colleges via an educational opportunity program, shows how a counselor might use the SRD model of counseling. For the first two academic semesters, Larry had performed exceptionally well in all his courses. During his sophomore year, however, Larry's grades began to drop drastically, and his counselor requested an interview with him. Larry told the counselor that he was depressed and that he found little meaning in his academic studies. He confided that he felt as if he were "selling out" to the white Establishment and forgetting about the plight of his own people. Upon further talking with Larry, the counselor found out that Larry had little social life on the college campus, that most of his time was spent either in classes or in his room studying. He felt isolated from the majority of the students and had not dated one person on the campus since he had enrolled in college.

Larry also explained that he had recently joined the Black Muslims and that he resented college because it detracted from the work he needed to do as a member of his new-found religious group. As he talked about his work in the Black Muslim restaurant on Saturdays, Larry seemed to come more alive. "What I'm learning here is just not meaningful any longer, Mrs. Johnson. It's like a whole new world has been opened to me, and I can't take advantage of it because of school. For the first time in my life, I'm found something that's meaningful."

The counselor, who happened to be Black, tried to talk with Larry about his religious involvement and what it seemed to be doing to his academic studies. She pointed out that of all the students whom she had known who switched from their early religious teachings to that of the Black Muslims, not one of them had been able to succeed in college. All had either chosen to leave the college or had flunked out.

"You're not going to dissuade me, Mrs. Johnson," Larry responded. "I know what I want." Mrs. Johnson replied that she wasn't trying to dissuade him from his religion, that she only wanted to point out to him what her experience had been with other Black students who had followed the same course as he had. Mrs. Johnson also confided that at one time in her life she had dated a Black Muslim and had seriously considered converting to the religion.

"What stopped you?" Larry asked. "A lot of things," Mrs. Johnson replied. "My parents, my own conflicts. . . . I became cut off from all of the friends with whom I grew up. I found it difficult to give up all of the simple pleasures—like not wearing lipstick, not going to the movies, and trying to stick to one type of diet while my family followed another one. I found it difficult relating to my white friends in high school. There were just a lot of different things that stopped me," Mrs. Johnson said. "But I guess when I look back on it all, the main problem was that I was trying to be something I was not. . . . I was trying to change my entire life-style and upbringing, and it was just too much for me.

"That's the way I feel about you, too," Mrs. Johnson said. "If you had been raised as a Black Muslim, there probably wouldn't be any problems. The religion would be a part of you. You're trying to find yourself, Larry. I think you're kind of searching for your own self-identity."

Larry listened silently but skeptically to Mrs. Johnson. He didn't want to hear about all the other students who had failed. He would succeed where they hadn't been able to; all he needed was time away from the college. Larry also told Mrs. Johnson that he probably wouldn't run into some of the same problems as she did because he had never had much of a family. He saw his father only infrequently and said without much elaboration that he was ashamed of how his mother was now living. Upon further questioning from Mrs. Johnson, Larry refused to talk about his mother. Instead, he left the counseling session with the promise that he would return for another meeting with Mrs. Johnson.

During the second interview, Mrs. Johnson asked Larry if he would mind if she contacted the Black Muslim Brother responsible for Larry's area. Larry refused to give her such permission. He did agree, however, to let Mrs. Johnson put him in contact with several other Black Muslim students on campus. The major difference between these students and Larry was that they had been raised as Muslims and were doing well in their academic courses. The students seemed to have a positive effect on Larry, for his grades began to improve.

After seeing Larry for several sessions, the counselor identified Larry's problem as stemming from an interaction of intra- and extra-psychic factors. His overriding difficulty seemed to be intrapsychic, that is, related to his search for identity and self-esteem. His erratic and negative family life also appeared to have had a significant impact on his life. Larry was searching for the stable family life he never really had, and his religious group constituted the regularity of family life he had always wanted.

The counselor's first step, then, was to explore the nature of Larry's problem and to help him with his feelings of isolation and depression by putting him in contact with other followers of his religious group. The second major thrust of counseling entailed getting Larry to explore his feelings about himself—both before and after his religious conversion. In the ensuing counseling sessions, for example, Larry explained that deep inside he had really hated himself because he had always felt that he was different from everybody else. He despised and was ashamed of both his mother and his father.

Getting these feelings to the surface helped Larry temporarily. The peer role models also helped. By the end of the academic year, Larry's grades had risen to a C+. Larry told the counselor that he was proud of his academic and personal comeback and that he was going to take the summer off from college. The counselor suggested that Larry still come in to visit her once a week. She said that she also wanted to make provisions for him to see a clinical psychologist. During the summer, Larry met with the clinical psychologist four times. He dropped in to see Mrs. Johnson occasionally and thanked her for her assistance. While Mrs. Johnson was away on vacation, Larry committed suicide by hanging himself. The note simply said that he was tired of fighting and couldn't face life any longer.

The case of Larry demonstrates what happens when deep-seated emotional problems are allowed to fester. Larry's problems with his own self-identity, his Blackness, and his family background were at the core of his suicide.

THE CASE OF ELAINE THOMAS

The case of Elaine demonstrates a young Black woman's attempts to come to grips with her view of herself as a Black woman and the factors of racial discrimination and cultural contradictions on a predominantly white campus.

The first thing one noticed about Elaine was that she was overweight and had probably been at one time an attractive young lady. The next thing that one noticed was that she changed her style of dress and appearance from day to day. On one day, Elaine might come in with an Afro wig. The next day she would wear her own hair, and the following day she would have on a shoulder-length straight hair wig. The same thing went for her clothing. While at times Elaine would come to class dressed appropriately in slacks or a skirt and blouse, on other occasions she would come to class dressed as if she were going to a cocktail party. On the surface, Elaine's manner of dress seemed to reflect her many moods and her efforts to come to grips with how she wanted to be seen as a woman.

Elaine had completed her undergraduate degree in sociology against great odds. She had been a high school student dropout and had attended a local high school to obtain her high school equivalency diploma. She was also the mother of two out-of-wedlock children. To support herself, Elaine worked at one of the community action centers in her neighborhood. Before completing her undergraduate degree, Elaine applied for the master's program in social work. She was accepted as an alternate, after another student had decided at a late date to attend another university. Elaine came to the Department of Social Work knowing this. At age 33, Elaine also had some doubts about her ability to compete with the younger students.

After her first semester in the master's program in social work, Elaine was referred to counseling because of her apparently aggressive manner and her number of incompletes. Her advisor told her that he felt that she really didn't belong in social work because she was much too direct in her dealings with people and because she lacked the type of personality the department thought important for counselors to have. He also pointed out that several of her professors considered her to be argumentative and that she intimidated both the white students in her class and her professors by wearing an emblem of the Black colors (red, green, and black) and a pin of the most vocal Black community action group.

Elaine came to counseling dejected and angry. She felt that she was being penalized for her involvement in Black community groups. She also indicated that every time she talked in class the white students would laugh and make fun of her speech. On the two occasions that she was supposed to work with small groups of students on a joint presentation, Elaine said that the students gave her either the wrong meeting time or the incorrect address and met without her. She felt that she was fighting both the students and the professors just to remain in graduate school.

After listening to Elaine, the counselor asked her how she felt about being counseled by a white male. Did she feel that she was going to experience the same type of discrimination she had just described? Elaine responded that she was uncertain about how things would work out with him and that she had no alternative other than to see him if she wanted to remain in graduate school. The counselor's question opened the door for Elaine to reveal some of the negative experiences she had had with white people. Elaine concluded her remarks on this topic by saying that she didn't hate whites but that her experiences had taught her to be careful of them. She wasn't sure whether the counselor would be like some of the other whites she had known. The counselor responded by saying that he was not going to ask Elaine to trust him, but instead he wanted her to judge his trustworthiness on the basis of his actions.

During the ensuing counseling sessions, Elaine began to let down her guard. She discussed her problem of being overweight and confided that she felt unattractive. "I want to look," she said, "the same way that I did ten years ago." The counselor pointed out that none of us could look exactly the way we did when we were younger but that he would do his best to encourage her to stick to her diet. The counselor also explored the reasons for Elaine's overeating. Elaine indicated that she tended to overeat when she was under a lot of stress and when she felt rejected by men.

"Is that why you also change your style of dress so often?" the counselor asked. "It's like you're trying to find the magical combination that will make men attracted to you, Elaine." At this point, Elaine began to cry. She talked about the father of her two children born out of wedlock and how she had let herself be used by him because she wanted his love. "I guess I tried to buy his love with my body," she said, "and now that I'm overweight, I can't even do that."

Elaine saw the counselor once a week until the end of the semester, only now she came of her own volition. She indicated that she wanted to learn more about herself and why she did some of the things she did.

The counselor also helped Elaine to understand some of the cultural contradictions she was facing at the college. He pointed out the different styles of communication that whites had and how variance from these styles might cause problems for her. In doing so, he made reference to some of the comments that Elaine had made in class and told her how he would have commented as a white student. "It's not that you're too aggressive," the counselor said. "It's just your directness and honesty. Part of succeeding in graduate school is learning tactful diplomacy. You've got to learn how to negotiate the system for your benefit."

As Elaine began to understand what she was up against—both from within and without—her grades began to improve. The counselor suggested that she talk with the few other Black students in the program to see if they could form a support group for each other and share ideas regarding how to meet the academic requirements and deal effectively with their professors. Elaine agreed and implemented the counselor's suggestions. By the end of the semester the white students and professors were praising Elaine for the marked changes she had made in her attitudes. What the students and professors did not know was that Elaine had also learned how to negotiate the college environment for her own survival. She had changed, but not necessarily in the manner that others believed. From Elaine's perspective, the most important changes in her life were coming to grips with her feelings about herself and men, losing weight, and learning how to get around the obstacles that were placed in front of her. The Black student support groups was also helpful insofar as she now had people to turn to, listen to her, and help her deal with a discriminating environment.

SUMMARY

In counseling Black individuals, it is important that counselors have an understanding of the former's historical background, cultural values, and conflicts. True cultural insight may help both clients and counselors to break down the barriers of communication and to reduce their chances of misinterpreting each other's behavior. Yet knowledge of another person's cultural and historical background does not automatically guarantee the counselor insight or understanding. In the final analysis, we must remember that each individual is like all other people, like some other people, and like no other person. If we are to be effective in counseling minorities, we must concentrate on these three fronts.

REFERENCES

Arnez, N. L. Enhancing the Black self-concept through literature. In J. A. Banks & J. D. Grambs (Eds.), *Black Self-Concept*, New York: McGraw-Hill, 1972, 93–116.

Astin, H. S. *Educational Progress of Disadvantaged Students*. Washington, D.C.: Human Service Press, 1970.

Astin, H. S., & Bisconti, A. S. *Career Plans for College Graduates in 1965 and 1970*. Bethlehem, Pa.: The CPC Foundation, Report No. 2, 1973.

Astin, H. S., & Panos, R. J. *The Educational and Vocational Development of College Students*. Washington, D.C.: American Council on Education, 1969.

Axelson, L. J. The working wife: Differences in perception among Negro and white males. *Journal of Marriage and the Family*, 1970, 32, 457–464.

Babcock, J. W. The colored insane. *Alienist and Neurologist*, 1895, 16, 423–447.

Bartee, G. M. *The perceptual characteristics of disadvantaged Negro and Caucasian college students*. Unpublished doctoral dissertation, East Texas State University, 1967.

Bayer, A. E., & Boruch, R. F. Black and white freshmen entering four-year colleges. *Educational Record*, 1969, 50, 371–386.

Billingsley, A. *Black Families in White America*. Englewood Cliffs, N.J.: Prentice-Hall, 1969.

Bogle, D. Black humor. *Ebony*, 1975, 30(10), 123–129.

Brazziel, W. F. Occupational choice in the Negro college. *Personnel and Guidance Journal*, 1961, 39, 739–742.

Briggs, V. M. The employment and income experience of Black Americans. In J. S. Picou & R. E. Campbell (Eds.), *Career Behavior of Special Groups*. Columbus, O.: Charles E. Merrill, 1975, 382–403.

Burrell, L., & Rayder, N. F. Black and white students' attitudes toward white counselors. *Journal of Negro Education*, 1971, 40, 48–52.

Calnek, M. Racial factors in the countertransference: The Black therapist and the Black patient. *American Journal of Orthopsychiatry*, 1970, 40, 39–46.

Caplan, N., & Nelson, S. D. Who's to blame? *Psychology Today*, 1974, 8, 99–104.

Chansky, N. M. Race, aptitude, and vocational interests. *Personnel and Guidance Journal*, 1965, 43, 780–784.

Cicourel, A. V., & Kituse, J. I. *The Educational Decision-Makers*. New York: Bobbs-Merrill, 1963.

Clark, K. The effects of prejudice and discrimination on personality development. In Helen Witmer & Ruth Lotinsky (Eds.), *Personality in the Making*. New York: Harper & Row, 1952.

Clark, K. *Dark Ghetto*. New York: Harper & Row, 1965.

Cleaver, E. *Soul on Ice*. New York: McGraw-Hill, 1970.

Coleman, J. S., et al. *Equality of Educational Opportunity*: U.S. Department of Health, Education and Welfare. Washington, D.C.: U.S. Government Printing Office, 1966.

Comer, J. P. *Beyond Black and White*. New York: Quadrangle Books, 1972.

Davis, A., & Dollard, D. *Children of Bondage: The Personality Development of Negro Youth in the Urban South*. New York: Harper & Row, 1964. (Originally published in 1940 by the American Council on Education, Washington, D.C.).

DeBow, J. P. D. The interest in slavery of the southern non-slaveholders. In E. L. McKitrick (Ed.), *Slavery Defended: The Views of the Old South*. Englewood Cliffs, N.J.: Prentice-Hall, 1963.

Delaney, L. T. The other bodies in the river. In R. L. Jones (Ed.), *Black Psychology*. New York: Harper & Row, 1972, 335–343.

Deutsch, A. The first U.S. Census on the insane (1840) and its use as pro-slavery propaganda. *Bulletin History of Medicine*, 1944, **15**, 469–482.

Deutsch, M., & Brown, B. Social influences in Negro-white intelligence differences. *Journal of Social Issues*, 1964, **20**, 24–35.

De Vore, I. The new science of genetic self-interest. *Psychology Today*, 1977, **10**(9), 42–51, 84–88.

Douglas, L. Negro self-concept: Myth or reality? *Integrated Education*, 1971, **9**, 27–29.

DuBois, W. E. B. Three centuries of discrimination. *The Crisis*, December 1947, **54**, 262–265, 379–380.

Elkins, S. M. *Slavery*. Chicago: University of Chicago Press, 1959.

English, W. H. Minority group attitudes of Negroes and implications for guidance. *Journal of Negro Education*, 1957, **26**, 99–107.

Erickson, F. Gatekeeping and the melting pot: Interaction in counseling encounters. *Harvard Education Review*, 1975, **45**, 78–87.

Eysenck, H. J. Race, intelligence, and education. *Intellectual Digest*, 1972, **11**, 33–35.

Foster, B. G. Toward a definition of black referents. In V. J. Dixon & B. G. Foster (Eds.), *Beyond Black or White: An Alternate America*. Boston: Hettle, Brown, 1971, 9–20.

Frazier, E. F. *The Negro Family in the United States* (rev. ed.)., Chicago: University of Chicago Press, 1948. (Originally published in 1939.)

Frazier, E. F. *Negro Youth at the Crossways: Their Personality Development in the Middle States*. Washington, D.C.: American Council on Education, 1940.

Gardner, L. M. The therapeutic relationship under varying conditions of race. *Psychotherapy: Theory, Research, and Practice*, 1971, **8**, 78–87.

Gibby, R. G., & Gabler, R. The self-concept of Negro and white children. *Journal of Clinical Psychology*, 1967, **23**, 144–148.

Gilbert, J. Counseling black inner-city children in groups. In M. M. Ohlsen (Ed.), *Counseling Children in Groups: A Forum*. New York: Holt, Rinehart & Winston, 1973, 147–169.

Gochros, J. S. Recognition and use of anger in Negro clients. *Social Work*, 1966, **11**, 28–34.

Golightly, C. L. Counseling, culture, and value. In C. E. Beck (Ed.), *Philosophical Guidelines for Counseling* (rev. ed.),. Dubuque, Iowa: W. C. Brown, 1971, 310–316.

Gordon, M. *Assimilation in American life.* New York: Oxford University Press, 1964.

Grantham, R. J. *The effects of counselor race, sex, and language variables in counseling culturally different clients.* Unpublished doctoral dissertation, State University of New York at Buffalo, 1970.

Grier, W., & Cobbs, P. *Black Rage.* New York: Basic Books, 1968.

Grob, G. N. *The State and the Mentally Ill: A History of Worcester State Hospital in Massachusetts, 1830–1920.* Chapel Hill, N.C.: University of North Carolina Press, 1966.

Hager, P. C., & Elton, C. F. The vocational interests of Black males. *Journal of Vocational Behavior*, 1971, **1**, 153–158.

Hall, E. T. *Beyond Culture.* New York: Anchor Press/Doubleday, 1976.

Hall, E. T. How cultures collide. (Edward Hall with Elizabeth Hall). *Psychology Today*, 1976, **10**(2), 66–74, 97a.

Hare, N., & Hare, J. Black women, 1970. *TRANS-ACTION*, 1970, **8**, 65–68.

Harrison, D. K. Race as a counselor-client variable in counseling and psychotherapy: A review of the research. *Counseling Psychologist*, 1975, **5**, 124–133.

Hays, W. C., & Mendel, C. H. Extended kinship relations in Black and white families. *Journal of Marriage and the Family*, 1973, **35**, 51–56.

Heacock, D. R. The Black slum child and the problem of aggression. *American Journal of Psychoanalysis*, 1976, **36**, 219–226.

Herkovits, M. J. *The Myth of the Negro Past.* Boston: Beacon Press, 1958.

Herzog, E. *About the Poor: Some Facts and Some Fictions.* U.S. Department of Health, Education and Welfare, Children's Bureau. Washington, D.C.: U.S. Government Printing Office, 1968.

Herzog, E. Who should be studied? *American Journal of Orthopsychiatry.* 1971, **41**, 4–12.

Howard, J. H. Toward a social psychology of colonialism. In R. L. Jones (Ed.), *Black Psychology.* New York: Harper & Row, 1972, 326–334.

Jensen, A. R. How much can we boost I.Q. and scholastic achievement? *Harvard Educational Review*, 1969, 1–23.

Joint Commission on Mental Illness and Health, 1961. *Action for Mental Health.* New York: Basic Books, 1968.

Jones, B. E., Lightfoot, O. B., Palmer, D., Wilkerson, R. G., & Williams, D. H. Problems of Black psychiatric residents in white training institutes. *American Journal of Psychiatry*, 1970, 127, 798–803.

Jones, E. Psychotherapists shortchange the poor. *Psychology Today*, 1975, **8**(11), 24–28.

Jones, S. E. A comparative proxemics analysis of dyadic interaction in selected subcultures of New York City. *Journal of Social Psychology*, 1970, **84**, 35–44.

Kimball, R. L. Sedlacek, W. E., & Brooks, G. C., Jr. Black and white vocational interests on Holland's Self-Directed Search (SDS). *Journal of Negro Education*, 1973, **42**, 1–4.

Kincaid, M. Identity and therapy in the Black community. *Personnel and Guidance Journal*, 1969, **47**, 884–890.

King, M. L., Jr. The role of the behavioral scientist in the Civil Rights movement. *American Psychologist*, 1968, **23**, 180–186.

Kramer, B. M. Racism and mental health as a field of thought and action. In Charles V. Willie, Bernard M. Kramer, & Bertram S. Brown (Eds.), *Racism and Mental Health*. Pittsburgh: University of Pittsburgh Press, 1973, 3–24.

Lerner, B. *Therapy in the Ghetto*. Baltimore: Johns Hopkins University Press, 1972.

Lieberson, S., & Fugitt, G. V. Negro-white occupational differences in the absence of discrimination. *American Journal of Sociology*, 1967–1968, **73**, 188–200.

Lorion, R. P. Socioeconomic status and traditional treatment approaches reconsidered. *Psychological Bulletin*, 1973, **79**(4), 263–270.

Mack, D. E. Where the Black matriarchy theorists went wrong. *Psychology Today*, 1971, **4**(24), 86–87.

Miller, C. H. *Foundations of Guidance*. New York: Harper & Row, 1961.

Mitchell, H. The Black experience in higher education. *Counseling Psychologist*, 1970, **2**, 30–36.

Moses, E. G., Zirkel, P. A., & Greene, J. F. Measuring the self-concept of minority group pupils. *Journal of Negro Education*, 1973, **42**, 93–98.

Moynihan, D. P. *The Negro Family: The Case for National Action*. Washington. D.C.: Office of Policy Planning and Research, U.S. Department of Labor, 1965.

Myrdal, G. *An American Dilemma: The Negro Problem and Democracy*, 2 vols. New York: Harper & Row, 1944.

Payne, Z. A. *Race, sex, and age related differences in academic counseling as they exist or are believed to exist among second-year students in three selected community colleges*. Unpublished doctoral dissertation, Michigan State University, 1971.

Pettigrew, T. F. Racism and the mental health of white Americans: A social psychological view. In C. V. Willie, B. M. Kramer, & B. S. Brown (Eds.), *Racism and Mental Health*. Pittsburgh: University of Pittsburgh Press, 1973, 269–298.

Pinderhughes, C. A. Understanding Black power: Processes and proposals. *American Journal of Psychiatry*, 1969, **125**, 1552–1557.

Powell, G. H. Self-concept in white and black children. In C. V. Willie, B. M. Kramer, and B. S. Brown (Eds.), *Racism and Mental Health*, Pittsburgh: University of Pittsburgh Press, 1973, 299–318.

Proshansky, H., & Newton, P. The nature and meaning of Negro self-identity. In M. Deutsch, I. Katz, & A. Jensen (Eds.), *Social Class, Race, and Psychological Development*. New York: Holt, Rinehart & Winston, 1968.

Pugh, R. W. *Psychology and the Black Experience*. Monterey, Calif.: Brooks/Cole, 1972.

Riessman, F. *The Culturally Deprived Child*. New York: Harper & Row, 1962.

Rosenthal, D., & Frank, J. D. The fate of psychiatric clinic outpatients assigned to psychotherapy. *Journal of Nervous and Mental Disorders*, 1958, **127**, 330–337.

Ruiz, R. A., & Padilla, A. M. Counseling Latinos. *Personnel and Guidance Journal*, 1977, **55**(7), 401–408.

Russell, R. D. Black perceptions of guidance. *Personnel and Guidance Journal*, 1970, **48**, 721–728.

Ryan, W. *Blaming the Victim*. New York: Pantheon, 1971.

Sattler, J. M. Racial "experimenter effects" in experimentation, testing, interviewing and psychotherapy. *Psychological Bulletin*, 1970, **73**, 137–160.

Seward, G. *Psychotherapy and Cultural Conflict*. New York: Ronald Press, 1956.

Sexton, P. Negro career expectations. In H. J. Peters and J. C. Hansen (Eds.), *Vocational Guidance and Career Development*, 1971, 352–365.

Shockley, W. Negro I.Q. deficit: Failure of a "malicious coincidence" model warrants new research proposals. *Review of Educational Research*, 1971, **41**, 227–248.

Simon, P. Literary review of *Roots*. *Buffalo Evening News*, January 26, 1977, 25.

Simpkins, G., Williams, R. L., & Gunnings, T. What a culture a difference makes: A rejoinder of Valentine. *Harvard Educational Review*, 1971, **41**, 4, 535–541.

Skolnick, A. The Myth of the vulernable child. *Psychology Today*, 1978, **11**(9), 56–60, 65.

Smith, E. J. Counseling Black individuals: Some stereotypes. *Personnel and Guidance Journal*, 1977, **55**(7), 390–396.

Smith, E. J. *Counseling the culturally different black youth*. Columbus, O.: Charles E. Merrill, 1973.

Soares, A., & Soares, L. Self-conceptions of culturally disadvantaged children. *American Educational Research Journal*, 1969, **6**, 31–45.

Sommers, U. An experiment in group psychotherapy with members of mixed minority groups. *International Journal of Group Psychotherapy*, 1953, **3**, 254–269.

Staples, R. The myth of the Black matriarchy. *Black Scholar*, 1970, **1**, 8–16.

Sue, S. McKinney, H., Allen, D., & Hall, J. Delivery of community mental health services to Black and white clients. *Journal of Consulting and Clinical Psychology*, 1974, **42**, 794–801.

TenHouten, W. The Black family: Myth and reality. *Psychiatry*, 1970, **33**, 145–173.

Thomas, A., & Sillen, S. *Racism and Psychiatry*. New York: Brunner/Mazel, 1972.

Tobias, P. V. Brain-size, grey matter and race—facts or fiction? *American Journal of Physical Anthropology*, 1970, **32**, 3–26.

Toldson, I. L., & Pasteur, A. B. Therapeutic dimensions of the Black aesthetic. *Journal of Non-White Concerns*, 1976, **4**, 105–117.

Torrey, E. F. *The Mind Game: Witchdoctors and Psychiatrists*. New York: Emerson Hall, 1972.

Tucker, R. N., & Gunnings, T. S. Counseling Black youth: A quest for legitmacy. *Journal of Non-White Concerns*, 1974, **2**, 208–217.

Valentine, C. Deficit, difference, and bicultural models of Afro-American behavior. *Harvard Educational Review*, 1971, **41**, 131–157.

Vontress, C. E. Counseling Blacks. *Personnel and Guidance Journal*, 1970, 48, 713–719.

Wallace, M. *Black Macho and the Myth of the Superwoman*. New York: Dial Press, 1979.

Walters, O. S. Metaphysics, religion, and psychotherapy. In C. E. Beck (Ed.), *Philosophical Guidelines for Counseling*. Dubuque, Iowa: W. Brown, 1971, 298–311.

Warner, W. L., Junker, B. J., Adams, W. A. *Color and Human Nature: Negro Personality Development in a Northern City*. New York: Harper & Row, 1969. (originally published in 1941 by the American Council on Education, Washington, D.C.)

West, E. H. *The Black American and Education*. Columbus, O.: Charles E. Merrill, 1972.

Whiteman, M., & Deutsch, M. Some effects of social class and race on children's language and intellectual abilities. In M. Deutsch, I. Katz, & A. Jensen (Eds.), *Social Class, Race, and Psychological Development*. New York: Holt, Rinehart & Winston, 1968.

Wilkinson, C. B. The destructiveness of myths. *American Journal of Psychiatry*, 1970, **126**, 1087–1092.

Williams, R. L., & Kirkland, J. The white counselor and Black client. *Counseling Psychologist*, 1971, **2**(4), 114–177.

Wilson, P. U.S. Commission on Civil Rights. *Racial Isolation in the Public Schools*. Washington, D.C.: U.S. Government Printing Office, 1967.

Witty, P., Garfield, S., & Brink, W. A. A comparison of the vocational interests of Negro and white high school students. *Journal of Educational Psychology*, 1941, **32**, 124–132.

Woodson, C. G. *Education of the Negro Prior to 1861*. Washington, D.C.: Associated Publishers, 1919.

Woofter, T. J., Jr. *Negro Problems in Cities*. New York: Negro Universities Press, 1928.

Yamamoto, J., James, Q. C., & Palley, N. Cultural problems in psychiatric therapy. *Archives of General Psychiatry*, 1968, **19**, 45–49.

STUDY QUESTIONS

1. What part has the enslavement of Black people played in the development of their cultural identity and world views? Give supporting data/examples.

2. What does the author mean when she states that "the mental health field has only mirrored the racism of white American life?" Please be specific.

3. How has Black American culture been analyzed in the past? What implications do each of the approaches have with respect to (*a*) a view of Black Americans, (*b*), a view of white society, and (*c*) implications for counseling?

4. What damaging myths have arisen concerning the Black family? How might accurate information/knowledge of the Black family structure/experience aid in counseling?

5. How may the "myth of sameness" be a major problem in counseling Black Americans?

6. What are some major barriers to effective cross-cultural counseling identified by the author in working with Black clients?

7. What were some strategies and approaches identified by the author in working with Black clients? How may these be more relevant and appropriate (please give rationale)?

8

Cultural and Historical Perspectives in Counseling Hispanics

RENE A. RUIZ

The guiding purposes of this chapter are to show that Hispanics are "different" enough to sometimes require culturally relevant methods of counseling and to help you decide when and how. To achieve these goals, the chapter begins with a brief historical sketch that shows how the colonization of the New World resulted in the development of several regional subcultures often referred to collectively as the "Hispanic culture." The chapter sometimes focuses on Hispanics, sometimes on other specific subgroups, but the distinction is always explicit. Current and future population estimates are presented, followed by data on education, employment, income, and residence. These population estimates and demographic data are used to support the idea that Hispanic needs for counseling services are high and will continue to increase. Next comes a discussion of the Hispanic and Anglo cultures, with emphasis on differences relevant to counseling, language, marriage, and the family. A discussion follows on the key variables of assimilation, acculturation, and their measurement. At this point, the chapter shifts from theory to practice. There are case histories that include critiques on treatment planning.

The author is currently on sabbatical leave at the Spanish Speaking Mental Health Research Center of the University of California at Los Angeles. This Center, the author's sabbatical, plus the preparation of this manuscript, were supported in part by National Institute of Mental Health Research Grant MH 24854.

WHO ARE THE HISPANICS?

The term "Hispanic" is gradually replacing the synonym "Latino," which was defined in earlier work as a "generic label including all people of Spanish origin and descent" (Ruiz & A. Padilla, 1977, p. 401). Thus, as used here, "Hispanic" replaces terms used by the U.S. Bureau of the Census or others that denote ethnicity ("Spanish origin"), language skill ("Spanish speaking"), family name ("Spanish surname"), or ancestry ("Spanish American").

Ethnohistory and Culture*

The issue here is that Hispanics are members of a single culture group in the sense that they share a fairly common history, beginning with the Spanish conquest. More important, Hispanics share language, values, and customs. These facts have misled some to assume that the Hispanic culture is homogeneous, whereas in actuality, it makes more sense to conceptualize Hispanic culture as an aggregate of distinct subcultures, each emanating from a different geographic area. The importance of this logical error for counseling is that intragroup cultural differences among Hispanics have been ignored or minimized. As a result, the need for culture specific methods of counseling have gone unrecognized, and many Hispanics have subsequently received inferior treatment (Ruiz, Casas, & Padilla, 1977). Let us look at Chicano history and culture as a means of making these points more clear.

The Spaniards arrived in the New World in the early sixteenth century and brought with them a fairly European homogeneous culture. The conquest of Mexico was followed by exploration and colonization. By the middle of the sixteenth century, the original immigrants from Spain, native Indians from Mexico, and their "mestizo," or "mixed blood," progeny had founded permanent settlements in what is today northern New Mexico. This process continued, and soon all of what today is known as the Southwest was settled. Thus contemporary Chicano culture is the end point of this historical, genetic, and cultural interaction.

This complex process of Indo-Hispanic marriage, exploration, colonization, and cultural fusion was occurring simultaneously throughout the New World. But differences were so great in some geographic areas that different Hispanic subcultures emerged. In some places,

---

*A more extended version of material summarized in this section appears in Ruiz & A. Padilla (1977).

instead of genetic merger and cultural fusion as in Mexico, genocide destroyed both the native inhabitants and their cultures. In some of these newly depopulated areas, slaves from Africa were imported for labor, and yet other genetic and cultural strains were introduced. The point is that all these people are "Hispanic" but that the intragroup differences are large enough to warrant the application of different methods of counseling. It is illogical to assume that the European-based methods of counseling that are effective with Anglos are adequate for Hispanics, and it is even questionable whether the different subgroups of Hispanics will respond equally well to the same treatment. Now let us move to an elaboration of how many people we are talking about.

HOW MANY HISPANICS?

The 1971 report of the U.S. Bureau of the Census estimated the presence of 9.0 million Hispanics, with the majority claiming Mexico as their country of origin (5.0 million). Almost immediately, however, both figures were described as inaccurate underestimates on the bases of the "alleged omission of migrant farm workers from census polls, casual enumerative practices among the barrio poor, and the misidentification of some Mexican Americans as Mexican citizens" (A. Padilla & Ruiz, 1973, pp. 2–3). A second and later analysis of census data (1975) shows an increase in the total number of Hispanics from 9.0 to 11.2 million, with Mexican Americans, still the largest subgroup, increasing from 5.0 to 6.7 million. Even these later and larger estimates, however, are considered by many to represent significant underestimates of the numbers of Hispanics and Mexican Americans in the United States.

A recent analysis by Macias (1977) is directly relevant to this discussion. Macias begins with the census figure of 11.2 million Hispanics in 1975. He reports the opinions of unidentified "Latino leaders" that 4.8 million Hispanics were erroneously omitted from this census. According to these sources, a more accurate figure should be 16.0 million Hispanics "just including citizens and legal residents." Next, Macias cites a recent survey by the Immigration and Naturalization Service that estimates the presence of an additional 7.4 million "illegal residents" of Hispanic origin in 1975. This analysis indicates that the actual number of Hispanics in the United States in 1975 was 11.2 million (census), plus 4.8 million (omissions), plus 7.4 million (illegal residents). This total equals 23.4 million Hispanics for an impressive 9% of the total 1975 U.S. population of 206.7 million.

Macias reports a mean age of 20.1 years and family size of 4.0 among Hispanics compared to figures of 28.5 and 3.4 for the general population. These discrepancies contribute to differences in natural increase rates based on births minus deaths per year—1.8% for Hispanics compared to 0.6% for the total population. Macias estimates that the actual increase is 3.5% since the "natural" rate fails to include population growth due to migration. Of relevance to those of us planning future needs for counseling services are population projections by Macias. By the year 2000, Macias estimates that the number of Hispanics will range from a minimum of 17.5 million (1975 census at 1.8% natural increase) to a maximum of 55.3 million (largest 1975 estimate at a 3.5% growth rate." Now that we have an idea of "how many" Hispanics there are, let us look at what Hispanic clients "will be like."

WHAT ARE HISPANIC DEMOGRAPHICS?

These census data on Hispanic demographics help us anticipate what to expect as the number of Hispanics increases and as their need for counseling services grows. Sources are identified in A. Padilla, Ruiz & Alvarez (1975) and in Ruiz, A. Padilla, & Alvarez (1978).

Education

The median number of years of formal schooling for males 25 years of age and older is as follows: Hispanics, 9.3 years; general population, 12.2 years; and Blacks, 9.6 years. The number of Americans who have completed five years of school or less breaks down by ethnicity as follows: Hispanics, 19.5%; general population, 5.0%; and Blacks, 13.5%. These are the data on graduation from high school: Hispanics, 32.6%; general population, 56.4%; and Blacks, 34.7%. The conclusion is inescapable, Hispanics are a significantly undereducated group, compared both to the general population and to Blacks, as measured by median years of education, percentage with five or less years of school, and graduation from high school.

Employment and Unemployment

With education so limited, it should come as no surprise to find Hispanics overrepresented in occupations that are menial and low paid; 76% of Hispanics are blue-collar workers. The unemployment rate among Hispanics during the third quarter of 1974 was 8.0%, which was greater than the national level of 5.0%, but less than the Black rate of 10.5%. Ruiz & A. Padilla (1977, p. 402) argue that "these data are somewhat deceptive . . . unless one considers the increase in unemployment during the preceding year was 29% among Latinos, compared to 22% among the general population and 8% among Blacks." Thus the conclusions are that Hispanics—relative to the general population and to Blacks—have high rates of unemployment; but among those employed, they tend to have blue-collar jobs with high probabilities of abrupt termination.

Earned Income

In 1970, median income for Hispanic males was $2000 per year less than that of non-Hispanic males ($6220 vs. $8220). Data on family income are skewed in the same direction. Among Hispanic families, 23% report annual incomes less than $5000 compared to 14.7% of the non-Hispanic families, whereas only 18.4% of the Hispanic families earned more than $15,000 per year compared to 35.5% among the general population. The significance of these data is perhaps better communicated by the fact that 21.9% of the Hispanic population was described as "low income" compared to 11.1% of the general population according to the 1973 census (Ruiz, A. Padilla, & Alvarez, 1978). At the risk of belaboring the obvious, the conclusion is that Hispanics represent one of the most impoverished segments of American society.

Areas of Residence

Census data reveal a relationship between ethnicity and area of residence (Ruiz, A. Padilla, & Alvarez, 1978). At the most broad level of analysis, for example, Hispanics, in general, are urban dwellers—82.5% compared to 67.8% for the total population and 76.0% for Blacks. With regard to within group differences, 87% of the Chicanos reside in the Southwest of the United States (California, Texas, Arizona, New Mexico, and Colorado); 76% of the Puerto Ricans reside in one of three states: New York, New Jersey, or Connecticut; and most Cubans are to be found in Florida.

HOW IS HISPANIC CULTURE UNIQUE?

Language Skill and Preference

An earlier analysis of two key questions from the 1969 census indicates that a significant percentage of Hispanics are Spanish monolingual or English and Spanish bilingual, with Spanish dominant (Ruiz, A. Padilla, & Alvarez, 1978). A clear majority of Hispanics (68.9%) identify Spanish as the "mother tongue," with English a remote second-place choice (28.8%). When asked to indicate the "language usually spoken in the home," 48.7% of the Hispanics answered Spanish and 50.3% English. Responses to these two questions equal slightly less than 100% each, because not all response categories are included in the present analysis (i.e., "other" and "not reported"). When one considers that a significant number of Hispanics are not included in census data and that migration of Spanish monolinguals continues, it is clear this range of preference for Spanish among Hispanics (48.7 to 68.9%) is almost certainly an inaccurately low figure. These language data are important, of course, because they provide a base rate minimum estimate of how many Hispanics may require culturally relevant counseling.

Sex Roles and Marriage*

The mistaken notion that Hispanic culture is homogeneous and that all Hispanics are "alike" is clearly reflected in discussions appearing in the scientific and the lay literature on Hispanic sex roles and marriage. These writings seem to suggest that sex roles for Hispanics are defined as unique and rigid. That is, that Hispanic men and women behave in very different ways ("unique") and never behave alike ("rigid"). As discussed next, some real differences between Hispanic men and women have been recognized by non-Hispanic commentators but distorted beyond recognition.

Nowhere is this distortion more evident than in discussions involving the word *macho*. This term translates from Spanish as "male" and is used among Hispanics as a flattering term to denote masculinity. It connotes physical strength, sexual attractiveness, virtue, and potency. In this sense, the label "macho" has many of the same connotations it has in English, where it is widely used in advertising to communicate an

---

*A more elaborate discussion of the theoretical issues summarized here appears in Ruiz (1978) and Ruiz & A. Padilla (1973).

element of "masculine power" (for example, "boss" sports cars) or the "masculine essence" (for example, "manly" shaving colognes). At a more subtle level of analysis, "real" masculinity among Hispanics involves dignity in personal conduct, respect for others, love for the family, and affection for children. When applied by non-Hispanics to Hispanic males, however, "macho" often is defined in terms of physical aggression, sexual promiscuity, dominance of women, and excessive use of alcohol. In reaction to this abuse, Hispanic women are assumed to be submissive, nurturant, and virtuous thereby maintaining the unity of the Hispanic family despite all this disruption from their fathers, husbands, and sons.

People who describe Hispanics in such unrealistic and unflattering terms often argue that a combination of the extended family and rural customs somehow "cause" and maintain this pattern of morbid interactions between Hispanic men and women. Such a description is difficult to accept, even logically, in view of so many changes in recent times that could influence family life and adherence to tradition among Hispanics: acculturation, assimilation, urbanization, and the transition from an agricultural to a technological society. In any event, more extended versions of this analysis of Hispanic family life appear in Madsen (1964), Murillo (1971), Ruiz (1978), and Ruiz & A. Padilla (1973). Caveats against naive acceptance of unsubstantiated assertions on this topic appear in Hawkes & Taylor (1975), McCurdy & Ruiz (1980), A. Padilla & Ruiz (1973), Ruiz (1978), Ruiz & A. Padilla (1973), and Staton (1972).

A recent study (McCurdy & Ruiz, 1980 on ethnicity, sex role, and decision making is relevant here. The sample included 128 married couples living together, all from a lower socioeconomic status group. The basic findings that concern us here are that 48 Chicano husbands and wives agreed in denying "traditional" sex roles, including male dominance in the marriage. Chicano marriages were no more or less traditional than those of comparable samples of Anglos and Blacks.

Family Structure and Dynamics

The term "nuclear family" refers to parents and children living together apart from other relatives, and the term "extended family" describes a living situation that includes other relatives in the home. In general, the nuclear family unit is more common in cities and is thought to be better fitted to cope with the stresses of urban, technological society (Goode, 1963; Parsons, 1943), whereas extended family structures are consid-

ered more characteristic of, and effective in, rural, agricultural settings (A. Padilla & Ruiz, 1973).

It has been suggested by others that the Hispanic tradition of an extended family structure has a stress resistant quality when it comes to the formation of emotional problems. This argument is most common as an attempt to explain Hispanic underutilization of mental health services. Other than using vague generalizations such as "emotional support systems," no notions have been forwarded to explain with any precision how family structure can offset the destructive influences of the poverty cycle and societal discrimination. Furthermore, this approach ignores factors that discourage Hispanic self-referral, the most obvious being geographic distance of the service agencies, inadequate transportation, and service delivery personnel who lack Spanish fluency or familiarity with any of the Hispanic cultures. This general situation has been examined in much greater depth, and several positive recommendations for both service and research appear elsewhere (A. Padilla & Ruiz, 1973; Padilla, Ruiz, & Alvarez, 1975; Ruiz, 1977; Ruiz, Casas, & A. Padilla, 1977; Ruiz, A. Padilla, & Alvarez, 1978).

Part of a recent study by Mindel (1980) on ethnicity, "visiting" and "recreation" with kin, and many other aspects of family life seems relevant here. Subjects were 455 lower-socioeconomic class Anglo, Black, and Chicano residents of a midwestern metropolis, but our major interest is in Mindel's subsample of Chicanos. One index of the vitality of the extended family is the frequency of interactions among kin. What Mindel found was that the relative number of self-reported interactions with kin was the same among Anglo, Black, and Chicano respondents, but that the absolute number was largest among Chicanos because they had the most kin.

Earlier, reference was made to the non-Hispanic stereotype of Hispanic life with regard to the macho, other sex role behavior, and the nature of the Hispanic family. We think this stereotype conflicts sharply with Mindel's general impression of the Chicano family based on his research. But you examine it, and decide for yourself. On the basis of data analysis too complex to report in this brief summary, Mindel (1980) reports these conclusions about the Chicano families he studied:

. . . very close to their parents and siblings, but less so with non-nuclear kin . . . they enjoyed (these visits), although there was an element of dependence . . . very little aid and support with kin outside the nuclear family of orientation . . . more matrilocal . . . more likely to be surrounded by and

in more frequent contact with kin of the wife . . . much greater level of exchange of aid and support with the kin of the wife.

HISPANIC OR ANGLO?

Acculturation and Assimilation

Some people seem to think that culture group membership for Hispanics in the United States is essentially dichotomous. As an alternative, it makes much more sense to conceptualize culture group membership for Hispanics in the United States as a continuum. One extreme of this hypothetical continuum might be designated "completely Hispanic" and the other "completely Anglo." An exemplar of total commitment to, and membership in, the Hispanic culture might be the newly arrived immigrant who is totally lacking in personal experience with the United States. Likewise, total commitment to, and membership in, the Anglo culture could be exemplified by the progeny of immigrants to the United States who have abandoned the cultures of their ancestors. In other words, these people no longer follow the "old ways" of their forefathers; they speak only English, follow no Old World traditions, consume an American diet, and so on.

The process just described—in which people migrate and their progeny give up "old" ways and adopt "new" ones—is labeled "acculturation" for the remainder of this chapter. This definition is too simplistic for theory and research in cultural anthropology, psychology, or sociology but is quite adequate for this discussion. It should be stated here that the history and social science of the United States is replete with the myth that acculturation represents a universal goal toward which ethnic minority group people voluntarily strive. In more common language, this is the allegory of the "American melting pot." The facts reveal the fallacy of the myth. Despite centuries of "voluntary" acculturation, Hispanics in the United States have retained Spanish fluency and other traditions of Hispanic culture. Furthermore, Spanish fluency and the Hispanic culture have survived centuries of "involuntary" acculturation—such as, the "English only" rule that characterized the educational system of the Southwest until very recently. And finally, anomaly of anomalies, despite all this pressure for acculturation, data reviewed earlier confirm that Hispanics receive relatively less education, employment, income, health care, and other societal rewards.

To return to a discussion of the hypothetical continuum of cultural group membership with its two extreme points (Hispanic at one end and

Anglo at the other), it is now clear that it is the "degree of acculturation" which determines placement on this variable. A given Hispanic
may be "completely Hispanic" (the example was given earlier of a new
immigrant) or may be "completely Anglo" (that is, totally acculturated
to the general culture of the United States). But almost certainly, the
majority of Hispanics fall at some intermediate point between these two
extremes; that is, most are "bicultural." This observation that most
Hispanics are only partially acculturated to the dominant culture of the
United States is very important to the main thrust of the entire chapter.
As is demonstrated later, this variable of biculturality, as measured by
the degree of Latinization or, conversely, the degree of Anglicization, is
used to determine treatment. Now, however, it is helpful to continue to
define key terms.

The concept of "assimilation" must be considered in conjunction
with acculturation. Basically, "assimilation" refers to the extent to
which an individual enters a given culture and becomes a part of it. In
this sense, the two terms are highly similar in meaning. Assimilation,
however, transcends individual motivation and includes societal "acceptance." In other words, the degree of assimilation for any given Hispanic (and possibly, other ethnic and racial minorities in the United
States) is a dual function of how motivated the person is to enter the
Anglo culture as well as the extent to which members of the Anglo
culture welcome, or prevent, the introduction of that person into the
majority Anglo culture.

The relevance of these two concepts as used here is that a given
Hispanic may be very acculturated in the sense that he or she is
conversant with the Anglo culture in terms of English fluency, costume,
diet, and tradition. Some very acculturated Hispanics, however, may
simultaneously vary widely with respect to the degree of assimilation.
Some may prefer and feel themselves a part of Anglo culture; others
may reject it, and still others may retain a bicultural identification.

The complexity of the interaction between acculturation and assimilation is potentiated by the fact that cultural identification may be
situational for many Hispanics by virtue of their bicultural life adjustment. For example, some Hispanics may be very Anglo at school and on
the job but very Hispanic at home or with the family. Furthermore,
different complexes of life experiences, emotions, cognitions, and even
language preferences may be associated with different environmental
situations.

Now imagine the vast implications of this issue of bicultural membership, with underlying differences in acculturation and assimilation,
for counseling. A given bicultural patient may think, act, and feel more

like an Anglo than an Hispanic during treatment of a work or school problem, while the very same person (or another person of equivalent acculturation and assimilation) may respond more like an Hispanic than an Anglo in dealing with problems associated with home and family. Granted, people are not compartmentalized and do not generally refer themselves for treatment for a single problem that is totally unrelated to any other aspect of their life adjustment. Nevertheless, this artificial distinction among reasons for referral facilitates consideration of some of the special problems associated with the treatment of people seeking help who may be bilingual and bicultural. Some bicultural clients with certain types of problems may respond best to bicultural counseling. Thus the important question is how to decide whether a given patient is bicultural and whether that patient and that particular set of problems will respond better to a bicultural counseling program.

How to Decide

The uninformed reader might erroneously assume that bicultural counseling programs are readily available and that service delivery agencies are providing the needed help. The situation is quite different. Universities are not meeting their responsibility of educating bilingual, bicultural counselors, psychotherapists, or researchers. The number of mental health professionals, or even paraprofessionals, both on the job and in training, is infinitesimally small. Furthermore, all available data indicate that the situation is very likely to continue to worsen (El-Khawas & Kimzer, 1954; E. Padilla, Boxley, & Wagner, 1953; Ruiz, 1951). Of equally morbid impact is the general impression that service delivery agencies are providing neither training programs in bicultural treatment nor services for their catchment population (A. Padilla & Ruiz, 1953; Ruiz, 1955).

There are several consequences to this situation. The pool of biculturally trained counselors is small, the number of agencies that deliver culturally relevant counseling is extremely limited, and the vast majority of Hispanics are thereby deprived of the bicultural services which could facilitate resolution of their problems. As a result, in those rare agencies in which culturally relevant treatment methods are available, treatment decisions may be made in a highly informal manner. Possession of a Spanish surname, for example, may be the sole criterion used to refer someone for culturally relevant counseling.

A second method may be to ask Hispanics to state a preference. This latter approach may present some unknown risks, however, since the limited available data suggest that Mexican Americans hold generally favorable attitudes toward psychotherapy and psychotherapists but tend to place less trust and credence in expert therapists of their own ethnicity (Acosta, 1955; Acosta & Sheehan, 1956). This research asked college students to pretend they were seeking treatment. Videotapes were viewed and rated of "potential" psychotherapists who varied along dimensions of ethnicity, stated degree and experience, and accent. These findings and conclusions, however, have not been accepted uncritically. Herrera (1958) points out that this is an "analogue" study of undergraduates rather than actual psychotherapy candidates. This disagreement leaves unresolved the larger question of whether Hispanics themselves are the best qualified to judge whether they would respond best to a culturally relevant treatment program. This same dissertation (Acosta, 1975) also found that this group of Mexican Americans was more reluctant than the Anglo undergraduates to disclose personal information to a strange person such as a mere therapist (Acosta & Sheehan, in press).

The implications of making treatment decisions on such a limited data base are immense. To assign all Spanish-surname clients to the same bicultural treatment program implies that all these people are somehow alike with regard to culture group membership. The logical absurdity of this assumption becomes obvious whenever operational definition is initiated. No one would seriously defend the premise, for example, that all Hispanics are alike in the sense that they possess Spanish fluency to the exact same degree. Furthermore, data are accumulating which indicate that Chicanos are part of a heterogeneous culture group (J. Martinez, 1977; Murillo, 1976; Ramirez & Castaneda, 1974).

If service delivery begins to respond to the needs of its bicultural clientele by providing relevant programs, there are more sophisticated measurement approaches available to aid in the assessment of the degree of acculturation. The significance of this variable, of course, is that the degree of acculturation can be used to maximize the relevance of a treatment program for a given individual. The Spanish-monolingual or Spanish-dominant client with a family or marriage problem is almost certainly a prime candidate for a biculturally oriented approach, while the Hispanic who is acculturated to the Anglo system and who presents school or work problems would probably respond better to the same type of treatment programs used with Anglos. A much more detailed analysis of the decision-making process involved in referral to culturally relevant treatment appears in Ruiz, Casas, & A. Padilla (1977) and in Ruiz, A. Padilla, & Alvarez (1978).

There exist at least two measurement approaches for acculturation that are relevant to Hispanics. First, there is the work of Mercer (1972,

1973, 1976), who basically counts how many of five sociocultural characteristics a given ethnic minority group child has in common with the Anglo middle class. The more characteristics manifested by a given subject, the more that person is considered to be acculturated in terms of greater similarity to the criterion of acculturation, that is, the Anglo middle class. These sociocultural characteristics include residence in a household in which there are five or fewer family members living together and in which the head of household was reared in the United States in an urban environment, has a skilled or higher occupation, and has a white-collar job. The demonstration that group mean IQ scores vary as a function of the number of sociocultural characteristics validates the use of this approach to measure acculturation, while simultaneously raising questions about the validity of IQ tests for the measurement of intelligence within ethnic minority groups. An extended discussion of the validity of tests of intelligence and academic achievement for ethnic minority group children at the third- and sixth-grade levels appears in Kent & Ruiz (1978).

A second approach to the measurement of acculturation among Hispanics that is also based on highly sophisticated research methods appears in the work of J. Martinez (1977), S. Martinez, J. Martinez, & Olmedo (1977), J. Martinez et al. (1976), and Olmedo, J. Martinez & S. Martinez (1978). Following a double cross-validation technique, the research team of J. Martinez & Olmedo was able to identify a group of 20 items that discriminated between Anglo and Chicano adolescents. Eleven of these items were sociocultural variables very similar to those used by Mercer. One such item, for example, is "only English spoken at home." The remaining nine items include the affective meanings assigned to certain culturally sensitive concepts using the Semantic Differential Technique. "Affective meaning" is measured by mean ratings (seven-point scale) of 15 pairs of bipolar adjectives (e.g., "hard-soft," "weak-strong") as they apply to culturally sensitive concepts such as "mother," "father," "male," and "female." The reader interested in using this scale is referred to Olmedo, J. Martinez, & S. Martinez (1978) who present the item pool and report means and standard deviations in both raw and standard scores. The breakdown of scores by ethnicity and sex (Table 4 of Olmedo, J. Martinez, & S. Martinez, 1978) can be extremely useful to the clinician interested in measuring the degree of acculturation among Chicano adolescents.

Solution of the Problem

There are several main points that emerge from this section. First, the majority of Hispanics are bicultural in the sense that they are members of both the Anglo and Hispanic cultures. Second, the range of commitment to the Anglo and Hispanic cultures varies widely. Some Hispanics are "very Hispanic," some are "very Anglo," and most are at various points between these two extremes. Third, it seems eminently reasonable to assume that Hispanics whose cultural identification is more Hispanic than Anglo will almost certainly benefit more from culturally relevant counseling methods than Hispanics whose cultural orientation is more Anglo. To provide an obvious illustration of this point, the Spanish-speaking person who seeks help for a problem perceived as related to culture group membership will probably not respond well to a treatment program conducted by someone who is ignorant of both the language and culture.

The fourth point is critical. Culturally relevant methods are extant and viable. Furthermore, a body of knowledge and affiliated technology is already available that makes it possible to measure the degree of acculturation among Chicanos in a valid and reliable fashion. Such information is critical in deciding whether a given Hispanic will respond better to traditional treatment methods conducted exclusively in English and that are oriented around an Anglo, middle-class value system, as opposed to a culturally relevant approach. There is no longer any justification for assigning Hispanic patients to inadequate or inappropriate treatment programs on the basis of such a weak prognostic criterion as a Spanish surname. Furthermore, asking Hispanics to make the decision appeals to the democratic principle but has yet to be demonstrated as the best way to make the choice. All things considered, it seems best to move in the direction of referring Hispanics for culturally sensitive treatment on the basis of their scores on objective questionnaires designed to measure the degree of acculturation. To the best of my knowledge, this ideal approach of basing treatment decisions on objective measurement is not being actualized anywhere. Decisions are being made, of course, but on the basis of data of dubious validity.

CASE HISTORIES

The concluding section of this chapter may be used as an exercise workbook by any reader interested in determining how well he or she has integrated the theoretical principles presented earlier. The material provided includes a series of historical comments on the lives of some real people who are already clients or who are potential candidates for counseling. The life events described here are essentially factual, although there are some slight modifications to lower the risk of subject identification. For example, pseudonyms are used to enhance confidentiality.

The best way to use this historical material as a "test" of comprehension is to examine each individual case carefully and then to outline a counseling program if one is called for in your opinion. To determine whether a bicultural approach would provide the best prognosis, you are encouraged to review the variable discussed earlier. While each case differs, some general questions of relevance might be these: Is this client more Hispanic or Anglo? What are the degrees of assimilation and acculturation? Is the client English or Spanish dominant? Will the client feel more comfortable discussing the problems presented in English or in Spanish? After these questions are answered, the next logical question is; How shall I counsel this person?

Following each case history is a brief statement by the author presenting his opinion concerning what intervention is called for (if any) based on his consideration of relevant variables. Each reader may compare his or her evaluation of the case and treatment plan with that provided by the author.

CASE ONE: FERNANDO AND REFUGIO ESCOBEDO

While Fernando is the identified client, information on his wife, Refugio, is also presented to facilitate more complete understanding of the situation. The couple has been married more than 35 years, are in their mid-fifties, and have 10 children. Both were born in the same small village in Mexico and resided there until three years ago when they moved permanently to a barrio in southern California. Since Fernando has labored as a "bracero" for most of his adult life, he has visited the United States annually during harvest seasons.

The Escobedos currently reside in a small, old, unpainted, and rented house on the back of a dirt lot. The house is sparsely furnished, and their belongings are old but serviceable and clean. They do not own a car, and public transportation is not available in their neighborhood. The couple's standard of living is far below poverty levels for this country, but the Escobedos are pleased at their relative affluence compared to life in Mexico. The couple's gross income is variable, ranging from $250 to $400 per month, and the source of income is disability, welfare, and help from their children.

In response to direct questions, both Escobedos are unequivocal with regard to self-identified ethnicity; they are Mexicanos, not Mexican Americans, Chicanos, Americans, or Anglos. Since their community is exclusively Mexican and Mexican American, their cultural value system remains essentially intact in terms of language, religion, food, and even home remedies for nontraumatic injuries. To make explicit what may already be obvious, both Mr. and Mrs. Escobedo are monolingual, and neither speak nor understand any English.

The presenting complaints concern Fernando. He hears threatening voices, is often disoriented, states the belief someone is planning to kill him and that something evil is about to happen to him. As a result, he refuses to leave home unless coerced. The years of heavy labor have taken their toll. Mr. Escobedo appears much older than his stated age. His psychological maladjustment, poor physical health, and generally decrepit appearance render him essentially unemployable.

Treatment Planning: The Escobedos   Data presented seem to support without dispute the opinion that the client and his wife fall at the "most Hispanic" extreme of the hypothetical continuum of bicultural identification. Every aspect of cultural identity proclaims their "Mexicanness," with an absolute minimum degree of acculturation to, or assimilation in, the Anglo majority culture. These are the factors of major significance in determining how to plan counseling. No mental health professional or paraprofessional—however well educated or trained— can hope to initiate any type of intervention without Spanish fluency and awareness of Mexican culture. This case *requires* service delivery personnel who are bilingual and bicultural, because counseling will consist to some extent of information gathering and dissemination. The use of translators is possible, but this approach can cause problems as President Jimmy Carter learned during his 1977 visit to Poland when his official statement that he had "great affection" for the Poles was translated as "lust."

The evaluation of Mr. Escobedo should start with a detailed medical history, with special attention paid to exposure to pesticides and other dangerous agricultural chemicals, especially those known to influence central nervous system function. Obviously, any illnesses of an unusual nature should be explored carefully. A concurrent physical examination is also highly recommended.

The etiology of Fernando's paranoid reaction and subsequent social isolation must be explored to determine prognosis. Obvious questions to begin with concern onset, duration, and response to ameliorative techniques. Some might argue that such questions transcend culture group membership. Be that as it may, one should not lose sight of the possibility that the patient's fears may symbolize realistic concerns. Fernando's fear that someone may "kill" him, for example, could reflect fear of deportation, creditors, the police, or others who often harass barrio dwellers. Whether one agrees or disagrees with this latter speculation, or even the possibility of its being true, please remember that its validity can be checked only through meaningful communication with, and concerning, the person whose life we are discussing.

The extended family can be extremely helpful in the evaluation and treatment of the Hispanic client. Distant cousins, "compadres," and other age peers may be more reliable informants concerning work history, for example, than people more closely related by blood. Members of the nuclear family, whether residing with the patient or not, may know more about symptom formation and behavior on a day-to-day basis. People who actually reside with the patient can also be extremely helpful in monitoring a whole range of treatment programs, from behavior modification to the regular ingestion of ataractic medication. Incidentally, this patient is on regular medication (type and dosage level unknown) and is described as showing a "good" response.

One final comment concerning Fernando and his family is that since the extended family may serve a stress-reduction function for Hispanics, I would recommend consideration of family-oriented treatment approaches with Hispanics more often than with non-Hispanics. I think it is premature in this particular case to be more specific in recommending "treatment" in the sense, for example, of psychodynamically oriented psychotherapy versus behavior modification. Nevertheless, whatever recommendations emerge from the necessary evaluation, the potential contribution to problem solving that can be provided by the Hispanic family will not be overlooked by the sophisticated counselor.

Up to this point, the analysis of the Escobedo family has been fairly traditional, even conservative. But the skilled counselor, especially one sensitive to human needs, recognizes that certain key aspects of this case are missing. These omissions were deliberate and for didactic purposes. I intend to cover them now, and urge the neophyte counselor of Hispanics to pause, reflect, and attempt to anticipate the next few points to be covered.

First, construct a hierarchy of needs for these people. Do they need brilliant insights into the etiology of Fernando's alleged paranoia? Would familiarity with Fenichel's theories be helpful? Do they need to become more introspective or psychodynamically oriented? The answers to these questions are negative. These people are aliens in a new land in more than one sense. They don't read or write English, they are not conversant with the Anglo culture, they may be unaware of their legal rights, and they may be "fearful" with due cause. They are poor and would probably benefit from any information that would help them cope with the Anglo system. For example, Fernando doubtless paid taxes to the U.S. government for 30 summers of picking crops. Are he and his dependents receiving their full share of benefits paid for by his tax dollars? Since the family's mobility is limited, is there any way transportation can be arranged for them? The point is that these people need "help"—not in the sense of understanding the roots of character formation—but rather in dealing with the realistic and irksome problems which daily confront people who are poor, undereducated, foreign looking and sounding, and old.

Second, I ask you to explore your attitudes toward these two people. They almost certainly live on a smaller income than most readers of this chapter. Does this make them your socioeconomic inferiors? They wear patched clothes and live in an old house in a poor part of town. Does this make them your social inferiors? Would you feel differently toward this couple if you were informed they were swarthy with Indian features as opposed to being fair and of European countenance? They have less formal education than you. How does this make you feel? Did you note I sometimes referred to them by first names and other times as Mr. and Mrs.? Which form of address do you prefer and why? What would you ask them to call you? Basically, I am asking how you feel about working with Hispanics, and only you can answer that question.

CASE TWO: CARMEN MUNOZ

This 54-year-old woman was born in a major city of northern Mexico. She describes her early years as relatively affluent but states that her family became bankrupt just before she entered her teen years. Because of this, she terminated her formal education at the approximate equivalent of the seventh-grade level in the United States. She married her first husband when she was 16 years of age, and bore six children in 16 years. This was a very unpleasant marriage for Carmen, which she terminated by migrating to the United States with her children. For the next eight years, Carmen provided the sole support for her children by holding down two jobs at a time. She met her second husband to be (Miguel), who was seven years her junior; at the age of 44, she bore her seventh and final child.

The Munoz family resides in a middle-sized redwood frame house in a lower-middle class, multiethnic neighborhood. This home and others around display lawns, shrubs, trees, and flowers. The inside of the Munoz home looks comfortable and lived in, although the furniture is old and well-worn. The sole source of income is Miguel's wages as a cook, which approximates $8500 per year. Perhaps the Munoz style of life can best be illustrated by commenting that they are paying off a car and a home, own insurance policies on both the car and home, possess a credit card from a local department store, and contribute regularly toward a savings account, retirement benefits, and unemployment insurance. The Munoz family does not, however, possess a life or health insurance policy, use a checking account, or vote, since neither has become a citizen of the United States.

Both Carmen and Miguel were born in Mexico; the couple's native tongue is Spanish, and their ethnic identification is Mexicano. Interestingly however, both are adept in English. The reasons seem to be related to Miguel's English conversations with co-workers, Carmen's chats with neighbors and others who are ignorant of Spanish, and the fact that the two children who still reside at home are young enough to attend school. The family cuisine is predominantly, but not exclusively, Mexican. The family structure is of the extended type, with Carmen's married children and grandchildren frequent visitors in the Munoz home.

Carmen's chief complaint is described by others as "melancholia and depression." This phrase is deceptive, however, because it is said to mask a complex and long-term process of "strong somatic pre-occupation . . . with frequent references to deteriorating physical health." The evaluation implies that this process is essentially "psychoneurotic."

This author cannot agree totally with the diagnostic formulation just cited for several reasons. First, the woman supported six children for eight years solely by her efforts at two jobs. There is no evidence during this period of her life of "somatic pre-occupation" or of significant physical illnesses. These life experiences seem to contradict allegedly lifelong tendencies toward hypochondriasis. Second, it is only within the last three or four years that Carmen has been discovered to be suffering from several serious illnesses which occured serially. After a fair-to-good recovery from meningitis, she developed a hernia that is inoperable because of a cardiac complication. More recently, Carmen has begun to experience recurrent headaches. Thus it seems much more reasonable to conceptualize (i.e., to diagnose, in more formal parlance) her "melancholia and depression" as a bona fide and reality-based reaction to a series of painful, debilitating, and restrictive physical illnesses.

Treatment Planning: Carmen Munoz   This woman's self-designation as Mexicana is unnecessary to deduce she is not a typical WASP. Her physical appearance, her country of nativity, and her accented English all support this inference. Thus it is easy to deduce we will almost certainly recommend a culturally relevant approach. But this designation, however accurate, can be refined further.

Note, for example, how much more acculturated and assimilated Carmen is than either Fernando or Refugio. Without arguing cause and effect, note that Carmen migrated at a younger, much more plastic age than did the Escobedos. Currently, she is conversant in English and familiar with many of the nuances of the Anglo majority culture, whereas the Escobedos are not. For example, Carmen uses a credit card, whereas the Escobedos subsist in a cash economy as do most of the very poor. It also seems important that Carmen's formative years were spent in a middle-class family in a Mexican metropolis, whereas the Escobedos emerged from an aspect of Mexican society that is rural, agriculturally based and impoverished.

To help the reader understand my opinion concerning Carmen's degree of acculturation, I would assess that the Escobedos are above the 95th percentile toward the "very Hispanic" extreme and that Carmen is at about the 75th percentile. In addition to the life experiences and historical events cited in the preceding paragraph, there are several differences between Carmen and the typical Hispanic. Specifically, she seems more independent, at least in the sense that she was willing to divorce, emigrate, and support her children with no known financial support from her former husband, family, or friends. While she has created her own extended family here in the United States, she has survived with only minimal emotional support from her family of origin. Carmen's husband is younger than she, which is definitely atypical in both cultures under discussion. This is a very unusual person, and a special bicultural program will have to be tailored to suit her unique set of needs.

First, Carmen must be counseled by someone who is truly fluent in both English and Spanish and who can switch from language to language with comfort. The prediction is that Carmen will choose to discuss different problems in different languages and her counselor must be able to follow along. Second, whoever counsels Carmen must be sensitive to her true biculturality: her roots are in Mexico, but her home, husband, children, grandchildren, and future life are in the United States. This may—or may not—create a problem of confused loyalty for Carmen. The skilled counselor will explore this possibility and help her resolve it if necessary.

The third recommendation concerns "melancholia and depression" and possible etiological explanations. I have already stated my opinion that the hypothesis of long-term, psychoneurotic "somatic pre-occupation" lacks verification and have suggested the alternative explanation that her sadness may be a realistic response to recent physical illness, chronic pain, and decreased motility. My opinion is theoretical only, however; and this is an issue the skilled counselor will explore and decide. If Carmen's behavior is truly maladaptive, then self-exploration and insight may be helpful. If, on the other hand, Carmen is responding normally to excessive stress, then emotional support may be more helpful.

Without belaboring the obvious, the fourth recommendation concerns medical consultation. I would seek verification that the painful hernia is in fact "inoperable" and that the cardiac condition which makes surgical intervention dangerous is actually immutable. It is a truism that the ethnic minority poor, and perhaps especially those who are less than fully articulate in English, receive second-rate medical care. For these reasons, I am unwilling to take for granted that the medical information available is accurate. In fairness to the medical profession, it should be noted that second-class citizens consistently receive a variety of second-rate services, not just medical care.

The fifth recommendation relates to the fourth. It is well known that depressions of psychotic proportions respond well to electroconvulsive treatment and that those of lesser severity are often lifted following the prescription of mood-elevating medication. Thus psychiatric consultation has the potential to provide significant relief. It goes without saying, or course, that this consultant should be fully apprised of possible cardiac and other physical pathology which could influence the choice of drug and ideally should be fluent in both English and Spanish and have some familiarity with Hispanic culture.

The sixth recommendation is thematic but is spelled out nonetheless for thoroughness. I would strongly recommend that someone explain to this woman what is going on when the fourth and fifth recommendations are being implemented. The client needs to be told why physical examinations are being readministered, why her medical history is being explored so meticulously, why drugs are being prescribed, and what relief and side effects to anticipate. Furthermore, all this must be explained in terms she can fully grasp, and directions must make sense to her or she will not follow them. Many antidepressive medications, for example, must be ingested routinely to be maximally effective rather than only when one "feels bad." The point is that information of this type must be communicated to her in terms she can integrate on the basis of her bicultural experience. It should be obvious by now that it is the author's bias that communication of this type can be transmitted, and positive motivation instilled, by a counselor who shares the same language skills and cultural experiences as the patient.

The seventh and eighth recommendations concern a culture specific approach to the alleviation of depression. It is generally recognized that depression is associated with apathy, inactivity, and social withdrawal.

Furthermore, the reverse is true; depression is alleviated by increases in interest, activity, and interpersonal interaction. It is possible that the Hispanic family may have curative powers non-Hispanic families lack. Basically, the seventh suggestion is that Carmen's family be used as "consultants" to recommend the kinds of activities that might make her feel better. Assuming Carmen's health and energy level is up to the task, she might feel better if she were to play a more significant role within the context of her cultural and family values. One example might be for her to baby-sit her grandchildren more frequently and a second example might be to encourage her to play a more active role at family gatherings such as planning and preparing a meal for a fiesta. The point is that members of Carmen's family are probably in the best position to suggest what activites she can carry out to feel better.

The eighth recommendation, like the preceding one, is designed to involve Carmen in some type of meaningful behavior that will enhance her enjoyment of life. The culturally sensitive counselor will perceive Carmen as a unique person with special skills she can use to help others while simultaneously helping herself. Imagine, for example, the tremendous lift a "depressed" person such as Carmen would experience by writing letters in Spanish for aged Hispanics in a home for the elderly, or serving as a teacher's aide in a bilingual/bicultural program for elementary schoolchildren, or helping divorced women with families to support learn how to acquire survival skills. I could go on, but these examples suffice to make the point.

CASE THREE: MIKE CABRAL

For reasons that will soon become clear, the available history is sketchy, occasionally inconsistent, and almost certainly inaccurate in part. Nevertheless, there is significant information here that is helpful in making the main points of the chapter more clear. Wherever possible, some attempt is made to assess the "truth value" of data imparted.

It is factually certain that Mike is 30 years old, is married to a 33-year-old Jewish woman, and that they have two children. He and his wife were both born in the United States, but Mike's father is a native of Mexico. Mike and his wife have a documented history of at least 10 years of addiction to heroin (off and on), but both claim to be "clean" for the past eight months and are faithful participants in a methadone maintenance program. It is the notorious unreliability of addicts as informants, plus Mike's "psychopathic" life-style (more on this later), that makes the veracity of this reported information uncertain.

Mike describes an extremely traumatic childhood, with serious physical abuse directed by the father primarily toward Mike, secondarily to Mike's mother, rarely to Mike's younger brother, and never toward Mike's younger sister. The intensity of this abuse can be inferred from an anecdote in which Mike states he was once "floored while in my Mom's arms." The father attacked one or both—Mike's recall is less than perfect—and both mother and son were "floored."

Mike describes a school adjustment that was equally turbulent and almost as violent. Punishment was frequent for a variety of offenses. At the elementary school level, he fought with the boys, teased the girls (for example, sprayed them with water), and threw chalk at the teachers. By the time of junior high and high school, the offenses escalated to more serious fighting, skipping classes, and "hustling pills." In one year alone, according to Mike, he was suspended 10 times. Mike also states he was labeled a "sociopath" by one school counselor and an "underachiever" by several teachers. Apparently, Mike had the potential to succeed academically, since he reports earning an "A" in a tenth-grade math class he liked, the year *after* receiving a failing grade in a prerequisite math course he disliked.

Available history describes his past school adjustment as following an "almost stereotypic path of deviance." Reference is made to a military enlistment at age 18, followed one year later by an undesirable discharge for possession of drugs and stolen goods. Mike has held a large number of jobs and lived in 13 places in seven different cities during one five-year period of heroin addiction. He supported his habit in the customary manner: menial and sporadic employment, sale of narcotics, transporting drugs for dealers, and petty thievery.

During the same eight-month period that Mike has been off hard drugs, he has held the same job, which is the longest period of continuous employment of his entire life. He is beginning to make short-range future plans, such as enrollment in a junior college as possible preparation for a career in radiography. Mike began counseling at a public health agency but quit after a few months. Thus Mike's current life adjustment—however unimpressive it may appear to some—is the most stable and productive it ever has been.

With regard to socioeconomic status, the Cabral family occupies the lowest group. The family has a history of moving frequently and currently resides in a moderately sized rented house. Mike's brother is a permanent resident and helps pay the rent. The house is furnished in a manner that reflects the family's past and current life. Most of the furniture is old, battered, and essentially worthless, although there are a few new pieces. Until very recently, they routinely supplemented their income by selling their possessions.

Mike Cabral is an excellent example of the tremendous potential for error intrinsic in deciding ethnic identification on the basis of surname, language facility, physical appearance, or even casual conversation with the candidate for treatment. Mike is bilingual, with English obviously dominant and Spanish described as "adequate." At least partially, Mike fits the Anglo stereotype of a Mexican. He is tall, broad shouldered, medium swarthy, black haired and has facial features such as high cheekbones that reflect his Indian heritage. Certain comments imply an Hispanic identification—for example, "I want a Mexican American doctor, but all I ever get is white therapists who don't know what's going on with me." Accurate or not, Mike clearly attributes his heroin addiction as a frustrated response to prejudice and discrimination by the majority culture toward ethnic minority group members. The bicultural counselor can quickly detect the superficiality of what appears to be a Chicano identification because of Mike's surprising ignorance of Hispanic values or customs.

Inconsistency and contradiction also characterize Mike's perceptions of his family of origin and his relationships with them. Mike claims to be "alienated" from his family, yet he visits them frequently and requests, expects, and receives emotional and financial support from them. In the context of differences in families across cultures, it is interesting to note that Mike's family "helped" him during his period of addiction by providing money, while Mike's wife's family "helped" her by disinheriting her. Who is to say which response was more "helpful"?

Mike visits none of his secondary kin. Since, however, he has no friends outside of his immediate family, this may reflect his general social isolation rather than familial estrangement. He also minimizes verbally the intensity of intrafamilial relationships, yet his behavior supports the opposite inference. For example, he traveled over 1000 miles round-trip to attend the wedding of his sister, and Mike's brother continues to reside with him and his family.

My opinion is that Mike is truly a "marginal" person (Stonequist, 1937; also see discussion by Ruiz, Casas, & A. Padilla, 1977). There is no strong sense of commitment to either the Anglo or Chicano culture, yet there are nonintegrated elements of both in Mike's life-style. Furthermore, these traits of inconsistency and weak commitment seem to permeate Mike's character. Perhaps these traits are related to Mike's ready boredom, lack of enduring motivation, and recourse to so-called immediate gratification by numbing his senses with drugs rather than confronting life directly. To be consistent with the designation system used with the preceding cases, I would place Mike at about the 25th percentile toward the Anglo side on the hypothetical continuum of commitment to Hispanic versus the Anglo cultures.

Treatment Planning: Mike Cabral   My bias is to give priority to helping this man continue to avoid heroin and, if possible, other illegal drugs that are addictive. While the substitution of methadone treatment for heroin addiction is not without controversy, it does have the distinct advantage of reducing social deviance. While on methadone and off heroin, Mike and people like him are less motivated to engage in overt criminal behavior. This increases the probability of a different life adjustment that is closer to what Mike says he wants and which society will condone. Specifically, I am referring to Mike's goals of more education, better career planning, and eventually, a more satisfying job.

Mike represents what is termed in the mental health literature as a "poor risk" for constructive behavior change. Operationally, this refers to low motivation for personal insight as reflected by a pattern of tardy arrivals for appointments, skipped appointments, and premature termination (that is, quitting before the counselor thinks the client is ready). As a matter of fact, Mike's therapeutic history shows exactly this pattern. Thus I believe it would be folly to attempt to coerce Mike into treatment; but at the same time, I would not give up on him entirely.

My suggestion would be to attempt to arrange at least one appointment with Mike—not so much as to initiate "treatment"—as to offer an invitation for future sessions. It might even be possible to get Mike to agree to periodic (one a month) meetings to monitor his methadone treatment. If not, perhaps he would not object to occasional telephone calls to "see how he is doing." Whatever the specific method, I would attempt to set up a procedure whereby Mike is casually, gently, and persuasively reminded of a regularly scheduled opportunity to "talk things over." I would remind Mike that he must expect frustration, and even harrassment, and that talking with a trained person can sometimes reduce stress. For example, Mike has already experienced some police harrassment because of his record, has felt bored with his work, has been tempted to quit, and has been severely anxious about his future. Mike's wife enthusiastically endorses the success of her own treatment, and perhaps she and Mike's family might be useful in encouraging him to become involved. If, however, Mike were adamant in his refusal to enter counseling I personally would not be more aggressive than outlined here in attempting to motivate him further. If his current life adjustment should falter, then I might feel inclined to be more assertive in approaching Mike as a potential candidate for treatment.

It is my belief, for reasons presented here concerning weak ethnic identification, that a bicultural treatment approach might be slightly more helpful but is not essential. Were Mike to request a bilingual and/or bicultural counselor I would attempt to comply but would not search if he didn't ask for one. I have a similar opinion in this case concerning the value of family, marital, or other small group approaches. These approaches tend to be used more frequently with addicts, and are strongly recommended for Hispanics, but do not seem essential in this particular case. I hope it is clearly understood that I am applying generalizations about groups of people to a single individual, which naturally increases the possible margin of error. Whoever assumes treatment responsibility for Mike will obtain more information than I have or can present here, and that person will thus make decisions that are less vague.

I chose to explain my underlying philosophy of treatment (or "bias") to help the reader grasp more fully my ideas concerning this and other cases. I do not believe psychotherapy, counseling, medication, or any mental health treatment approach is a panacea for the kinds of human problems under discussion. Furthermore, whatever validity is associated with these approaches is diminished significantly when the patient or client lacks motivation for change. I would collaborate with Mike in his efforts to improve the quality of his life, but I am very pessimistic about how helpful anyone could be if he wished to remain the same.

CASE FOUR: SANDRA VALDEZ.

Despite this 30-year-old married woman's self-designated ethnic identification as "Spanish American" (based on a "South American" grandmother and a "Mexican Indian" great-grandparent) it is clear that her life-style is more Anglo than Hispanic. She was born in southern California and reared by monolingual English-speaking parents who themselves had long before lost any vestiges of Hispanic culture. Sandra's husband is a third-generation American of Mexican descent, and he—like her—neither speaks nor understands Spanish.

The Valdez family is in the low-to-middle income bracket, and they own their own home in an Anglo enclave of a community that has a large Mexican American population. Nevertheless, they are totally isolated from the Mexican American community and never visit other Mexican Americans with the exception of the husband's family. The family religion is Catholic, but it is an Anglo rather than an Hispanic version, as reflected in the nature of the ceremonies associated with baptism, marriage, and confirmation.

Sandy has had two different sets of interaction with helping agencies. The first problem began about five years ago when her mother,

Maria, began to manifest indications of addiction to prescription medication. Sandy threatened the physician with legal action unless he discontinued prescribing the abused drugs (he stopped), helped her mother during the withdrawal period, and encouraged her continuation in group counseling. The second problem began about two years ago when her oldest son, Michael (age 10 years), began to lie and misbehave at home (but not at school). It is reported that a psychiatrist at a local mental health agency examined Michael for "psyiological disfunction" (none was found), then interviewed Michael and his parents. The diagnosis reported was a "not terribly serious . . . discipline problem," and the solution was for Sandy to acquire skill in discipline by reading a book on behavior modification. Two of the four sessions involved the testing and interviews of Michael, and two were counseling sessions for Sandy. It is unfortunate that there is not more information available concerning this intervention strategy but suffice it to say that Sandy reports her anxiety about childrearing diminished when Michael's behavior improved and that family relations are generally more harmonious.

Treatment Planning: Sandra Valdez   This woman's life was sketched out primarily to illustrate the degree of acculturation and only secondarily to discuss counseling strategy. Despite biological heritage, all indications are that Sandy falls at the "most Anglo" extreme of the hypothetical continuum of bicultural identification. Thus models of counseling designed for Hispanics are clearly unnecessary, perhaps inappropriate, for her as they are for Anglos. My assumption and prediction is that any problems in adjustment presented by Sandy and her immediate family (or other Hispanics as acculturated as they) would respond better to traditional counseling approaches. Without minimizing this woman's anxiety, distress, and problems—and with no snide connotations intended regarding ethnic identification—I would recommend counseling her like an Anglo. And since the focus of the chapter is on culturally relevant counseling for Chicanos, I will leave it at that.

REFERENCES

Acosta, F. X. Effects of psychotherapists' ethnicity and expertise on self-disclosures by Mexican Americans and Anglo American. (Doctoral dissertation, University of California, Los Angeles, 1974.) *Dissertation Abstracts International*, 1975, **35**, 4157-B (University Micro films No. 75-2213,119).

Acosta, F. X. Ethnic variables in psychotherapy: the Mexican American. In J. L. Martinez, Jr. (Ed.), *Chicano Psychology*. New York: Academic Press, 1977.

Acosta, R. X., & Sheehan, J. G. Preferences toward Mexican American and Anglo American psychotherapists. *Journal of Consulting and Clinical Psychology*, 1976, **44**, 272–279.

Acosta, F. X., & Sheehan, J. G. Self-disclosure in relation to psychotherapist expertise and ethnicity. *American Journal of Community Psychology*, in press.

El-Khawas, E. H., & Kimzer, J. L. *Enrollment of minority graduate students at Ph.D. Granting Institutions*. Washington, D.C.: American Council of Education, 1974.

Goode, William. World revolution and family patterns. Glencoe, Ill.: Free Press, 1963.

Hawkes, G. R., & Taylor, M. Power structure in Mexican and Mexican-American farm labor families. *Journal of Marriage and the Family*, 1975, **37**, 807–811.

Herrera, A. Preferences of bilingual Mexican American psychotherapy candidates for psychotherapists who vary in ethnicity, language orientation, and status. Paper presented at the Third Annual Colloquium Series of the Spanish Speaking Mental Health Research Center at the University of California at Los Angeles, California, January 31, 1978.

Kent, J., & Ruiz, R. A. The prediction of reading ability from intelligence test scores. In R. A. Ruiz & R. E. Cromwell, (Eds.), *Anglo, Black, and Chicano, Families in the Urban Community*. Book in preparation, 1980.

McCurdy, P. C., & Ruiz, R. A. Sex role and marital agreement. In R. A. Ruiz & R. E. Cromwell (Eds.), *Anglo, Black, and Chicano families in the Urban Community*. Book in preparation, 1980.

Macias, R. F. U. S. Hispanics in 2000 A.D.—Projecting the number. *Agenda*, May/June 1977, 7, 16–19.

Madsen, W. Value conflicts in cultural transfer. In P. Worchel & O. Bryne (Eds.), *Personality Change*. New York: Wiley, 1964.

Martinez, J. L., Jr. Cross cultural comparisons of Chicanos and Anglos on the Semantic Differential: Implications for psychology. In J. L. Martinez, Jr. (Ed.), *Chicano Psychology*. New York: Academic Press, 1977.

Martinez, J. L., Jr., Martinez, S. R., Olmedo, E. L., & Goldman, R. D. A comparison of Chicano and Anglo high school students using the Semantic Differential Technique. *Journal of Cross-Cultural Psychology*, 1976, 7, 325–334.

Martinez, S. R., Martinez, J. L., Jr., & Olmedo, E. L. Comparative study of Chicano and Anglo values using the semantic differential techniques.

Mercer, J. R. *Labeling the Mentally Retarded*. Berkeley: University of California Press, 1973.

Mercer, J. R. IQ: The lethal label. *Psychology Today*, 1972, **6**(4), 44, 46–47, 95–96.

Mercer, J. R. Pluralistic diagnosis in the evaluation of Black and Chicano children: A procedure for taking sociocultural variables into account in clinical assessment. In C. A. Hernandez, J. J. Haug, & N. N. Wagner (Eds.), *Chicanos: Social and Psychological Perspectives* (2nd ed.). St. Louis: Mosby, 1976.

Mindel, Charles H. Kinship in a multiethnic community. In R. A. Ruiz & R. E. Cromwell (Eds.), *Anglo, Black, and Chicano Families in the Urban Community*. Book in preparation, 1980.

Murillo, N. The Mexican American Family. In C. A. Hernandez, M. J. Haug, & N. N. Wagner (Eds.), *Chicanos: Social and Psychological Perspectives*. (2nd ed.). St. Louis: Mosby, 1976.

Murillo, N. The Mexican Family. In N. N. Wagner & M. J. Haug (Eds.), *Chicanos: Social and Psychological Perspectives*. St. Louis: Mosby, 1971.

Olmedo, E. L., Martinez, J. L., Jr., Martinez, S. R. Measure of acculturation for Chicano adolescents. *Psychological Reports*, 1978, **42**, 159–170.

Padilla, A. M., & Ruiz, R. A. *Latino Mental Health: A Review of Literature*. Washington, D. C.: National Institute of Mental Health, 1973.

Padilla, A. M., Ruiz, R. A., & Alvarez, R. Community mental health services for the Spanish speaking, Spanish surname population. *American Psychologist*, 1975, **30**, 892–905.

Padilla, E. R., Boxley, R., & Wagner, N. N. The desegregation of clinical psychology training. *Professional Psychology*, 1973, **4**, 259–263.

Parsons, Talbott. The kinship of the contemporary United States. *American Anthropologist*, 1943, **45**, 22–38.

Ramirez, M., III, & Castaneda, A. *Cultural Democracy, Biocognitive Development, and Education*. New York: Academic Press, 1974.

Ruiz, R. A. La familia: Myths and realities. Unpublished speech, available on request from the author at the Spanish Speaking Mental Health Research Center, University of California at Los Angeles, California 90024, 1978.

Ruiz, R. A. Relative frequency of Americans with Spanish surnames in associations of psychology, psychiatry, and sociology. *American Psychologist*, 1971, **26**, 1022–1024.

Ruiz, R. A. The delivery of mental health and social change services for the Chicanos: Analysis and recommendations. In J. L. Martinez (Ed.), *Chicano Psychology*. New York: Academic Press, 1977.

Ruiz, R. A., Casas, J. M., Padilla, A. M. Culturally relevant behavioristic counseling. Spanish Speaking Mental Health Research Center, Occasional Paper Number 5, 1977.

Ruiz, R. A., & Padilla, A. M. Chicano psychology: The family and the macho. Unpublished manuscript, available on request from first author at the Spanish Speaking Mental Health Research Center, University of California at Los Angeles, California 90024, 1973.

Ruiz, R. A., & Padilla, A. M. Counseling Latinos. *Personnel and Guidance Journal*, 1977, **55**, 401–408.

Ruiz, R. A., Padilla, A. M., & Alvarez, R. Issues in the counseling of Spanish speaking/ surname clients: Recommendations for therapeutic services. In Walz, G. R., & Benjamin, L. (Eds.), *Transcultural Counseling: Needs, Programs, and Techniques*. New York: Human Sciences Press, 1978.

Staton, R. D. A comparison of Mexican and Mexican-American families. *Family Coordinator*, 1972, **21**, 325–330.

Stonequist, F. V. *The Marginal Man: A Study in Personality and Culture Conflict*. New York: Russell & Russell, 1937.

U. S. Bureau of the Census. Persons of Spanish Origin in the United States: Nov. 1969. *Current Population Reports*, Series P-20, No. 213. Washington, D.C.: U. S. Government Printing Office, 1971.

U.S. Bureau of the Census, Selected characteristics of persons and families of Mexican, Puerto Rican, and other Spanish origin: March 1971. *Current Population Reports*, Series P-20, No. 224. Washington, D.C.: U.S. Government Printing Office, 1972.

STUDY QUESTIONS

1. How might knowledge of Hispanic history and demographic data be of importance in cross-cultural counseling? Be specific and relate facts to counseling examples.

2. In what ways have Hispanic culture and family roles been distorted by U. S. interpretations? How might that affect the cultural identity of Hispanics as well as counseling?

3. How are the singular concepts of acculturation and assimilation too simplistic? Can you give examples of the complexity of these concepts with respect to the bicultural Hispanic?

4. If you were a counselor working with a Hispanic client, how would you (*a*) determine the importance of acculturation/assimilation in the client, and (*b*) select a culturally relevant counseling method?

5. Can you make a brief outline of important factors for a counselor to consider in working with the four cases presented in this chapter? Also, what were the major differences between the cases that dictated a somewhat different approach?

9

Cultural and Historical Perspectives in Counseling American Indians

EDWIN H. RICHARDSON

WICONI—WE WILL SURVIVE!

"Today is a good day to die."

This statement was made by LaDonna Harris, the Comanche Indian wife of former U.S. Senator Fred Harris. "Today is a good day to die" is a saying used by the American Indian people to express their frustrations with living in a society that denies them their basic rights. The statistics presented subsequently indicate that the life of the American Indian is one of hardships, incarcerations, degradations, exploitations and that of a second-class citizen which makes for problems of survival, low self-esteem, and rejection.

The plight of the Indian is appalling, as documented here (Richardson, Edwin H. *The Problems of the Indian in the Affluent Society*; papers presented at Region 8—Indian Health Meeting, Rapid City, S.D., May 1973; at the S.D. Senate Educational Committee Hearing, Pierre, S.D., August 1976; and at S.D. Indian Commission for Alcohol and Drug Abuse, Fort Thompson Indian Reservation, S.D., Spring 1975):

One out of three Indians will be jailed at sometime during his/her lifetime.

Every other Indian family will have a relative die in jail.

One county in Nebraska has 28% Indians, yet 98% of all arrests were of Indian people.

The life expectancy of Indians is 44 years.

Approximately 25 to 35% of all Indian children are separated from their families and placed in foster homes, adoptive homes, or institutions.

In South Dakota, 48% of all adoptions are of Indian children.

An average income per year for the family is $1500.

Between 40 and 80% of the tribal members are unemployed.

Something like 451 of our tribes, like my own, do not have federal recognition.

There are 29 tribes in the Rapid City, South Dakota, area; 42% of the members are unemployed, and the average income is $1200.

Suicide is seven times the national rate, and 75 to 80% or more of all suicides among Indians are alcohol related.

Until 1975, the Bureau of Indian Affairs (BIA), the only bureau in the world to "manage" a conquered people, was run by non-Indians.

To give some sense for the exasperation and intimidation of the American Indian I would like to cite a letter that epitomizes the deep-seated feelings of bitterness American Indians often hold toward white professionals. The professional may mean well, yet his or her superior-acting, holier-than-thou, savior-of-the-Native-American attitude is resented by American Indians. It is this kind of a rescuer, crusader, "leader" who robs the Native American people of their self-determination and puts them into a "not O.K. posture" of dependency, and to whom Anglos later say, "I was only trying to help you (you poor slob!)" (Richardson, 1976).

February 22, 1976

Dear Doctor Richardson,

On [President George] Washington's birthday it seems appropriate to write to you. You are the only one at the hospital I miss . . . I'd like to give some of the others hell. . . .

I am an American Indian. I am a soveriegn individual, even though I received my "U.S. Citizenship" through a tricky Congressional Act. . . . Being a "citizen" entitles me to travel the streets . . . hell holes for my people. Some doctors say . . . I certainly should not return to the "bad influences" of my reservation . . . Some of these doctors tell me I should not be so quiet and I should look people in the eye—and say what I feel. . . . Your doctors want me to apply for a job because then I can practice daily embarrassing myself as they turn me down and say, "I don't hire Indians. . . . they are unreliable."

. . . these doctors always give me "advice." . . . they love to "advise" me. I am a good listener and these . . . wicicu [white man] have "ready advice" for me . . . it's big words . . . and if I don't understand they tell me more with big words . . . they love to determine goals for me. They get paid for that too. . . . I'm told I have to become "civilized," . . . to "live like a white man." It is so nice to give me goals . . . their goals. . . . his . . . white man values, . . . and he tells me [what] I should do with my life if I want to amount to anything. . . . you have seen me drink . . . in Cheerio and Western [bars] and you are friendly. They tell me "why" I drink . . . you don't . . .

. . . they want to "help" me. They give me more "advice." It good they are making me so "well educated." I used to drink and be very dumb; . . . and now I even "know" why I drink. . . . When I asked if he could be wrong . . . he always has a reason why he is "right."

. . . they read many books . . . they know more about me than I do . . . I am so pleased. . . . They "understand" me now; even better than I understand myself. I now know why I am a "character disorder," a bad example to our people . . . He keeps notes on me and if I forget . . . he can always read the reports to me.

. . . they get excited like I do . . . only they pace the floor, scowl, fret . . . and say nasty little things. . . . They make themselves sick over making me well! . . . they conclude I need more advice. They write mountains of notes. . . . Sometimes they get carried away with the progress I am "making" and that gets them to believe in themselves . . . All the time I am learning all of these big words . . . I can pull them on my friends and they even think I am a "doctor" too . . .

Dr. Richardson—I am a good listener, a "professional listener," and I have listened for hours and hours. . . . The one who talks the most knows me the least. He doesn't know our people. He doesn't know the reason why I drink, because I don't need a reason. I wish he would practice all that advice on himself before he goes to sleep. It might bore him like it does me.

On this great day that the mighty George Washington started spoiling our ecology by cutting down cherry trees, polluting our rivers by throwing stuff into them (like [non-biodegradable] metal coins), surveying our land and giving it to his friends, and finally catching pneumonia while chasing a Black woman—let me say I WILL ONLY GET WELL IF I WANT TO GET WELL. I WILL GET WELL INDIAN WAYS—NOT WHITE WAYS. I WILL LISTEN TO MY OWN PEOPLE. IF I DECIDE, I WILL FOLLOW THE WAYS OF THE PIPE AND NOT WHITE PREACHING.

Kola

HISTORICAL EXPERIENCE

The Wasichus (white) dominant society does not seem to be fully aware of what has happened to the Indian and Eskimo to create his/her feelings of distrust and resentment. Anthropological evidence indicates that the Paleo-Indian of North America arrived here some 40,000 years ago. Many of my people feel he came from the center core of the earth.

It makes little difference when you commence to focus your attention: on the Taber "man" in southern Canada, the Folsom "man," or the Abilene "man" (Satterlee & Malan, 1967). It seems that almost immediately after the arrival of the white "man," the greatness of the Indian people was distorted. Explorers and trappers noticed their generosity and also observed that tribal society seemed to be deteriorating with influence from the outside world, trade, rum, "imported diseases," and the loss of old skills. The tragedy of these observations is that they are misconstrued to mean that the Indian is inferior to the "civilized" white man.

Objectifying Guilt

This apparent "cultural lag" led to an attitude of superiority by the majority society. The white man had preconceived ideas, and, along with greed, there came a need to repress the guilt that was building up among the conquering settlers. There was a need to make every thing seem objective and rational. The extermination of the Indian tribes seemed to be the simplest way of settling land title claims. A chilling statement that epitomizes the feeling of many was summarized by General de Trobriand (1872), "The majority were convinced that the simpliest and only means of settling the 'Indian question' was to exterminate 'all the vermins.' This opinion prevails."

The "Magnanimous" Manipulator

The obsession to eliminate the Indian compelled the white man to compartmentalize the Indian into reservations, and to atomistically repress any feelings of sympathy or understanding about the Indians. Perhaps no one did more to encourage an atmosphere of hate toward the Indians than President Andrew Jackson. As early as 1826 Jackson referred to the treaty process as "an absurdity." Caselli (1970) claims that between 1829 and 1837 Jackson was involved in six important events:

1. Men, women, and children numbering 125,000 from five major tribal groups were forced to move over the "Trail of Tears" from the Atlantic states to Oklahoma.
2. Over one-third of these people were forced to relocate on useless land, and it cost 40,000 lives over the seven-year period! This represents more loss of life than occurred in the Civil War.
3. There were massacres for those who were "uncooperative," much

like what happened to Chief Black Hawk. [Can you imagine massacreing uncooperative white people who would not want to annex their home into a city zone?]

4. President Jackson's flagrant violations of the principle of separation of powers were shown as he openly encouraged Georgia to *defy* the Supreme Court against the Cherokee nation.

5. Jackson introduced five major legislative acts, including the Indian Removal Act!

6. There were 55 treaties that were masterpieces in intimidation, bribery, threats, misrepresentation, force, and fraud during Jackson's two terms in office.

There were constant attempts to make the persecutors appear guilt-free and to displace the blame onto the innocent Indian. Note the sanitized posture of General O. O. Howard in cheating the North American native while representing the "virtue of the service" with a slogan of "duty, honor, and country" that sanctions cheating, deception, and subterfuge (Holford, 1975): "First acknowledge and confirm to the Indians a sort of title to vast regions. Afterward, we continue, in a strictly legal manner, to *do away* with both the substance and the shadow of the title. Wiser heads than (Chief) Joseph's have been puzzled by this manner of balancing the scales."

Current Conditions of the American Indians

The present-day problem is one of continued suppression of Indians, since about all the land that could be taken has been taken. There are many examples of the white people imposing their bias on the Indian. An Ottawa Indian youth of Michigan gave up wearing a beautiful eagle feather bonnet that he had made to wear on state occasions because "those damned anthropologists are always telling me it isn't typical of my tribe's headdress and I just couldn't stand their 'holier than thou' comments all the time" (Howard, 1975).

THE SIGNIFICANCE OF U.S. OPPRESSION AGAINST AMERICAN INDIANS LIES DEEPER THAN THE LEGAL ACTIONS

It is more a matter that the white people have never seen fit to want to understand the Indian. In fact, in their compulsion to make the Indian into a white person they have never stopped to appreciate those beliefs that are important to American Indians. In economics, Indian beliefs hold that to kill an animal or to reap the produce of a wild plant beyond one's daily needs is to exploit Mother Earth, a violation for which there would be retribution. This economic belief is tied closely to Indian religion in which we feel that we must pay retribution through a sacrifice.

Superiority Justifies Exploitation

Anglos feel superior to all other life forms, and for this reason they feel no guilt in the exploiting Mother Earth. Note the whites' indifference to conservation of energy, to the ecology pleas of President Carter, and their desire for "success" at almost any cost!

"We Are All Living Creatures of Mother Earth"

As in the past, Indians today still believe that Mother Earth gave birth and sustained life for all living creatures. They do not make the marked contrast between humans and animals that others do. They find the animal capable of planning, thinking, loving, and caring; and they have many legends. to emphasize the wisdom and greatness of animals. They feel, in fact, that people and animals and all living creatures are akin, all possessing equal rights. Even urban Indians see the white man, the "invaders," as indiscriminately hewing down the forests; exterminating all animals and some in the name of "predators," killing the beavers and dynamiting their wonderfully constructed dams, allowing flood waters to wreak havoc; poisoning the holy bird, the Eagle; poisoning the crops with insecticides; and, in many ways, causing his/her own destruction. Native people cannot conceive of a zoo that pens up their "brothers and their sisters," the four-legged, the two-legged, and the creatures that crawl. They feel that all that walk, fly, and swim must live in harmony with one another—it is God's wish.

Indian people have long memories, and they feel that history will repeat itself and before long all people will recognize the need to live like Indians in harmony with everyone else.

To Be Native Is to Sacrifice

To most Indians, leadership is almost always a required sacrifice. Contrast this to the Anglos who excuse the scandals of their leaders by using the "logic" that it is the temptations of the high office. I can honestly say that I have never seen a wealthy Indian. This concept fits in with all levels of Native life. To be a parent, the parent must suffer if it is expected that the parent is to set an example. The parent, like the chief, is always taking a risk, a risk that her/his actions may not be approved by those she/he loves. This kind of openness results in added trust and strengthens the family and the tribe.

The main problem of reservation management is that the administration has set itself above the people, and thus the people feel disillusioned. The people have the same feeling that anyone with such great power as Uncle Sam should be open and honest and do well for all peoples.

"If You Force Us to Be Like You, You Should Reward Us!"

There has historically been a feeling that the Indians did *not* want to be white people, but since the government insisted on making them so, it was logical for the Indians to believe that they should be supported while being forced to act like whites. The more the Indians found that federal agents were letting them down, the more they found it intriguing to spy on the agents, and, consequently, the more they found that the agents were indifferent to them and stealing from them, and thus the greater became the Indians' distrust. Since Indians have been taught informally through example, they did not accept blindly the fact that the federal agents demanded respect from them. These federal agents were at all levels, including teachers, principals, lawyers, administrators, doctors, and even the "federally tax exempt religious element" of the reservation. Indians have seen Watergate, the Tonsun Park payola, the Hays sex scandals, the Bert Lance Office of Management and the Budget money scandal, and countless other transgressions by government officials and others. On the local level they have witnessed grant rip-offs, misuse of school funds and total disregard for their cultural needs, sterilization of their women without consent, goon-squad terrorism, scrutinty by the Central Intelligence Agency (CIA), and almost constant surveillance by the federal government in the name of the Federal Bureau of Investigation. Consequently, the American Indian feels that there should be a "fair return" for all the misery he/she has experienced while attempts have been made to turn him/her into a white person. The "take-over" of the BIA building in 1972 and the rifling of files by Indian people was a relief to the inequity of being a white person.

Indians Beginning to Recognize the Honor of Being Indian

It is quite apparent to the Indian that whites live not by example but by expectations. Indians see the old ways as the safest model to perpetuate their culture, and more and more they talk of their religion, because they are no longer ashamed. More and more they openly admit that it is a privilege to be Indian. Indians are now looking back at 300 years of resistance to their culture, and they are more convinced than ever that their culture has strong points.

Along with this, more and more, Indians are turning to their own people. Although "self-determination" started out as a political appeasement by the federal government, the Indians are increasingly becoming convinced that they are going to make it, and their pride in their history will remain intact. The important religious ceremonies, like the Sun Dance, are coming out in the open. No longer do Indians consider piercing and self-sacrifice as acts that make them animalistic. In fact, they are becoming more and more adept at shifting from one religious perspective to another, and they are able to shift from Christian to non-Christian practices—all with no apparent difficulties. The reason for this is shown in Figure 9.1. All religions, all things, and all living creatures fit into "the Indian Hoop of Life"—it is all part of the Indians' giving respect to everything. Thus they respect all religions.

Even the Indians' diet is improving, and less and less are they living on junk foods. In previous years of white supremacy Indians were given diseased cattle, moldy flour, and rancid bacon in government rations. A more severe problem has been actual starvation, and that still persists. The one advantage of living on the reservation or in a boarding school is that the children are given at least one good meal a day—a real need for

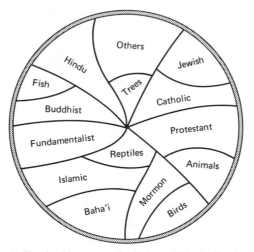

Figure 9.1   How an Indian is able to see all religions. "The Indian hoop of life" embraces all things and all religions.

children. Smallpox, scarlet fever, measles, diphtheria, and other diseases introduced by the invaders are still somewhat prevalent. Sickness among reservation people will continue for some while, until the economic level is better than the substandard one of today.

The Indian Hoop of Life is round and is thought of as a lariat that encircles the universe; it includes Father Sky, Mother Earth, and all things therein. The Indian has respect for all things, alive and dead, that are within the hoop. It is because of this concept that it is so easy for the Indian to adapt—so easy for the Indian to move from one religious belief to another and, consequently, to have respect for all things living and dead as brothers and sisters. Indians and Eskimos are proud that they are the only ones to have this holistic view of the universe. They never rap one religion or one group; they feel all are equal and should be so treated. Unfortunately, the Anglo has seen fit to compartmentalize, to place "in rank order," and to show supremacy.

Reasons to Distrust

Historically, we can see that Indians have many reasons to distrust the federal government, professionals, and white people in general. It is because of this that the Indian counselor will more often do a better job of counseling Indian people.

CULTURAL INFLUENCES

Following a tracing of the historical experiences, it is appropriate that we address ourselves to the cultural influences. Value systems will obviously vary among tribes, but many are shared. Keep in mind that there are 541 tribes unrecognized by the BIA. There have been 55 tribes that have received federal recognition in this century alone (Deloria, 1975).

To Be Indian Is to Have a Value System

Part of the dilemma in understanding the Indian is that the Anglos have never thought out their own value system. One exists for the Anglos, but because they do things so compulsively they do not recognize the noxious qualities of their values to themselves or others. Oftentimes the Anglos' values are in direct opposition to those of the Indians. The majority society has a stereotype of Indians and Eskimos that does not reach beneath the surface. The Anglos do not listen, and they have been too busy pushing what they consider important to be able to listen. They are preoccupied (Good Tracks, 1973). Perhaps the best way to understand the Indian value system is to study the Medicine Man (Richardson, 1977a) and books and papers on Indian religion (Brock, 1971; Richardson, 1973b, the *Weewish Tree*, 1974; Black Elk, 1971; Lame Deer, 1971, & Richardson, 1973a). No two races could so grossly differ in value systems than the American Indian and white. In fact, the phrase "value system" is hardly used in the white culture; but it appears constantly when Indian people are talking. Some of the major differences of the two are listed in Table 9.1 (Richardson, 1975a).

There are many more contrasts in the value system, such as patience versus impatience, indifference to hardship versus compulsion to eliminate pain, and an acceptance of time versus desire not to waste time and to keep busy while watching the clock. I want to hasten that some Indian and Eskimo value systems are changing. For example, some have come to recognize that the only way to survive is through education. In the past, the school, along with the church and BIA, did much to thwart, hinder, and intimidate the Natives ("Voices from Wounded

Table 9.1 Differences in Indian and Anglo values

Indians	Anglos
1. Happiness—this is paramount! Be able to laugh at misery; life is to be enjoyed	1. Success—generally involving status, security, wealth, and proficiency
2. Sharing—everything belongs to others, just as Mother Earth belongs to *all* people	2. Ownership—indicating preference to own an outhouse rather than share a mansion
3. Tribe and extended family first, before self	3. "Think of Number One!" syndrome
4. Humble—causing Indians to be passive-aggressive, gentle head hangers, and very modest	4. Competitive—believing "If you don't toot your own horn then who will?"
5. Honor your elders—they have wisdom	5. The future lies with the youth
6. Learning through legends; remembering the great stories of the past, that's where the knowledge comes from	6. Learning is found in school; get all the schooling that you possibly can because it can't be taken away from you

Indians	Anglos
7. Look backward to traditional ways—the old ways are the best ways; they have been proved	7. Look to the future to things new—"Tie Your Wagon to a Star and Keep Climbing Up and Up"
8. Work for a purpose—once you have enough then quit and enjoy life, even if for just a day	8. Work for a retirement—plan your future and stick to a job, even if you don't like it
9. Be carefree—time is only relative. Work long hours if happy. Don't worry over time; "I'll get there eventually"	9. Be structured—be most aware of time. "Don't put off until tomorrow what you have to do today." Don't procrastinate
10. Discrete—especially in dating. Be cautious with a low-key profile	10. Flout an openness—"What you see is what you get." Be a "Fonz" character
11. Religion is the universe	11. Religion is individualistic
12. Orient yourself to the land	12. Orient yourself to a house, a job
13. Be a good listener—and it is better if you use your ears and listen well	13. Look people in the eye—don't be afraid to establish eye contact It's more honest
14. Be as free as the wind	14. Don't be a "boat rocker"
15. Cherish your memory—remember the days of your youth	15. Don't live in the past—look ahead. Live in the here-and-now
16. Live with your hands—manual activity is sacred. "Scratch an Indian—you'll find an artist." (Natives are also intelligent)	16. Live with your mind—think intelligently. Show the teacher how well you know the answers to questions he/she might ask of you. Good at books
17. Don't criticize your people	17. A critic is a good analyst.
18. Don't show pain—be glad to make flesh sacrifices to the Spirits	18. Don't be tortured—don't be some kind of a masochistic nut
19. Cherish your own language and speak it when possible	19. You're in America; speak English
20. Live like the animals; the animals are your brothers and sisters	20. "What are you—some kind of an animal? A Pig or a Jackass?"
21. Children are a gift of the Great Spirit to be shared with others	21. "I'll discipline my own children; don't you tell me how to raise mine!"

Indians	Anglos
22. Consider the relative nature of a crime, the personality of the individual, and the conditions. "The hoe wasn't any good anyway"	22. The law is the law! "To steal a penny is as bad as to steal 10,000! Stealing is stealing! We can't be making exceptions."
23. Leave things natural as they were meant to be	23. "You should have seen it when God had it all alone!"
24. Dance is an expression of religion	24. Dance is an expression of pleasure
25. There are no boundaries—it all belongs to the Great Spirit "Why should I fence in a yard?"	25. Everything has a limit—there must be privacy. "Fence in your yard and keep them off the grass!"
26. Few rules are best. The rules should be loosely written and flexible	26. Have a rule for every contingency, "Write your ideas in detail"
27. Intuitiveness	27. Empiricism
28. Mystical	28. Scientific
29. Be simple—eat things raw and natural. Remember your brother the Fox and live wisely	29. Be sophisticated—eat gourmet, well prepared, and seasoned. Be a connoisseur of many things
30. Judge things for yourself	30. Have instruments judge for you
31. Medicine should be natural herbs, a gift of Mother Earth	31. Synthetic medicines—"You can make anything in today's laboratories"
32. The dirt of Mother Earth on a wound is not harmful but helpful (Sun Dance, mineral intake)	32. Things must be sterile and clean, not dirty and unsanitary
33. Natives are used to small things, and they enjoy fine detail (Indian fires)	33. Bigness has become a way of life with the white society (compulsion for bigness)
34. Travel light, get along without	34. Have everything at your disposal
35. Accept others—even the drinking problem of another Indian	35. Persuade, convince and proselytze—be an evangelist/missionary
36. The price is of no concern	36. "You only get what you pay for!"
37. Enjoy simplifying problems	37. "Nothing in this world is simple."

Knee," 1953; BIA, "I'm Not Your Indian Any More," 1976; and
"Indian Educators Told Public Schools Irrelevant," 1975).

White Imposition

Suffice it to say that "Manifest Destiny" (sometimes termed "Divine
Destiny"), a white man's way of ripping off Indian people, must change
and recognize Indian value systems. Examples of cultural conflict in
Indian versus Anglo value systems are many. A few examples will
demonstrate the tremendous gap between the two races. An Indian had
been feeding his dog with food supplements and vitamins, much the
same way that the white person fattens cattle for market. To the Indian
people the Tatonka (buffalo) and Shunka (dog) are holy animals and to
eat the meat of these animals gives certain special powers to the Indian
person. This Indian had killed his dog to eat, gutted it, and built a fire to
singe the hair—much the same way we singe the feathers of poultry. A
priest came upon this Indian and presumptuously assumed that the dog
had been diseased and that the Indian was attempting to cremate his
dog. The priest took over and "helped" the Indian to burn up the dog.
The passive Indian, made to feel ashamed of his "primitive values" by
the culture of whites, indifferently watched as his dog was burned to
ashes. This is the imposing of one culture on another, and I would
hasten to say that many Asian cultures eat dog meat. Dog meat is a very
succulent meat that we eat at our Yuwipi (holy) meetings. It so
happened that this Indian was a Medicine Man, and he was preparing
this dog meat for a holy meeting. The priest was new to the reservation,
and the Medicine Man did not want to embarrass him.

Another example that may be equally shocking to the reader concerns the Indian's indifference to money. A Minniconju Sioux Indian at
the Cheyenne River Eagle Butte Indian Reservation had just received a
large allotment of money, when he saw a big truck filled with beer.
With a twinkle in his eye the Indian had a great idea: he would buy that
truck loaded with beer, lock, stock, and barrel, and then share it with
the entire tribe. That is exactly what he did, and he spent his entire
allotment money, much to the profit of the trucker and the amusement
of his brother and sister Indians.

This is appalling to most white people, because it is seen as lacking in
logic and common sense and as irresponsible management of money;
but to the Indian it represents something that was fun (happiness) and a
way of sharing with the entire tribe, had a very distinct purpose, and
was as free as the wind. Many Indians are, of course, becoming "better"
at handling money.

Whites Learn from Indians

Surprising as it may seem, people are coming to see that many of the components of the Indian value system are very meaningful. Some of this is indirectly fostered by conservation groups, some by religious leaders with a sense of guilt, and some by the medical profession, which is coming to recognize the worth of the Indian value system. Jack Lewin, a physician, told a story (to Richardson) about his own innocent poor judgment concerning Indian values. He related a case where he advised a leather-skinned Southwest Indian woman with a large, ugly sore on her leg, to "Soak it in a tub three times a day." The woman giggled and said nothing. The point was that the woman lived on the top of a mesa where there was no water and she and her people carried water a long distance. The Navajo Indian nurse, who had overheard, said, "The next time she'll go see the Medicine Man."

Illness Is Disharmony

Frequently, Anglo doctors can give only symptomatic relief. They have no effect on the cause of the disease, which can be discovered and cured only by a traditional healer. In the Indian value system there is no separation between culture, religion, and medicine, which are all interrelated. In the Native value system, any illness encountered, whether physical, mental, emotional, or social, is thought of as a disharmony with other forces (Looney & Dale, 1972; Petty, 1974; Brock, 1971; Stuckey, 1975; Hays, 1974; Lewis & Ho, 1975; *Native Heritage*, 1975; Ridley, 1973; & Richardson, 1973d).

It would seem that if medicine, the schools, and the colleges commence to recognize the importance of the Indian value system, inroads will be made and will eventually pay off. However, even more essential is the need for legal, political, and social agencies to begin honoring the Indian value system. As the Indians become more skilled, more businesslike, and more professionally educated they will exert a more positive influence for their own welfare.

EFFECTS OF CULTURAL CONFLICTS

Perhaps the most severe conflict between the Native people and the Anglo people grows out of cultural oppression. All the numerous laws, countless treaties, and the day-in-day-out policies concerning Native people reflect disrespectful unilateral action. It is unbelievable that a magnanimous country steeped in a history of humanitarian concern for human rights all over the world can so defiantly disregard the views of Native people. Representing the highest office in the land, President Jimmy Carter spoke at the Berlin Wall in Germany and again later lambasted the Russians for their conduct in human relations with their own Jewish dissidents, and yet he refused to see the spiritual leaders of the Longest Walk, who had trudged all the way from Alcatraz Island in California to Washington, D.C. It has been said by Carter friends that if Russian Jews had walked from Siberia to Moscow and asked for an audience with President Carter, he would have flown there to see them. Yet here in America he ignored the Indians! It was truly unbelievable. Little wonder that the Indians were resentful and felt that the effects of cultural conflicts are intensified by the pompous, holier-than-thou, and assertive indifference of the Anglos (Richardson, 1973d)!

It is more complex than that: I feel that the dominant society is obsessive-compulsive, arrogant, with a fetish for the all-or-nothing approach to life, and past masters at discounting their own inadequacies, which they partly suppress and partly project as an inadequacy of other people (Richardson, 1975b). Remember, the Indians frequently feel misunderstood and on the losing side of almost everything (Earle, 1975) *South Dakota State University Collegian*, 1975; Roubideaux, 1973). We would therefore recommend that one of the things counselors do is to minimize their authoritarian role, be cautious about giving advice, and avoid stereotyping. There is a commonality among minorities: they all have endured being forced to feel bad about being different. It is as if they have been "controlled" in their role. Minorities actually enjoy being different. This is seen when Indians call themselves "skins" and refer to a bureaucratic Indian who sides with white people as a Macintosh apple (red on the outside and white inside). An Indian may, on meeting another Indian, raise one arm straight up above his/her head and then, bending the wrist, let the fingers point down toward the top of his/her head in what is the sign of "broken treaties."

Why Must There Be "White Supremacy"?

This leaves questions in the blending of the two cultures: Must we consider the white's culture more desirable? Is it better to emphasize competition, success, exactness, materialistic achivement, control over the environment, and other measures of individual greatness? Do the Indians lose in blending their culture with that of the white's? Is it better to concentrate on being happy, sharing, honoring the family, being humble, honoring your elders, listening to great legends, being carefree, honoring nature, recognizing the universality of religion, being able to work with your hands, not criticizing others, respecting animals, not being squeamish, being simplistic with few rules, and not having a phobia about the soil being "dirty." Could it be that in the struggle to be more of a white person the Indian is losing both ways? In a very real sense, Indians were nonalcoholic, nonmalnourished, and reasonably disease free before the white people arrived. Drinking problems, for example, were a white people's problem that was passed on to the Indians (Thompson, 1974).

Now It's Your Time to Listen

What may be a solution to the problem of cultural conflicts, no matter what the cause, would be for the counselor to attend Native workshops. The recent workshop that included Dr. Virginia Satir, along with the Indian Medicine Men at the University of South Dakota, was a tremendous success, and Dr. Satir called it her best workshop. It concerned the "tiyospaye," or the extended family, and made family therapy more meaningful for non-Indian people by focusing on the cultural factors in the family system. Perhaps another approach would be for the counselor to consult Indian friends frequently for advice, visit Indian and Eskimo homes, and *not attempt to solve the cultural conflicts but rather to make it more acceptable for the Natives to have one foot in both cultures*. That way the Natives can preserve their own culture and still be able to function in white culture.

IMPLICATIONS FOR COUNSELING

In dealing with Indians, the implications for counseling must be refocused. Traditional counseling has bits and pieces that are applicable; yet as an isolated technique couched in the framework of a white man's field of reference, it leaves much to be desired. Counseling and psychotherapy, from the textbook approach, emphasize Western values and are antagonistic to the Indian value system. As such, they are tools of cultural oppression. As an innocent counselor you may be oriented to be most understanding; however, subtle aspects like the tone of your voice, the manner in which you study the client with your eyes, and innocent little comments may be met with resistance. You must be aware of the fact that suggestions seem like orders to Native people when they come from authority. Ideas at times appear as exploitation. A simple question like, "Do you think. . . ?" can be misconstrued as questioning the individual's ability and thus denying that individual's rights (The Continuing Denial of Our Existence, *Akwesasne Notes*, July 1977). The *Denver Post* (February 8, 1974) cautions that a well-meaning attempt to speak the Indian's language may be met with mixed emotions, because Indians are sensitive to the fact that many of them do not speak their own language well. I am aware of a woman counselor who was condemning the roughness of games, and she touched on lacrosse, wrist wrestling, and ear wrestling. All these games were developed by Indians and Eskimos. The counselor almost immediately lost all the rapport she had previously enjoyed.

Admit Your Ignorance

One can commence by indicating that he/she may say something offensive because of ignorance on his/her part and then indicate that if this does occur he/she would like the client to correct the error that has been made or the offensive statement. There is hardly an area that is not offensive to Native people, whether concerning the police, delinquency, family, future opportunities, education, alcoholism, Indian courts, emergency situations, pollution, fines for having Eagle feathers, water and mineral rights, abuse to South American and Canadian Indians, adoptions, Christianity, politics, ceremonies, vocational opportunities, the Alaskan pipeline, housing, grave digging, and, of course, treaties, which are always a sore spot.

See the Positives

It will suffice, at this point, to say to all counselors who have a "feeling for others" that they may become capable of working with American Indians. As we have already stressed, it is essential to appreciate the "greatness" of the Indian and his or her culture. It is important to know that the phrase "war bonnets" was a white distortion for a symbol of leadership and honor; that peanuts, chicle, chocolate, corn, squash, beans, tomatoes, potatoes, and countless other products were grown and used by the Natives long before whites arrived; that cracker jacks without the prizes were here for thousands of years; that the wheel, as a part of a toy, was first made in the United States by indigenous people and not by the Greeks or someone else; that the buffalo provided everything the Indian needed until they were slaughtered by whites for tongues alone; that antibiotics, curare, quinine, herbs, birth control, and other aspects of medicine were practiced by the American Indians many years ago; that the Iroquois were using psychotherapy before some PhD from an accredited university "invented" it; that tin, rubber, bronze, and other industrial processes were practiced by Native Americans; that the Palomino horse was developed by the Indians; and that there are many famous contemporary Native Americans: Will Rogers, America's greatest humorist, honored in the "Cowboy" Hall of Fame; Johnny Cash and Wayne Newton, singers, known throughout the world, along with Cher Bono Allman and Buffy Sainte Marie, plus South Dakota's Billy Red Bow; Billy Mills; America's great Olympic track and field star, Jim Thorpe; Joe Guyon and Joe Kapp, football players enshrined in the Football Hall of Fame; the Tallchief sisters were prima ballerinas; and there are numerous others. Too much prejudice has been expressed and too little has been said about the greatness of these people. Too much has been expressed about the so-called "radical" Indian, whatever assertive Indian that is supposed to chastise, and too little has been understood about the traditional Native American. Too much time has been wasted in trying to "wipe out," "convert," and "condemn" the Native American who is here to stay!

Best Help by Listening

Deloria (1973; 1975) and the *Indian Affairs Newsletter* (1975) assert that it is now time for Indians to speak and for others to listen. Assume the attitude that you can best help by listening.

The tendency to ignore the need to listen and to tell "too much" have blinded Anglo counselors. Native Americans will give you clues with their bodies, eyes, and tone of voice; but do not expect them to be as ostentatious, flamboyant, and dramatic as white clients. Rather, the clues they give are on a subliminal basis that many people miss. If you want to learn and listen, then I recommend that you visit the reservation and villages, attend cultural centers, visit with American Indians in their homes, watch the performance of Indian children in the classrooms, talk with Indians in college, take courses in Indian culture, go to Indian rodeos, and when you visit an American Indian bar sit where you can inconspicuously observe all around you. Don't stare. Most American Indian people have a disdain for being stared at,—so simply sit with an American Indian friend and stare at your drink. You will learn a lot by listening to your friend and observing others. Be inactive and concentrate on listening. After you have attended several Pow Wows then join in the dancing, not as an exhibitionist but as one who is sincerely interested in American Indian culture. Don't be afraid to make a fool of yourself if you are sincere.

Be Realistic and Accepting

After you have participated, again be ready to listen. Certainly, do not "lecture" to us about our own culture. If, by chance, when you visit an American Indian bar you see Indians whom you have had for clients for alcoholism treatment, or for whatever reason, *do not lecture to them.* A simple, inoffensive statement is permissible, such as "Pete, you are epileptic, and I wish you weren't drinking, because that can trigger off a seizure." That's enough. Unfortunately, the majority society is compulsive. They cannot settle for saying one simple sentence; they are most comfortable with tirades. They are super salespeople who do not like to miss a point in their presentation or take no for an answer. Be realistic and permit your expectations to wane. Grant the American Indian the dignity of self-determination, self-appraisal, and realistic actualization.

Honoring and Respecting Indians

If you expect to be effective, you must respect the traditional ways of Indians. You must know that they are people who have endured for thousands of years. *They expect to endure!* They can withstand tremendous hardships, and *they will never succumb!* They are determined, and they will survive. They are, of course, as we have stated, changing. They are asking that their culture be preserved, that ceremonies not be distorted, that there is tribal conformity to rules and standards, and that their language be revived. At the same time, they recognize the need for education and training, so that they are able to have the best of two worlds and can compete better with the majority society.

"Enjoy Us!"

You can well realize that Indians are going to want to work with you, now try enjoying them. Indians will not be the patsies as they used to be—but rather *they want you to honor them.* Therefore, many of you will have to undergo personality changes before you can be good psychologists or counselors for American Indian people. American Indians, like myself, feel that if you are so smart and well trained that you can serve as a psychologist or counselor for us, then the slightest thing we do you should observe. We are observing and listening to you intently, you owe the same respect, and we do not mean stare at us. We mean "feel," "sense," a certain perceptual alertness about us. American Indians do not focus on themselves. They do not spend hours analyzing their actions, recognizing polarities, developing goals, and being overly concerned with unfinished business. Consequently, the psychologist/counselor must start with the same humility and get out of his or her mind the need to be "effective," "establish priorities," and be "goal oriented." Relax, settle back, and enjoy the client. It is best to start off with a soft voice; if you must stare, focus your gaze at the floor or the desk, and listen.

Self-Actualization is a Personal Choice!

Although for years the majority society has enjoyed the "freedom" of careless prejudices, you are going to have to become "more Native American" and less white (Richardson, 1971a). Remember, some psychologists and counselors are so insecure, so threatened, and so intent on their own needs that they forget the needs of others (Richardson, 1973c). You must be casual and natural. The perfectionist even thinks that he or she can give the client the ingredients of self-actualization. This is ludicrous. Self-actualization is a privilege of the individual to obtain personal insight (Richardson, 1973). The individual sets the pace, and you humbly follow along. To this natural, easy manner you may try to add a sense of humor. This is a psychological trait not always seen in the white world; among the American Indians it is a spontaneous eruption of pleasure.

Greeting the Indian Client

Since we have stated that the American Indian is perceptually alert we suggest that you take advantage of this fact. Perception and mental interaction, as I see them, are the processes by which people see and react to the things about them. Since the American Indian is humble, quiet, and unpretentious, we suggest you have a small, homey, and lived-in office. Certainly, you should not have an "auditorium" that is cold and resembles a page from a decorating magazine. The office could be a bit cluttered. We also recommend that you intentionally have pictures of American Indians, posters, or artifacts that are genuine and not too showy. This will tell your Indian clients that you respect their way of life. Do not feel that you have to sit side by side with Indian clients, for this may make them most uncomfortable. Indians may appreciate your hiding behind your desk to equally "protect them from you" and your aggressive, confrontive, and demanding ways.

Be Honest and Direct

Do not hem and haw. Get right to the point of why the client has been sent to see you, and then go back and fill in the details. This will reduce any suspiciousness of the typically circumventing bureaucratic individual who sneaks up on the client, or tries to, by taking 10 minutes to a half hour to get to the point.

Honor Their Presence

When you first greet the American Indian do not try to impress the individual with your "friendliness" by acting like a traveling salesperson, and do not feel you have to use your politician's handshake. I always shake hands "softly" with an American Indian brother or sister. You may call it the "sissy," "limp," or "dead fish" handshake; yet it is typical of humble people to shake hands in such a manner. Very soon after you have greeted the person, offer him or her something, preferably a cup of coffee or tea. Cola or ice water may be acceptable, depending on the area and the weather. Do not tell your secretary to "go to the coffee dispenser" unless you give her the money in the Indian client's presence. American Indians are givers, and that is why reciprocal courtesy will help establish rapport: honor your client by giving something that is acceptable, and you will put her or him at ease.

Settle Back

Do not lean toward the client and commence giving the "third degree" or studying him or her with piercing eyes. Do not be upset with long pauses, but, on the other hand, do not try "seating out the client" to see who can be the winner. A loud and overbearing manner is exceedingly irritating and makes Indians feel subservient, and this will cause them to shut you out as they clam up and remain quiet. After indicating why the client has been sent to you, if it is not a self-referral, then ask if you may take notes. Make these notes short, a mere word here and there. Then summarize at the end of the session. This way the client knows if you have been listening intently. This will reinforce the credibility of your sincerity and counseling technique.

Be Accepting

American Indians are unlike white people in that they do not mind if a brother or sister comes by and wants to listen. As a counselor you should ask permission for the new arrival to sit in, and then allow this to happen. Oftentimes, the client feels more comfortable, and it enhances the esprit de corps, to provide the client with another "skin's" impression of you. The Indian client is telling you this: I trust my brother and sister, because I know nothing will be said; I hope I can trust you the same way. If the Indian client invites you to visit his or her home, eat his or her food, go to a place where there are only skins, then do everything to accept this opportunity. The Indian is sensitive to rejection. By accepting the Indian client's offer, you will be afforded an opportunity to learn about his or her home life, children, parents, and way of life. Some counselors show their interest too by taking courses in American Indian studies. If you do this, even when the instructor invites you to talk freely, be reticent, humble, and soft spoken; do not use that as an invitation to open up and talk. This is a gesture on the part of the instructor: do not abuse it. By the same token, if you are invited into a home and you sense that the Eskimo or Indian family is expecting you to talk, and talk, and talk—don't! The family may be placing you at the center of attention. Again, this is the Eskimos' or Indians' way of being hospitable and friendly; yet if you want to become accepted as one of them you will *act as they act*. You will not act as they expect you to act or as they provide you an opportunity to act. *You will honor their culture by becoming more like them*!

Learn by Observing

By talking too much to the American Indian you may very well drop one seemingly simple statement which shows that you look on them as a "novelty." Some of the questions I have heard are "Don't Indians believe in God?" "Why do Eskimos eat Muktuk?" "Why do the Indians all speak different languages?" "Do Eskimos still make love by rubbing noses together?" "How do Eskimos shower or take a bath in their igloos?" And "How do you scalp people?" If you reread these questions—and there are many others—you can easily see why they are offensive. They all are, or imply, put-downs. The best thing to do is just to listen to them, discuss items with them, and show them you honor and appreciate them. You will learn by listening.

Do Not Inform People

Commence in a very sincere way to become more like an Indian—and less like a compulsive white who knows all the answers about most of the conditions in the world. I am not saying this just as an idle statement. I have taken college students all around the world by ship and then later extensively throughout Europe on several occasions, and it never seems to fail that American whites are always informing other people. It is utterly amazing how the American people feel that they know the answers to all the problems throughout the world. They may even be "right" and the indigenous people "wrong"; yet no one likes to have someone else telling them how they should live. Culturally different people want to make that decision for themselves.

Do Not Be Condescending and Deceptive

Do not patronize the Indian. Do not say, "I have a good friend who is an Indian." Equally damaging are sentences like "What does your dad think of the restrictions on hunting the bowhead whale?", or "What do you Indian people think of . . .?" Don't ask Indians to commit themselves about their leaders. Don't say, "I know what it's like to be poor, but what's it like for Indians?" Indians have no way of knowing how, when, and why you may use their statements for your own benefit, even if it is just for your own attention-getting purposes. Recently, a biased Anglo from Washington State was arguing with me, and, in the course of the conversation, he said, "Why, I even know a Chief So-and-So who just admitted to me that . . ." And I thought, if Chief So-and-So only knew he were going to be "used" he would never have made a negative statement about his own people. This is again why we do not trust the majority society, because the majority society always uses information it has about minorities against them. And stay away from pseudosecrecy statements like "Feel free to tell me . . ."; "You can rest assured I won't say a thing to a soul!"; or "My role as a professional is to observe 'privileged communications' . . ." Indians (and other minorities) have all been told these things a million times before. They have heard this from the Great White Father, the federal bureaucrats at every level, and the school and church, and they have been deceived at every level, and still they are being told, "I understand your problems." Why should Indians trust you any more than they have all the others of your race? Besides, they would have had trust in you, in the first place, or they would not have come to you voluntarily; now they will question why you

felt so compulsive and insecure that you had to make these statements.

SPECIFIC DIMENSIONS OF COUNSELING RECOMMENDED

In the specific dimensions of counseling we wish to emphasize that the directive approach versus nondirective approach tends to be more description than actual and that the two schools of thought are not independent, nor are they always in opposition to one another. In general, the disagreements are not over goals but over the specific techniques to be used. It is the techniques that we discuss at this time.

Become Eclectic and Adaptable

Normally, there are aspects of the directive counseling technique that are counterproductive, and at other times the directive technique is most applicable. We feel that ordering, forbidding, exhortation, suggestion, advice, forcing conformity, and time structuring are to be avoided. Yet assisting in interpretation, reassuring, changing environments, and developing new attitudes may be advisable. Furthermore, the directive techniques of synthesis, diagnosis, and particularly follow-up will be part of an effective repertoire. I would caution against being too authoritative and striving for control of the relationship. Furthermore, the idea in a directive approach that the behavior is predictable, that quantification is necessary, and that objectivity must always be maintained, is ineffective with the American Indian and Eskimo.

Make Statements—Let Them Know Where You Stand

In many ways, the nondirective technique is valuable to individual growth and independence. Prodding and slapping around the American Indian to motivate him or her does not work, and the counselor must show great faith in the individual's capabilities, which is a nondirective point of reference. This, also allows the individual to participate more actively in finding a solution to his/her own problem. I would, however, caution that a completely permissive atmosphere is interpreted by the American Indian as another write-off. The Indian expects direction. I always let Indian clients know where I stand, occasionally scolding them, but I do not rub it in, or "brown stamp," by coming back to an "I told you so" posture, nor do I chide them into action. You have every right to show emotional concern, only do not overdo it. I see so many psychologists, counselors, nurses, social workers, and physicians who will be backing away from an American Indian who is obviously "stewed to the gills" and as he is talking he is spitting in their faces, he is flushed, slurring his words, staggering, and his eyeballs are bloody red, and they will ask a stupid question: "Have you been drinking?" What do you think the answer is? Of course, they say, "No!" Then the professionals are stymied, and where does the conversation go from there? The American Indian will play a game, if that is what the professionals choose. Instead, I look at the individual and simply say, "Cecil, your eyeballs look like they could bleed all over the floor." Then he says, "That's right. I've been drinking." I may then briefly add, "Yuh, I know." Or I may state, "I know it's not easy, certainly not as easy as people think, and that's why I wish the hell you didn't drink." Sometimes it is necessary to say, "Selo, I wonder if you have hepatitis?"—as I look at his yellow eyeballs. With alarm the response is generally, "Really?" This is all directive. It is appreciated, and the Indian client can handle it.

Concentrate on Problems Not on Personalities

It is true, of course, that under the privileges of self-determination we should be nondirective enough to permit the individual to begin to take action steps of his or her own accord and terminate the process of counseling at his or her own volition. There are fewer dangers in being nondirective, and it is thus possible to concentrate more on problem areas than on personalities. It provides the client the opportunity to develop his/her own goals, if any, and to make major decisions. Nondirective assists in rapport are flexible and are less likely to offend the client.

Techniques and Vignettes

Let us look at the least directive techniques: silence, acceptance, restatement, clarification, and summary clarification. I prefer to think of this as the first level of counseling and find some of these dimensions most appropriate. An analysis of each would be as follows:

Dimension of Counseling	Vignettes
1. Silence	Speechless, taciturn, and motionless. Maintain a state of inactivity, be reserved and

listen intently. However, do not see how cute you can be by forcing the client to sweat out his or her problem.

2. Acceptance

Consent to the client's thinking, receive with favor what is being said, verbally and in body action. Showing receptiveness

Use an utterance that merely indicates you are "with the client" like "umhm," "uh-huh," or "mmmh" or in Indian language "Oh-haa!" Occasionally, nod the head. To do this too automatically appears as if you are a broken record and simply grunting and not listening.

3. Restatement

To state again or in a new form the same implications with perhaps less words.

There is no attempt to clarify. One must listen closely to repeat the salient part of the very last sentence. Consider the following example:

CLIENT: I hate this damn school. The principal, the teachers, the students they all give me a hard-ass time, with just everything . . . everything.

COUNSELOR: Everyone gives you a hard time.

CLIENT: Yuh, that's right! I think they got it in for me 'cause I'm an Indian, that's why!

COUNSELOR: Being Indian makes it difficult.

4. Clarification

To make clear, to purify, to refine. The client is rambling along, covering many subjects or not seeming to see the relationships between what he or she is saying. This example illustrates:

CLIENT: You betcha boots! When I was a kid the teachers picked on me. I've had several jobs and the boss has to rub my face in it—that I'm Indian. It's all a pain. It makes me wonder at times.

COUNSELOR: All your life you feel being Indian has been a handicap.

5. Summary clarification

Consolidate the thinking over a period of time.

It is wise to crystallize the client's thinking after he or she has been talking for some while. Do not talk too long; make your sentences short and lucid; do not talk down to the client, and make it clear that your views are only general impressions, not gospel truths or facts. This example shows what *I* mean:

COUNSELOR: What I think I've been hearing you say is "You're locked into an impossible situation because you are an Indian, and you don't know what to do about it—is that true?"

Of these five different dimensions, feel free to use the first three: silence, acceptance, and restatement quite freely. However, do not get into a rut so that what you say sounds artificial and trite, as if you were more interested in a system or technique than in the client. Clarification and summary clarification may be applicable. At the end of a session I use some summary clarification and tentative analysis sparingly.

The middle group of dimensions of counseling is a slightly more forceful way of pushing the client. Perhaps various techniques represent an overlapping area between directive and nondirective counseling as appears in Figure 9.2.

Both the directivist and nondirectivist tend to use a considerable amount of approval and general lead. An analysis of the middle zone would appear as follows:

Dimension of Counseling   Vignettes
1. Approval   Sanctioning suitability of action, officially ratify, confirm as satisfactory, judge as favorable. Consider this example:

   CLIENT: I'm going to stay away from the reservation hassle.
COUNSELOR: That's good.

This technique is used by both the nondirectivist and the directivist: it is an act of "passing judgment" on the behavior of the client with the use of such comments as "good," "correct" or "right" and "right on."

2. General lead   This is one of the best techniques because it leads the individual like a quarterback tossing the ball to a receiver. It is lifelike; many are used to "leading" in bidding in cards; leading, like a blow in boxing, has the power of jarring the client into seeing himself or herself; leading goes toward a definite goal like leadership training; it guides and advances the individual into clearer thinking; it is one of the most inactive ways to direct the client if used with a soft and

nondemanding voice, or it can be one of the most challenging if used with an aggressive and demanding voice; therefore the technique is very flexible; it works with all classes of people and is excellent with minority peoples.

Use of the general lead requires the professional to pose the kinds of questions minority clients have been asked all their lives. In this sense, this technique is universal and generic to the whole person. It usually makes use of the words *you* or *why, when, how, whom, where*, "explain it," "Tell me." If skillfully used, it does not develop resistance, and the client feels that he or she is clarifying his or her own thinking. Note this example:

CLIENT: This whole damn school sucks!

COUNSELOR: Tell me why you say that.

CLIENT: Well, hell, man! The kids in class tease me because I'm an Eskimo and they want to know if I had my whale blubber for breakfast and how do you make love inside of an igloo, and Mrs. Philapijano, just sits and laughs along with all the others like it's a big joke. Wouldn't that get you?

COUNSELOR: Tell me more.

CLIENT: It's like I said, everyone teases me—teases the hell out of me, and no one including the Eskimo teacher sticks up for me. Hell, I'm tired of being laughed at. There is only so much . . .

COUNSELOR: What do you think we can do?

All the counselor's responses were general lead; note the effectiveness as the client talked freely.

There is a common tendency for counselors to dole out approval, since we all consider ourselves to sit on judgment's seat. However, doling out approval is one of the poorest techniques to use with American Indians.

American Indians have always been treated as little children who had to seek the approval of the Great White Father. General lead is also used rather universally, but, in contrast, if stated indifferently, with comments like "Tell me more," "You might look at it another way possibly," "Why do you say that?" or just plain "Why?" It is extremely potent. In brevity, it lets the individual be captain of his or her own thinking. It provides freedom, internal strength, and a nonthreatening way of directing the session.

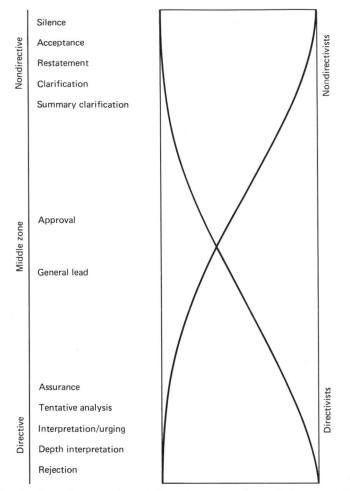

Figure 9.2 A schematic comparison of the various counseling techniques used by nondirectivists (on the left) and the directivists (on the right). Overlapping occurs, particularly in the middle zone.

Now we turn to the more direct techniques, which are the most difficult. Like many techniques in life, the ones that are the most difficult may also be the most productive. These techniques, which are the most precarious, are calculated to stir up some of the most painful and therefore the most suppressed material; in the long run use of these techniques may lead to the greatest areas of individual growth. I would tend to reserve these comments for the American Indian and Eskimo counselors to use with their own people. These counselors will be able to take liberties that other counselors are unable to enjoy—much the same way that a recovered alcoholic counselor can challenge another recovering alcoholic. In other words, the American Indian and Eskimo counselors can say to their American Indian and Eskimo clients: "Cut it out! I've been there, you know!" Let us now analyze the most directive techniques as follows:

Dimension of Counseling	Vignettes
1. Assurance	This guarantee of the client's action provides a pledge that everything will turn out satisfactorily. It causes a state of being sure and thus gives a sense of false security. It can develop a phony aura of safety and even seem legal if spoken with authority. It gives a spirit of confidence that may be reassuring in the hands of the professional. On the other hand this is also why professionals are not trusted by the Native Americans. This assurance technique has the counselor overreacting to the client, which tends to belittle the client's judgment, assuring him or her that there is no problem. It placates the Native American and has been frequently stated in these forms: "God will take care of you," "Everything will be OK; it always is," "You'll do all right if you can keep those militant Indians out." This example illustrates:

CLIENT: I don't know what "we" can do, but I know what I'm going to do—I'm going to drop out of school. You don't think I should stay, do you?

COUNSELOR: I'm sure everything will turn out OK. We all have a tendency to exaggerate these little problems when we are your age. You won't remember it 50 years from now.

2. Tentative analysis	Using various hypotheses the counselor, indicating uncertainty at that point, presents a new approach in a purely tentative manner so that the client is free to accept or reject the ideas. The new approach is an attempt to determine the nature of the relationship and breaks down aspects of the

individual's behavior to discover the true nature of any inner problems. When counseling the Native American the counselor's use of this new approach may get him or her into trouble. "You might look at it this way" is generally taken as a put-down by the American Indian. In skillful hands such an approach works well and is best presented as an option for consideration. Note this example:

CLIENT: I've been talking with you for twenty minutes and I still think the best thing for me to do is to walk up to this guy and punch him right square in the mouth. I hate his guts! He's just a wise guy like Kiyan Little Eagle, Terry Tananara, and Gilo Makicinjiin. All a bunch of slobs. I've talked with you . . . er, all this time.

COUNSELOR: You wonder why your friends turn into your enemies. Could it be (1) you expect too much, (2) you have a need to fail as you stated earlier, (3) a need to assert your masculinity as your sister stated, (4) you are "testing the limits" to see if people love you when you are obnoxious, or (5) you have a sado-masochistic need and you set the stage for getting negative strokes? I don't know. I'm not sure. All these possibilities do, however, go back to how you stated your family treated you. Do you think all of this is part of your early childhood—the expectation placed upon you, your role as a family failure, your shortness of size, etc.?"

3. Interpretation and urging   The counselor makes an inference generally in a positive manner, based on the client's behavior, and it is hoped that these remarks will speed insight.

Problems arise from the fact that this is oftentimes psychoanalytically oriented with a Freudian viewpoint. It may be more than the client wishes to accept. This example illustrates:

CLIENT: "Well, like you say, it probably is because of my childhood. I think at times I want to feel sorry for myself: The way I was raised. Well, when other people, my friends, don't appreciate it—I get kinda riled up and act out my problems. Like you say, I expect everyone to like me—and I had to do that with my folks. I ought to just rewrite my script I guess and tell myself I don't need my folks' approval anymore. I can get my own satisfaction from myself.

COUNSELOR: It sounds like you see the problem—why don't you write out a new script this evening and bring it in to me in the morning. This will be a positive step for you.

4. Depth interpretation

This is interpretation in terms of psychoanalytics, psychodiagnostics, typologies, psychogenesis, countertransference, repression, dream analysis, et cetra.

This is generally reserved for a psychiatrist, psychoanalyst, or clinical psychologist and can be dangerous if sufficient time is not available . . . with some individuals into depth interpretation for three to five years. Consider this example:

CLIENT: Yuh, you're right. I shouldn't delay things. I do that often though. I wonder why?

COUNSELOR: Maybe you want attention. You may have felt abandoned by your mother, almost castrated, and by ignoring what she wanted you to do you were punishing her. It may be that you had feelings of love and hate—and when she went out and ignored you at night. You then later ignored her. Sorta an eye-for-an-eye. Do you feel better when you punish other people?

5. Rejection

To throw back, to refuse to acknowledge, to decline to accept, to throw away as useless or unsatisfactory to the counselor. Sometimes it is appropriate to use this technique although it has the danger of enraging the client. Then all parties become highly emotional. Consider this example:

CLIENT: Why did you say my mother wasn't a good mother?

COUNSELOR: I didn't say that!

CLIENT: Well, you implied it.

COUNSELOR: You didn't listen.

CLIENT: Hell, man—I've been listening to you for six months! Don't give me that crap!

COUNSELOR: Well, let's quit for today!

Analyzing Direct Techniques

In these more direct techniques, there are some inherent dangers—some of the dimensions leave much to be desired. For example, assurance is meant to be helpful and reassuring, but really it is demeaning. The

American Indian is used to having people belittle his or her problems. Tentative analysis can imply that the client has not crystallized his or her thinking and that you are the expert who can put it all together. Thus it may be taken as a put-down. And what you suggest may not fit the framework of the American Indian's cultural references; and the American Indian may feel that she or he has to pick one of your answers to appease your needs. Interpretation and urging are techniques bureaucrats have been using for a long time, as they hurry the Native American to sell her or his birthright and gobble up her or his land. There is an element of coercion, or force, and it may make the Native American feel inadequate and slow. For many Native Americans, depth interpretation is scarey. Native Americans have a built-in resentment that is sort of like this: "If you think my Indian religion is a lot of hocus-pocus then how can you believe this crazy stuff by Freud, that if I climb a mountain I am struggling to overcome my mother, that if I like to catch a fish that it means I like to hold a penis, and that if I collect rocks I am anally fixated. My people have been picking up rocks for thousands of years and their bowel habits are no different from anyone else's! Man, your stuff is crazy—not Indian religion!" Rejection is oftentimes appropriate; yet it can be very destructive to the counseling process and can bring the counseling session to an abrupt ending.

CONCLUSIONS

Of the best dimensions of counseling for Native Americans, I would suggest the following: silence, acceptance, restatement, and general lead. At the end of the counseling session it may be advisable to make a verbal summary of what has transpired. Remember, you have to develop your own technique; a person who is sincere can utilize a very poor technique and be effective, whereas an insecure and insincere person will be a failure even with the best techniques. American Indians can almost feel a phony person. It is almost as if they had antennae that pick up signals, or as if the insincere person gave off a chemical that betrayed her or his insincerity, or maybe it is something like infrared or electrical vibrations. The point is this: American Indians can tell when you are game playing. Therefore, we recommend that you try to understand American Indians, that you understand this group's cultural values and achievements, and that you try to do your best to accept your own imperfections.

REFERENCES

The Acceptance Cost. *Akwesasne Notes,* July 1977, pp. 18–20.

Alcohol abuse and alcoholism among Native Americans. Unpublished manuscript, 1975. (Available from Edwin H. Richardson, PhD, Box 23504, Washington, D.C. 20024.)

American Indian Policy Review Commission Report. House Office Building Annex, Washington, D.C., April 1976, p. 6.

Batesland Siox testifies that CIA on reservation. *Rapid City Journal,* May 18, 1976, p. 10.

Bender, Ron. Indian participation in area discussed. *Rapid City Journal,* October 12, 1975, p. 1.

BIA, I'm not your Indian anymore. *Akwesasne Notes,* 1974.

Bigness of the White society: Has a craving for big cigars, long cigarettes, bigger and stronger drinks—all damaging to one's health. There is a vogue also for large homes, big airplanes, large colored TV, big weddings, large cars, luxurious tours, and scrumptious parties.

Black Elk. *The Sacred Pipe.* Baltimore: Penguin Books, 1971.

Brock, George. Hetahele—Magic or sense? *Journal of American Medical Association,* October 25, 1971, pp. 511–516.

Canada's Indians encounter urban bias. *Denver Post,* May 15, 1974, p. 32.

Carroll, Dennis. The League of the Iroquois: An Indian democracy. *American Indian Policy Review Commission Newsletter,* May 1976, pp. 1–2.

Caselli, Ron. Historical repression and Native Americans. *Indian Historian,* Fall 1970, pp. 44–45.

Cawte, John E. *A Study of Primitive Medicine in Australia: Basic Tools of Primitive Psychiatry.* (Technical Reports, Parts I–IV), New York: Smith Kline & French Laboratory News, June 1975.

Chief Joseph. *National Geographic,* March 1977, pp. 409–434.

Colleges: Pride of the reservation. *Time,* April 11, 1969, pp. 67–68.

Conaham, Virginia. *Hominology Handbook.* Manuscript submitted for publication, 1975.

The continual denial of our existence. *Akwesasne Notes,* July 1977, pp. 16–17.

Coulter, R. T. Might makes right: A history of Indian jurisdiction. *Akwesasne Notes,* Late Spring 1977, pp. 21–27.

Culver, Virginia. Indian tribal beliefs related to the real world. *Denver Post,* December 15, 1973, p. 7HH.

The darkening horizons. *Akwesasne Notes,* Summer 1977, pp. 4–9.

Dates in history. *The Weewish Three. A Magazine for American Indian Young People,* June 1974, p. 14.

Deloria, Vine, Jr. A better day for Indians. (Reprinted from *Field Foundation Newsletter,* 1975, pp. 7–11.)

Deloria, Vine, Jr. Indian lives, identity twisted, shaped by Wounded Knee. *Denver Post,* November 4, 1973, p. 23.

Denial of Indian civil and religious rights. *Indian Historian,* Summer 1975, pp. 38–40.

Denver manpower conference—Indians express wish to control own lives. *Denver Post,* December 11, 1970, p. 43.

Dirt of Mother Earth: At the Sun Dance, in sacred marriage, and other times the Lakota (Sioux) make "flesh sacrifices," in which the skin is pinched by the Medicine Man, a razor blade is used to quickly slice off the skin, and then the cut is smeared over with "unpurified dirt" from the breast of Mother Earth. There is never any infection—it appears we have to re-examine "sanitation."

Doyon raps pipeline. *River Times,* July 31, 1973, p. 1.

Earle, Jane. Another policy review—dealing with the "Indian problem." *Denver Post,* November 16, 1975, p. 19.

Earth as a food: In the homeostasis of body balance, the human body gives messages to its needs and is phenomenal with its accuracy. Particularly during pregnancy and at other times the body craves earth minerals. Eskimo, Indian, and other poverty women, unable to purchase from the store capsules, eat raw earth. This is more scientific than it may seem to some people.

Eskimos—We will hunt the bowhead whale, from Ketchikan to Barrow. *Alaska Magazine,* December 1977, pp. 34–43.

Evictions—OC25. American Indian Press. (Available from Edwin H. Richardson, PhD, Box 23504, Washington, D.C. 20024.

"Extended family" called basic difference in Indian culture. *Rapid City Journal,* November 30, 1973, p. 31.

Fenton, Ronald L., & Krueger, Michael. American's Bicentennial tragedy—The Indian. *Faces,* September 1976, pp. 40–58.

Foote, John. Christ and our Indian heritage. *Indian Life,* **10** (2), 6.

Fromm, Erich. *The Revolution of Hope.* New York: World Perspective Series, 1968.

The future is the family. *Akwesasne Notes,* Spring 1977, pp. 4–7.

The future of the Indians; analysis and opinion by Vine Deloria, Jr. *Akwesasne Notes,* Early Winter, 1975, pp. 36–37.

Garner, Van Hastings. The treaty of Guadalupe Hidalgo and the California Indians. *Indian Historian,* Winter 1975, pp. 10–13.

Good Tracks, Jim G. Native American non-interference. *Social Work,* November 1973, pp. 30–34.

Grinde, Donald. Cherokee removal and American politics. *Indian Historian,* Summer 1975.

Grinde, Donald. Cherokee removal and American politics. *Indian Historian,* Winter 1976, pp. 34–49.

Hansell, Deanna. Reburial for tribal ancestors. *Confederated Umatilla Journal,* June 1976, pp. 1–13.

Harjo, Susan Shown. Hearing—DC 291. American Indian Press Association News Service. (Available from Edwin H. Richardson, PhD, Box 23504, Washington, D.C. 20024.)

Harner, Michael. The enigma of Aztec sacrifice. *Natural History,* April 1977, pp. 84–96.

Harper, Chris J. Indians lack political clout on problems. *Rapid City Journal,* October 19, 1975, p. 33.

Harper, Chris J. Reservation migrants learn big-city living isn't easy. *Denver Post,* December 14, 1975, p. 57.

Hatch, Steve. The Eskimo: The miracle of the North. *Fourth Estate.* Denver: Colorado University, Denver Center, October 13, 1971, p. 1.

Hays, H. R. Strong medicine. *Physician's World,* May 1974, pp. 94–98.

Holford, David M. The subversion of the Indian land allotment system of 1887–1934. *Indian Historian,* Spring 1975, pp. 11–21.

Holman, Ben. Police and minorities. *Confederated Umatilla Journal,* October 1976, p.3.

Hopi education: The faith to the future. *Qua Togti,* November 7, 1974, p. 5.

Howard, James H. The culture-area concept: Does it diffract anthropology. *Indian Historian,* April 1975, pp. 22–26.

Indian activist claims government infringing on "our" civil liberties. *South Dakota State University Collegian,* October 15, 1975, p. 21.

Indian Affairs. Newsletter from the Association of the American Indian Affairs, New York City, September–December 1975 (No. 90).

Indian educators told public schools irrelevant. *Rapid City Journal,* November 9, 1975, p. 10.

Indian Health Service Discharge Summary, Fiscal Years 1967–1977. Rockville, Md.: Indian Health Service, 1978. (Publication No. HSA 75–12021).

Indian hiring festival schedule Tues. *Rapid City Journal,* October 11, 1975, p. 13.

Indian housing: A HUD failure. *Confederated Umatilla Journal,* July 1977, p. 2.

Indian medicine. *Spectrum,* March–April 1962, pp. 25–36.

Indian woman to meet. *Rapid City Journal,* June 13, 1974, p. 5.

Jones, C. David. *Hominology: Psychiatry's newest frontier.* Springfield, Ill.: Charles C. Thomas, 1975, Chapter 7.

Kahn, Theodore C. *An Introduction to Hominology: An Integrated View of Mankind and Self.* Pueblo, Col.: Nationwide Press, 1976.

Kahn, Theodore C. *A Study of Values: Hominology Workbook.* Pueblo, Col.: Nationwide Press, 1976.

LaCourse, Richard V. The Indian image. Paper presented at meeting of the *American Indian Press Assocation,* Sante Fe, N.M., December 8, 1974. (Available from Edwin H. Richardson, PhD, Box 23504, Washington, D.C. 20024.)

Lame Deer, John Fire. *Lame Deer seeker of vision.* New York: Simon & Schuster, 1972.

Lawrance, Olive. Dozens of languages: Information sunburst possesses Indian problems. *Denver Post,* February 8, 1974, p. 38.

Lewis, Ronald G., & Ho, Man Keung. Social work with Native Americans. *Social Work,* September 1975, pp. 8, 28, 38.

Locke, Ray Friday. History of Aztec medicine. *Nishnawbe News,* Fall, 1975, p. 7.

Looney, Ralph, & Dale, Bruce. The Navajo National Looks Ahead. *National Geographic,* December 1972, pp. 783–803.

de Los Angeles, Andy. International conference of world's indigenous peoples. *Northwest Indian News,* November 1975, p. 1.

Lovett, Vince. Maine officials say George Washington on state's side. *Indian News Notes,* August 16, 1977.

McKinely, Francis et al. *Who Should Control Indian Education?* Berkeley, Calif.: Far West Laboratory of Educational Research and Development, 1971.

Mafziger, Richard. A violation of trust: Federal management of Indian timber land. *The Indian Historian*, Fall 1976.

Mails, Thomas E. *The People Called Apache*. Englewood Cliffs, N.J.: Prentice-Hall, 1974.

Manuel, George. *Thanksgiving*. American Indian Press Association. (Available from Edwin H. Richardson, PhD, Box 23504, Washington, D.C. 20024.)

Marasmus: This is the story that denounces the fetish of the Anglo professionals for cleanliness. It points to the greatness of love. The story developed from the events that occurred on a maternity ward during the early part of this century when babies were placed in sterile incubators—and they died. The professionals were shocked to find that the infants who were thriving were being "molested" and handled by a filthy scrubwoman with stringy hair, dirty fingernails, and ragged clothes. The incident clearly proved that the fetish for cleanliness is not as important as the need for love.

Medicine Man underscores little understood practice. *Rocky Mountain News*, June 20, 1975, p. 24.

Miller, Virginia P. Whatever happened to the Yki!? *Indian Historian*, Fall 1975, pp. 6–12.

de Montellano, Bernard Ortiz. Empirical Aztec medicine. *Science*, April 18, 1975, pp. 215–220.

de Montigny, Lionel H. The bureaucratic game and a proposed Indian ploy. *Indian Historian*, Fall 1975, pp. 25–30.

Murdock makes NCAI history. *Confederated Umatilla Journal*, October 1977, p. 1.

Native American Elders Newsletter. Carson City, Nev.: Native American Elders United, May 1976.

Native Heritage. Minneapolis: Indian Youth News and View, May 1975.

Nelson, Bryce. Tension between Indians, whites build in area. *Standing Rock Star*, December 20, 1974, pp. 7–32.

Newsletter will focus on Indian children's welfare. *Rapid City Journal*, December 26, 1973, p. 14.

Old Coyote, Barney. The issue is not feathers. *Akwesasne Notes*, July 1977, pp. 21–23.

Ostar, Allan W. American Association of State Colleges and Universities for American Indians. *Black Hills State College/Indian Studies Newsletter*, January 1978, pp. 3–9.

Petty, Roy. Medical practice Navajo-style: White man's rules go out the window. *Denver Post*, December 8, 1974, pp. 37–46.

Phoenix Urban Center Dilemma: Cultural and multi-services program vie with constant emergency situations. *Native American*, March–April 1976, pp. 1–6.

The Prairie Potawatomie resistance to allotment. *Indian Historian*, Fall 1976, pp. 27–31.

Press has let Indians down delegates told. *Rapid City Journal*, November 17, 1972, p. 2.

Quigley, Pat. A child can affect his parents. *Choctaw Community News*, December 1975, p. 16.

Religious significance of Sioux Sun Dance described at seminar. *Black Hills Press,* July 9. 1977, p. 2.

Reservation vs. hospital treatment environment in patient rehabilitation efforts, 1976. *Pine Ridge Research Bulletin No. 9.* Pine Ridge Agency, S.D. *Resolution to permit the Medicine Man to practice medicine in any hospital in USA where there are Indian patients.* Resolution passed at the National Indian Education Association Annual Conference in Phoenix, Ariz. Minneapolis: National Indian Education Association, November 17, 1974 (Resolution).

Resolution to teach local Indian language in public schools. Resolution passed at the National Indian Education Association Annual Conference in Phoenix, Ariz. Minneapolis: National Indian Education Association, November 17, 1974 (Resolution).

Resource development on Indian reservation is subject to talk by Mrs. LaDonna Harris. *Indian Travel Newsletter,* Fall 1975.

Richardson, Edwin H. Complexities of creative thinking. (Chapter IX, *Human Relations: How to Get Along with People*). Unpublished manuscript being prepared for publication, 1971b.

Richardson, Edwin H. Counseling the alcoholic Indian (parts I and II). Paper presented at the meeting of the South Dakota Psychological Association, Rapid City, S.D., May 28, 1976.

Richardson, Edwin H. Counseling Indian alcoholics and the state-wide problem. Paper presented at the Education Committee of the State Legislature of South Dakota, Pierre, S.D., May 1973a.

Richardson, Edwin H. Counseling minorities. Paper presented at the meeting of the Sixth International Congress of Group Psychotherapy, Philadelphia, August 1, 1977a.

Richardson, Edwin H. *Development Aspects of Counseling Minority Clients.* Unpublished manuscript, 1975a. (Available from Edwin H. Richardson, PhD, Box 23504, Washington, D.C. 20024.)

Richardson, Edwin H. *Educating Indians to Appreciate Their Culture and Traditions.* Unpublished manuscript, 1973c. (Available from Edwin H. Richardson, PhD, Box 23504, Washington, D.C. 20024.)

Richardson, Edwin H. Indian philosophy and tradition and how to teach this to the Indian people. Paper presented at the meeting of the Black Hills State College Indian Studies Group, Spearfish, S.D. 1975b.

Richardson, Edwin H. Mental interaction and perception. (Chapter IX, *Human Relations: How to Get Along with People).* Unpublished manuscript being prepared for publication, 1971d.

Richardson, Edwin H. Motivation, what causes us to act. (Chapter X, *Human Relations: How to Get Along with People).* Unpublished manuscript being prepared for publication, 1971a.

Richardson, Edwin H. The problems of the Indian in the affluent society. Paper presented at the meeting of Region 8—Indian Health Meeting, Rapid City, SD, May 1973b.

Richardson, Edwin H. Psychology of the North American Indian. Paper presented at the meeting of the Rocky Mountain Psychological Association, Las Vegas, May 11, 1973d.

Richardson, Edwin H. Religion as psychotherapy. Paper presented at the Pastoral Counseling and Psychiatry Workshop, Fort Meade, S.D., October 25, 1971c.

Richardson, Edwin H. The role of the Medicine Man as a part of the modern therapeutic team in psychotherapy for Indians. Paper presented at the Sixth International Congress of Group Psychotherapy, Philadelphia, August 5, 1977b.

Richardson, Edwin H. Standards for Indian alcohol counselors. *Monograph of the South Dakota Indian Commission on Alcohol and Drug Abuse*, 1974, **32** (2, Whole No. 1).

Ridley, J. F. Protecting Indianness. *American Indian Culture Center Journal*, Winter 1973. (Available from Room 3221 Campbell Hall, 405 Hilgard Avenue, UCLA Campus., Los Angeles, Calif.)

Roubideaux says Indian problems dwarf Watergate. *Rapid City Journal*, July 8, 1973, p. 41.

Satterlee, James L., & Malan, Vernon D. *History and acculturation of the Dakota Indians*. Brookings, S.D.: South Dakota State University, 1967.To secure operational funds—Indian businessmen's group start "White Brother" membership drive. *Rapid City Journal*, May 19, 1973, p. 2.

Senator Harris's wife says new image creates problems. *Rapid City Journal*, May 6, 1973, p. 27.

Separate Department of Indian Affairs almost created a century ago. *American Indian Policy Review Commission Newsletter*, June 1975, pp. 1–2.

Sitting Bull, Donald. An escape from alcoholism. *Indian Life*, **7** (4), 3.

Springer, W.F. The Omaha Indians: What they ask of the United States government. *Indian Historian*, Winter 1976, pp. 30–33.

Standing Bear, Luther. *Land of the spotted Eagle*, p. 244.

State-Indian relations at crisis stage? *Rapid City Journal*, June 14, 1974, p. 9.

Stefon, Frederick J. Significance of Meriam Report of 1928. *Indian Historian*, Summer 1975, pp. 3–5.

Strauss, Joseph H., Jensen, Gary F., & Harris, V. William. New research report: Crime, delinquency and the American Indian. *Native American*, February 1975, pp. 5–8.

Stuckey, William. Navajo Medicine Men. *Science Digest*, December 1975, pp. 34–41.

Survival—Wiconi. Rapid City, S.D.: Intertribal American Indian Association (Use-of-Time Handout).

Ted [Kennedy] urges parley on Indian reforms *Denver Post*, October 7, 1969, p. 37.

Thompson, Terter. Indian alcoholism: A "National Disaster." *The Journal of Indian Affairs*, December 1, 1974, p. 15. (Available from the Simon Fraser University in British Columbia, Vancouver, B.C.)

Training opportunities open for Indian leaders. *CINA Trail Blazer*, December 1975, p. 4.

de Trobriand, Philleppe. *Army life in Dakota*, 1892, pp. 12–13.

Victims of progress. *Akwesasne Notes*, July 1977, pp. 24–27.

Voices from Wounded Knee 1973: The people are standing up. *Akwesasne Notes*, June 1973.

Wah-Shee, James J. The white man must change. *Indian Truth* (The Indian Rights Association), September 1975, pp. 3–4.

Wasson, John Stuart. The Nimipu War. *Indian Historian*, Fall 1970, pp. 5–9.

STUDY QUESTIONS

1. What has been the historical experience of Native Americans in the United States (cite statistics and facts) In what ways might this experience affect the Native Americans' perceptions of the white counselor (world view)?

2. How might cultural values of Native Americans be distorted by U.S. society? Can you compare and contrast these values with one another?

3. In what ways may Native American cultural values be at odds with the values of traditional U.S. counseling?

4. The author outlines several general and specific suggestions in working with Native Americans. How do these suggestions derive from the earlier discussion?

5. Of the counseling suggestions given, which would be most difficult for you to do? Why?

III
Critical Incidents in Cross-Cultural Counseling

In the next chapter, a series of case vignettes on American Indians, Asian Americans, Blacks, and Hispanics are presented for student analyses and discussions. Each case is presented in a counseling context and raise cross-cultural counseling issues described in Parts I and II. We encourage students to also review appropriate chapters in Part II that correlate with the client's minority group.

10

Critical Incidents in Cross-Cultural Counseling

Critical incidents have been shown to be effective means of highlighting and illustrating crucial issues/concerns/decision points likely to arise in certain characteristic situations. I have found such incidents useful in cross-cultural counselor training and evaluation because they require people to (a) identify the factors operating in the situation and (b) suggest possible solutions that may be taken.

While the first two sections of this text have been devoted mainly to providing general and specific information about counseling and the culturally different, this chapter is concerned with analysis and application. In the following pages, you will be exposed to several cross-cultural counseling situations that involve people from different cultural/racial backgrounds. Each case is briefly described in some counseling, educational, or mental health framework. Your task is to do three things, as enumerated here:

1. First identify as many cross-cultural issues in the case vignettes as possible. Do not stop with one or two! Your ability to see the situations from as many perspectives as possible is important. In most cases, listing your answers with brief elaborations is needed.

2. Second, identify as many possible value differences between the interaction of the characters or the values of the characters and institutions. For example, restraint of strong feelings may be highly valued by certain Asian groups but not by many Anglo Americans. A possible value conflict may arise between individuals from each group. Conflicts can also arise between an individual and institution or another society. In this case, institutional and societal values need to be identified. Again, listing these conflicts with some elaboration to clarify your analysis is all you need do.

3. Third, committing yourself to a course of action in each case vignette forces you to examine your own values/priorities and those presented in the case. Address yourself to what you would do, how you would do it, and why? In other words, it is important to define your goals, approach, and rationale.

USING THE CASE VIGNETTES

These case vignettes when used as a teaching/training tool by a skilled and knowledgeable leader can (*a*) help you become culturally aware of your own values, (*b*) expand your awareness of other world views, (*c*) anticipate possible cultural barriers in counseling, and (*d*) generate and suggest alternative counselor intervention strategies more consistent with the life experiences of minorities. The instructor or workshop leader may wish to use the case vignettes in several ways. For example, these cases may be used to stimulate group discussion among participants or used for individual study and learning. Some of these cases are also conducive to role playing rather than a purely cognitive exercise. The cases may be used prior to reading the text, during each chapter as may be appropriate, or after the complete study of Parts I and II. The benefits derived from the critical incidents depend on the ingenuity and effectiveness of the facilitator. In my own classes and workshops, I have found that if a systematic approach is used for the express purpose of accomplishing these objectives, any combination will aid in learning. I have even used critical incidents to assess the effects of a course or workshop on participants (midterm examinations, take-home assignments, final examinations, etc.). A typical outline I follow in leading discussions and having students write an analysis of a case is shown in Table 10.1. This same form or some variant of it may be reproduced and used by students to study the cases.

Learning can also occur when trainees are asked to create a cross-cultural counseling situation. Creation of a good critical incident requires you to understand (*a*) alternative world views, (*b*) the generic characteristics of counseling, (*c*) value systems of the culturally different, and (*d*) social-institutional dynamics. Creating a critical incident requires active integration rather than isolated learning. Furthermore, these can be shared with other participants to enhance further learning. You may like to use the following form outlined in Table 10.2.

Table 10.1
Critical Incidents

Answer Sheet

Name _____

Critical Incident No. _____   Date _____

1. In the case vignette just read, please identify as many cross-cultural issues as possible. Please be brief, and list them (1, 2, 3, etc.) when possible.

2. Identify potential value differences/conflicts occurring or likely to occur in this case.

3. Supposing you are a counselor or mental health worker who finds himself/herself in the situation. What would be (*a*) your goals, (*b*) you course of action, and (*c*) your rationale for the goals and action you have chosen?
   (a) Goals:

   (b) Course of action

   (c) Rationale

Table 10.2
Critical Incidents in Cross-Cultural Counseling

Name _____   Date _____

As one aspect of cross-cultural counselor training, we are interested in compiling several counseling cases that deal with cultural/racial issues. These critical incidents may be used in future training. All of you are being asked to describe a cross-cultural counseling encounter that raises cross-cultural conseling issues. We are especially interested in the counselor-client interaction, but a broader description (teaching, colleague relationships, institutional dilemmas, etc.) is also permissible. The specific purposes of this assignment are to (*a*) identify cultural points of view and responses, (*b*) show how two cultural dictates may lead to misunderstandings, (*c*) reveal how traditional counseling may clash with cultural values, and (*d*) suggest alternative ways of dealing with the critical incident.

Your brief description should involve an actual or hypothetical event that took place over a limited period of time. The situation should be cross-cultural, involving people from two different cultures, and should place the counselor in an ambiguous position with no easy solution.

Please describe such a situation, answering the following questions. All information will be treated as confidential. If more space is required, use the reverse side to elaborate.

1. Describe a cross-cultural counseling situation you experienced, witnessed, or heard about.

    _____
    _____
    _____

2. Describe the events in sequence, indicating what, when, where, how, and why they occurred.

    _____
    _____
    _____

3. List the race/culture of the persons involved, giving their relationship to one another.

    _____
    _____
    _____

4. Describe how the counselor or main character handled the situation.

_____

_____

_____

5. What cross-cultural issues did this situation raise?

_____

_____

_____

6. How should the counselor have handled the situation and why?

_____

_____

_____

7. Please describe any additional information we might need in order to use this case as a training one.

_____

_____

_____

CRITICAL INCIDENTS

Each of the cases described next is placed on separate pages so that they may be reproduced for class or workshop use. The cases cover a diversity of racial/cultural minorities that raise general and specific counseling issues. Each is presented uninterrupted without commentary or analysis. However, the last part of this chapter does contain in question/outline form an analysis keyed to the cases. I suggest readers first attempt to analyze the cases before studying the last section. I hope you will find these cases helpful in integrating what you learned from the first two sections.

CRITICAL INCIDENT NUMBER 1

While working at a counseling center, a white female client (Mary) comes to you for help in sorting out her thoughts and feelings concerning an interracial relationship with a Black student. Although she is proud of the relationship and feels that her liberal friends are accepting and envious, her parents are dead set against it. Indeed, Mary's parents have threatened to cut off financial support unless she terminates the affair immediately.

Mary told of how she had rid herself of much bigotry and prejudice from the early training of her parents. When she left home, everything changed for her. She joined a circle of friends who were quite liberal in thought and behavior. She recalled how she was both shocked and attracted to her friends' liberal political beliefs, philosophy, and sexual attitudes. When she first met John, a Black student, she was immediately attracted to his apparent confidence and outspokenness. It did not take her long to become sexually involved with him and to enter into a long-term relationship. Mary became the talk of her dormitory but did not seem to care. Indeed, she seemed to enjoy the attention and openly flaunted her relationship in everyone's face. One night, she had the audacity to have him stay overnight.

Because Mary requested couple counseling, you decide to see them together. However, to really get a feel for John, you decide to see him for two sessions individually before holding joint counseling. In talking to John, he informs you that he came solely to please Mary. He sees few problems in their relationship that cannot be easily resolved. John seems to feel that he has overcome many handicaps in his life and that this represents just another obstacle to be conquered. When asked about his use of the term "handicap" he responds, "It's not easy to be Black, you know. I've proven to my parents and friends in high school, including myself, that I'm worth something. Let them disapprove, I've made it out of there and into a good school." Further probing revealed John's resentment over his own parents' disapproval of the relationship. While his relations with them had worsened to the point of near-physical assaults, John continued to bring Mary home during vacations. He seemed to take great pride in being seen with a beautiful white girl.

In the joint sessions, Mary's desire to continue and John's apparent reluctance became obvious. Several times when John mentioned the prospect of a "permanent relationship" Mary did not seem to respond positively. She did not seem to want to look too far into the future. Mary's constant coolness to the idea and your attempts to focus in on this reluctance anger John greatly. He becomes antagonistic toward you and puts pressure on Mary to terminate this useless talk "crap." However, he continues to come for the weekly sessions. One day, his anger boils over, and he accuses you of being biased. Standing up and shouting, he demands to know how you feel about interracial relationships.

Identify the issues. What would you do? Why? (Assume the race of the counselor is whatever race you are. Furthermore, assume that the time is 1968 and that this is a predominantly white institution.)

CRITICAL INCIDENT NUMBER 2

A white community social worker, Janet Myers, has recently been hired by the BIA to work with reservation Indian youth participating in an educational exchange program. Approximately 10 of the children (ages 12 to 14) attended predominantly white schools outside the reservation. The program is an experimental one, and Ms. Myers has been given the task of evaluating its effectiveness.

Approximately one month into the school year, the social worker receives several calls from teachers expressing concern over Johnny Lonetree's performance in class. The teachers state that Johnny is often as much as one hour late for classes and his contributions always seem tangential to the subject being discussed. One teacher, in particular, is concerned about how other children in the class react to Johnny. For example, the female teacher often divides her class into teams that compete against one another in spelling, mathematics, social studies, and so on. Scores obtained by the teams are dependent on individual students being the first to state the correct answer. When students are given the opportunity to choose members, Johnny is always chosen last.

CRITICAL INCIDENT NUMBER 3

Sylvia Echohawk is a 29-year-old American Indian woman who works for one of the major automobile manufacturing companies in the United States. The company has recently implemented an affirmative action program designed to open up jobs for minorities. The personnel director, a male Black counseling psychologist, is in charge of it. Sylvia, being hired under the affirmative action program, is referred to him by her immediate supervisor because of "frequent tardiness." Also, the supervisor informs you that other employees take advantage of Sylvia. She goes out of her way to help them, shares her lunches with them, and even lends them money. Several times during the lunch hours, other employees have borrowed her car to run errands. The supervisor feels that Sylvia needs to actively deal with her passive-aggressive means of handling anger (tardiness), to set limits on others, and to be able to assert her rights.

In an interview with Sylvia, the psychologist notices several things about her behavior. She is low-keyed, restrained in behavior, avoids eye contact, and finds it difficult to verbalize her thoughts and feelings. After several meetings, the psychologist concludes that Sylvia would benefit from assertion training. She is placed in such a group during regular working hours but fails to show for meetings after attending the first one. Additionally, Sylvia's supervisor informs the psychologist that she has turned in a two-week resignation notice.

CRITICAL INCIDENT NUMBER 4

David Chan is a 21-year-old student majoring in electrical engineering. He first sought counseling because he was having increasing study problems and was receiving failing grades. These academic difficulties became apparent during the first quarter of his senior year and were accompanied by headaches, indigestion, and insomnia. Since he had been an excellent student in the past, Dave felt that his lowered academic performance was caused by illness. However, a medical examination failed to reveal any organic disorder.

During the initial interview, Dave seemed depressed and anxious. He was difficult to counsel because he would respond to inquiries with short but polite statements and would seldom volunteer information about himself. He avoided any statements that involved feelings and presented his problem as a strictly educational one. Although he never expressed it directly, Dave seemed to doubt the value of counseling and needed much reassurance and feedback about his performance in the interview.

After several sessions, the counselor is able to discern one of Dave's major concerns. Dave does not like engineering and feels pressured by his parents to go into this field. Yet he is unable to take responsibility for any of his own actions, is excessively dependent on his parents, and is afraid to express the anger he feels toward them. Using the Gestalt "empty chair technique," the counselor has Dave pretend that his parents are seated in empty chairs opposite him. The counselor has Dave express his true feelings toward them. While initially very difficult to do, Dave is able to ventilate some of his true feelings under constant encouragement by the counselor. Unfortunately, the following sessions with Dave prove nonproductive in that he seemed more withdrawn and guilt ridden than ever.

CRITICAL INCIDENT NUMBER 5

Felix Sanchez is a second-generation 19-year-old freshman attending a major university in northern California. He is the oldest of five siblings, all currently residing in Colorado. Felix's father works as a delivery driver for a brewery and his mother is employed part time as a housekeeper. Both parents have worked long and hard to make ends meet and have been instrumental in sending their eldest son to college.

Felix is the first in his entire family (including relatives) to have ever attended an institution of higher education. It is generally understood that the parents do not have the financial resources to send Felix's other brothers and sisters to college. If they are to make it, they would need to do it on their own or obtain help elsewhere. As a result, Felix found a part time job, without the knowledge of his parents, in order to secretly save money for his siblings' future education.

During the last two quarters, Felix has been having extreme difficulties in his classes. Felix's inability to obtain grades better than C's or D's greatly discouraged him. Last quarter, he was placed on academic probation and the thought of failing evoked a great sense of guilt and shame in him. While he had originally intended to become a social worker and had looked forward to his coursework, he now felt depressed, lonely, alienated, and guilt ridden. It was not so much his inability to do the work but the meaninglessness of his courses, the materials in the texts, and the manner in which his courses were taught. Worse yet, he just could not relate to the students in his dormitory and all the rules and regulations.

At the beginning of his last quarter, Felix was referred by his EOP adviser to the University Counseling Center. Felix's counselor, Mr. Blackburne, seemed sincere enough but only made him feel worse. After several sessions, the counselor suggested possible reasons for Felix's inability to do well in school. First, it was possible that he was "not college material" and had to face that fact. Second, his constant "sacrificing" of his time (part-time work) to help his siblings contributed to his poor grades. Third, Felix's depression and alientation was symptomatic of deeper more serious intrapsychic conflicts.

CRITICAL INCIDENT NUMBER 6

As a newly hired counselor at a large public university, you are given the task of encouraging minority students to utilize the services offered at the counseling center. While the university is comprised of 12%

Asian Americans, 7% Blacks, and 2% others, very few minorities ever come for counseling. The center you work for is nationally known as a fertile training program for interns doing work in the area of socioemotional problems. The orientation of services is heavily clinical (personal/ emotional counseling) and uses the traditional counselor-client model. A recent survey taken of counselors at the center revealed that 85% of them listed a preference for clinical types of cases, while only 5% chose educational/vocational ones. Indeed, you quickly sense that a status hierarchy exists among the staff. At the top of the pecking order are those who do primarily clinical work and at the bottom are the educational/vocational counselors.

CRITICAL INCIDENT NUMBER 7

A white counselor at a community college is given an appointment with a male Black student. The client appears guarded, mistrustful, and frustrated when talking about his reasons for coming. He talks about his failing grades, about the need to get some help in learning study skills, and about advice on changing majors. The counselor, who has been trained in a nondirective approach, feels both uncomfortable and resentful that the student is demanding advice and information. It is the counselor's belief that the student's behavior is indicative of avoiding responsibilities for making decisions. Focusing in on feelings, the counselor adroitly reflects and paraphrases the client's thoughts and emotions. As the hour progresses, an increasing tension becomes evident in the session. Finally, the counselor decides to reflect the apparent tension and antagonism he feels. At this point, the Black student angrily retorts, "Forget it, man! I don't have time to play your silly games." The Black student abruptly gets up and leaves the office.

CRITICAL INCIDENT NUMBER 8

A male foreign student who had just arrived at the university from an extremely conservative culture was welcomed by a group of U.S. and foreign students and invited to move into their International House. One of the U.S. female students was particularly warm toward him, and the two of them enjoyed talking with one another alone for hours at a time. The female student felt sorry for the foreign student and wanted to help him feel more at home. He, on the other hand, had never been alone with any other female outside his family and was encouraged by her friendliness. One night after he had been here for about a week, he knocked on her door late at night and asked to talk with her. She had been sleeping and was wearing only a nightgown. Because he sounded so distressed she let him into her room to find out what was bothering him. Without a great deal of preliminary explanation he began to put his arms around hers and pushed her back on her bed. The more she resisted the more excited he became until finally another resident, wakened by the noise, came into the room and intervened. The girl was both frightened and angry, threatening to charge the foreign student with attempted rape. The foreign student was also angry and felt she had trapped him into an embarrassing situation. By letting him into the room at that hour he assumed she wanted to have sex with him. The other residents in the International House threatened to expel both persons.

CRITICAL INCIDENT NUMBER 9

Suppose that you are a counselor at a predominantly white high school. One of the teachers, Mrs. Sakamoto, has referred Jimmy Johnson, a Black student, to your office because of "abusive language" and "aggressive behavior." Prior to seeing Jimmy, you notice that his folder contains the results of several psychological tests. This personality profile, as interpreted by the scales, indicates a suspicious, mistrustful individual. Indeed, it is not infrequent for persons with this score to be labeled as paranoids.

CRITICAL INCIDENT NUMBER 10

A white female high school counselor has just undergone some group dynamics training seminars. She has received specialized training in conducting group counseling. She decides to run several groups in her own school along certain topical areas: study skills, career planning, and personal problems. While the first two groups are voluntary, the last one is formed on the basis of referrals from teachers. Since the counselor's high school is racially mixed, most of the groups also reflect this composition. However, the counselor notices that very few Asian American students are represented in the last group.

After several months of running two study skills, two career planning, and three personal problem groups, the counselor begins to see a pattern emerging. While the Black and white students tend to be fairly verbal in all their groups, the Asian American students do not participate (verbally) as often. This is especially true of groups dealing with personal problems. Another observation is that the Asian American students are not cooperating with her request that they confront others in the group and should freely express feelings in order to avoid misunderstandings.

As a result, the counselor redoubles her efforts to force participants from the Asian American students. This, she feels, will help them get over their shyness and inhibitions. To implement this goal, she devises several role-playing situations in the group.

CRITICAL INCIDENT NUMBER 11

A Chinese foreign student whose performance had been just barely adequate received a termination notice from graduate school after two quarters of being on probation. The student was very upset because he felt he could not go home as a failure and no other alternative seemed available. After several sleepless nights he reported to the student health service in a state of exhaustion and severe depression. Through conversations with his adviser, the counselor discovered that some of the faculty in his department felt that the student should be given some kind of degree to compensate for having come so far and to help him save face when he returned home. The student had been at the university for five years and had completed enough courses for a master's degree, but half of the courses were incomplete, and the other half were below average grades. Other faculty members argued that awarding him a degree would start a dangerous precedent. None of the faculty thought the student had any chance of completing his doctorate, especially not in his present state of depressed exhaustion.

CRITICAL INCIDENT NUMBER 12

Mark Bennett, a freshly graduated Black male school counselor, has just been employed by a school district in which the population is racially mixed. Although he enjoys counseling students, he becomes painfully aware that several white counselors are racially biased in their attitudes and behaviors.

While passing a fellow counselor's office one day, Mark overhears a conversation in which a white counselor recommends to a Black student that he enter a vocational training program. Mark knows that this particular student is extremely bright and, indeed, had hoped to go to college. He confronts his fellow colleague but is accused of eavesdropping and as being too young and idealistic to make adequate judgments. When Mark appeals to the principal, he suddenly realizes that what he considered to be a highly liberated and sensitive program is really quite rigid and opinionated.

Mark's anger becomes so intense that he voices his opinions strongly in a school meeting. Although the principal and teachers listen cordially and promise an assessment of the problem, nothing is done for several weeks. All inquiries are met with statements like "We are studying the situation." Besides this state of affairs, Mark notices that teachers and fellow counselors are extremely cold toward him. He no longer receives referrals and is told by the principal that his work will not be supervised by the head counselor.

In a fit of anger, Mark threatens to resign. In a cold tone, the principal asks for this in writing. That following night, several Black students come to his home and beg him to stay.

CRITICAL INCIDENT NUMBER 13

Martha Chan is a 20-year-old junior attending a prestigious university in which you are working as a counselor. Martha first came to the counseling center because of "help in making a vocational choice." During the first two interviews you notice that Martha seldom looks you in the eye and tends to avoid expressing her feelings. Indeed, she appears so dependent that she waits for you to do all the talking. You become suspicious that she is repressing many conflicts and suggest that she take a personality test. When she fails to show for her test-taking session, you feel correct in your analysis.

CRITICAL INCIDENT NUMBER 14

Elaina Martinez is a 13-year-old Chicana who was recently referred to Mrs. Johnson, a school counselor, for allegedly peddling drugs on school premises. The counselor is aware that Elaina has had minor problems in school (talking back to teachers, refusing to do homework assignments, and fighting with other students; and comes from a blue-collar Chicano neighborhood. The father is an immigrant from Mexico, and the mother is a natural citizen.

Elaina hangs around with a group of other Chicano students who are responsible for several schoolyard pranks. Mrs. Johnson has talked with her several times but was unable to "get through" to Elaina. Because of this incident, Mrs. Johnson feels that something has to be done and the parents need to be informed.

Mrs. Johnson calls the parents in order to set up an interview with them. When Mrs. Martinez answers the telephone, the counselor explains how Elaina had been caught on school grounds selling marijuana by a police officer. Rather than arrest the young lady, the officer turned the student over to the vice-principal, who luckily was present at the time of the incident. After the explanation, Mrs. Johnson asks that the parents make arrangements for an appointment as soon as possible. The meeting would be aimed at informing the parents about Elaina's difficulties in school and coming to some decision about what needed to be done.

Mrs. Martinez seems hesitant about choosing a time to come in and when pressed by the counselor excuses herself from the telephone. The counselor overhears some whispering on the other end and then the voice of Mr. Martinez. He immediately asks the counselor how his daughter was and expresses how upset he is over the entire situation. At that point, Mrs. Johnson states that she understood his feelings, but it would be best to set up an appointment for tomorrow and talk about it then. Several times Mrs. Johnson asks Mr. Martinez about a convenient time for the meeting, but each time he seems to avoid the answer and to give excuses. He had to work the next day and could not make the appointment. The counselor stresses strongly how important the meeting is for the daughter's welfare and that the one day of work was not important in light of the situation. The father states that he would be able to make an evening session, but Mrs. Johnson informs him that school policy prohibits evening meetings. When the counselor suggests that the mother could initially come alone, further hesitations seem present. Finally, the father agrees to skip work to attend.

The very next day, Mr. and Mrs. Martinez and a brother-in-law (Elaina's godfather) show up together in her office. Mrs. Johnson becomes slightly upset at the presence of the brother-in-law when it becomes obvious he plans to sit in on the sessions. At that point, she explains that a third party present would only make the sessions more complex and difficult to resolve. Again, the counselor sees this attempted maneuver on the part of the parents as avoiding the responsibility for dealing with Elaina's delinquency.

COMMENTARY ON CRITICAL INCIDENTS

Critical Incident Number 1

Issues

1. **Mary's motivation for relationship:** What is Mary's motivation in having the relationship with John?
   (a) To appear liberal with peers.
   (b) To rebel against conservative parents and parental upbringing.
   (c) For the attention she was getting (shock effect of dating a Black man).
2. **John's motivation for relationship:** What is John's motivation in having the relationship with Mary?
   (a) To prove he has made it in a white society by dating a white woman.
   (b) To prove self-worth and pride to himself, parents, and friends.
   (c) To defy his parents.
3. **Mary's motivation for counseling:** What reasons could Mary have for initiating and continuing the counseling sessions? Was it a desire to end the relationship or give her more time to think about it?
4. **John's reluctance to go to counseling:** Why is John reluctant to continue counseling? Is he afraid of losing Mary? Is he afraid of seeing himself in a true light (Oreo)?
5. **Permanent relationship:** Why does Mary not want to look too far into the future with their relationship—"her constant coolness?"
6. **Disclosure:** Should a counselor disclose personal values and beliefs to clients? If so, when and how much should be disclosed? What do you think would be the impact to John's question (How do you feel about interracial relationships?) if the answer was "No, I don't think it's right?" Or "There's nothing wrong with it." How would you respond and why?
7. **John's relationship to his parents:** How would John like to relate to his parents, and how does he relate to them now?

8. **Mary's relationship to her parents:** How would Mary like to relate to her parents, and how does she relate to them now?

9. **John's motivation for counseling (real reason):** Why does John continue to come to the counseling sessions, despite his antagonism toward it? Is it really just to please Mary and not lose her (breaking up)?

10. **Mary's identity:** Where does Mary draw her identity from?

11. **John's identity:** Where does John draw his identity from?

12. **Sociopolitical implications:** What are the sociopolitical implications of this case? How may cultural racism be a major influence on John's world view? How may it influence Mary? How may it influence the counselor? What can be done about this?

Conflicts

1. **Counseling:** Mary and the counselor value counseling and seem to believe it can help Mary with her problems. John does not seem to value counseling but came solely to please Mary. He sees few problems in their relationship that cannot be easily resolved between the two of them.

2. **Parental prejudice** (Mary's parents): Mary values interracial relationships. Mary's parents do not value interracial relationships. "Mary's parents have threatened to cut off financial support unless she terminates the affair."

3. **Parental prejudice** (John's parents): John values interracial relationships. John's parents do not value interracial relationships. John's parents disapprove of the relationship.

4. **Internal conflict in Mary:** Conflict between two values Mary holds
    (a) Conservative parental values.
    (b) Liberal peer values.

5. **Motivation for relationship:** Mary seems to value the relationship for the attention and feelings of liberalness it gives her. John seems to value the relationship because it represents another success in white society that he managed to obtain.

6. **Permanent relationship:** John values and would like a permanent relationship with Mary. Mary does not value a permanent relationship with John (at this time). Mary gives cool responses to John's mention of a permanent relationship.

7. **Interracial relationships:** John and Mary seem to value interracial

relationships. A conflict of values may arise if the counselor does not also value interracial relationships.

8. **Cultural oppression and racial self-hatred:** John may be the victim of cultural oppression and be experiencing culture conflict.

Critical Incident Number 2

Issues

1. **Teacher attitude:** Is the teacher's negative attitude toward Johnny affecting how the white children treat him? Could this be defeating the effectiveness of the program?

2. **Social worker's knowledge of her reporting staff:** Positive or negative evaluations of the program by the social worker may depend on her awareness and knowledge of Indian culture. Also, how aware is she of the attitudes held by teachers who give her feedback on Indian students in their classes?

3. **Interpretation of Johnny's actions by Anglo and Indian cultures:** What does Johnny's "tardiness and tangential contributions" signify in Indian culture versus Anglo culture?

4. **Johnny being a minority in the class:** What effect does being one of the few minorities, if not the only minority, in a class have on Johnny and the other students?

5. **Teacher's attitude and awareness of Johnny's cultural differences:** How willing is the teacher to deal with Johnny's cultural differences? The teacher continues to set up class exercises that are competitive. What is the teacher's attitude about Johnny being in her class?

6. **What should happen when two cultures meet?** How, if at all, should the teacher's classroom teaching style change to meet the cultural belief system of Johnny's Indian culture? Do minority students always have to do the adjusting?

7. **Psychological impact on Johnny:** What is the psychological impact on Johnny in trying to apply his Indian culture in an Anglo-ruled school? Could he be receiving double messages regarding his Indian culture: good on the reservation, bad at the white school?

8. **Biculturalism:** If the aim of the exchange program is to expose Johnny to an Anglo culture and to expose the white students to an Indian culture, it seems to be done from a nonbicultural point of view. Can Johnny maintain or achieve a positive bicultural atti-

tude when the teachers set up the class to be monocultural? If the aim of the program is to "acculturate" Johnny, is this being fair to him by putting down Indian values that Johnny holds?

Conflicts

1. **Anglo versus Indian culture interpretation of behavior:** The social worker may value the Anglo interpretations of Johnny's behavior (withdrawn, sullen) over an Indian interpretation of the same behavior (respect for authority or elders). Thus her evaluation would be a negative and culturally biased one.

2. **Punctuality:** The teacher values punctuality in her students. Johnny's Indian culture values a different time perspective, no strict adherance to time.

3. **Cooperation versus competition:** Anglo culture values competition. Johnny's culture values cooperation.

4. **Class participation:** The teacher values individual contributions; she states that Johnny is "withdrawn, sullen, and uncooperative." Johnny may not value the same system of teaching the teacher does and thus may not respond to this teaching system. The system may be more to blame than Johnny himself.

5. **Verbalness:** The teacher values verbalness and students speaking up in class. Johnny's culture may not put such a high emphasis on class participation as does the Anglo culture. It is possible that Indian culture does not speak to thinking aloud. Or Johnny's culture may believe that one speaks only when spoken to.

6. **Anglo versus Indian interpretation of Johnny's class contributions:** Johnny's contributions may be very relevant from an Indian point of view but tangential from an Anglo point of view. Or it is possible that Johnny's communication style is more subtle and indirect than that used by Anglos. Conflict in interpretation of Johnny's contributions may be causing many of these difficulties.

7. **Teaching system:** The teacher values the Anglo system of teaching and learning (competitive/verbal); she does not seem to value Indian methods of teaching and learning or even wants to know what would be the best method in reaching Johnny. Johnny values the teaching system he had at the reservation.

8. **BIA versus Indian parents:** BIA and Ms. Myers may value a program of integration that introduces Anglo cultural values to Indians. Indian parents may not value this integration and see it as corrupting the Indian value system by imposing Anglo values on

the Indian students, seemingly, without respect for Indian cultural values and traditions.

9. **Culturally enlightened evaluator and culturally ignorant teacher:** If the social worker is aware of Indian traditions and values and the teacher is culturally encapsulated, the social worker may not value the teacher's interpretation of Johnny's behavior.

Critical Incident Number 3

Issues

1. **Definition of "frequent tardiness":** What does Sylvia's immediate supervisor consider to be "frequent tardiness?"
   (a) Is he picking on her because of his disapproval of affirmative action?
   (b) If Sylvia does have a different perception of her "punctuality" will it
       (i) Cost her her job?
       (ii) Make her responsible for changing to meet the company's rules and time perspective?

2. **Sylvia's generosity versus "jealousy" of supervisor:** Are Sylvia's fellow employees taking advantage of her generosity and "naiveness" or is the supervisor jealous of Sylvia's popularity and comraderie with her fellow employees? The employees may respect and admire her willingness to help others and do not feel the same way toward the supervisor.

3. **Sylvia's idea of psychologists:** What are Sylvia's ideas and attitudes regarding psychologists and being referred by her supervisor? What does she think of their diagnoses? Does this shame her?

4. **Cultural enlightenment of psychologist and supervisor:** Are the supervisor and psychologist aware of cultural differences (Indian vs. Anglo) that could help them to explain Sylvia's actions and more accurately understand her?

5. **Resignation:** Why did Sylvia resign?

6. **Restraint of behavior, avoidance of eye contact, nonverbalness, Anglo versus Indian culture:** What does restraint of behavior, avoidance of eye contact and nonverbalization of thoughts and feelings mean in an Indian versus Anglo society?

7. **Affirmative action:** Does Sylvia's supervisor and personnel director approve of affirmative action hiring or not? Are they sincerely

trying to help minority employees by referring them? If they disapprove, what may be the effects?

Conflicts

1. **Cooperation and sharing versus "I" orientation:** Sylvia's culture may value sharing and cooperation with fellow employees. The supervisor values keeping what you have to yourself and not going out of your way to help others.
2. **Punctuality:** Anglo culture values being on time/punctuality. Indian culture does not have the same time perspective. It does not value punctuality as much as the Anglo culture.
3. **Generic counseling characteristics:** Psychologist values verbalness, expression of feelings. Sylvia does not value or is not accustomed to this type of encounter.
4. **Assertiveness:** Anglo culture in general values being assertive. Indian culture may not value asserting oneself to others but rather being in harmony with others.
5. **Eye contact:** Anglo society views eye contact as positive, attentive behavior; it is highly valued. Indian culture may view eye contact as a form of chastisement or disrespect, something negative; it is not valued as it is in Anglo culture.
6. **Affirmative action:** The supervisor may not value affirmative action and is harder on those employees hired under this policy. The psychologist may value the affirmative action program and may sincerely try to help minority employees survive in the Anglo work situation.

Critical Incident Number 4

Issues

1. **Technique of counselors—inappropriate:** How may the use of the Gestalt "empty chair technique" do more harm than good in the case of a traditional Asian client? It forces Dave to talk back to his parents, which he would not normally do (out of respect for them)?
2. **Expectations:** What are David's expectations of the counselor and of the counseling sessions? Is he seeking advice from the counselor, or is he there to learn how to take responsibility for his decisions?

3. **Restraint of feelings:** Does the counselor understand why David does not openly disclose his personal feelings (respect for authority)

4. **Individual versus family responsibility:** Does the counselor understand David's relationship to his parents and family (decisions include family—not solely an individual decision)?

5. **Resolution:** Can David and the counselor arrive at a resolution that will satisfy both David and his parents?

6. **The major-engineering:** What aspects of the major does David dislike, or what aspects of the major turn David off? Why do David's parents want him to become an engineer? Does David like any aspect of engineering?

7. **Maintenance of engineering major:** Can David remain in engineering without causing serious physical and emotional harm to his body (somaticizing)?

8. **Parental confrontation:** Can David confront his parents about his dislike of engineering, or will his parents refuse to hear him?

9. **Timing of symptoms:** Why did the headaches, insomnia, and indigestion begin to show up during his senior year of school and not earlier?

Conflicts

1. **Internal conflict within David:** David values his parents' approval on his major (do what his parents want). David values changing majors (do what David wants).

2. **Generic characteristics of counseling:** The counselor values openness and elaboration of personal feelings. This is an Anglo value. David's Chinese culture values restraint of feelings; his "short and polite statements" reflect respect for elders and authority. David's culture also does not value telling personal problems to "strangers."

3. **"I" versus "we" decisions:** Anglo culture values taking responsibility for one's life (individual responsibility and decisions). Chinese culture values a family decision; the family is harmonious, and one is part of the family, not separate from it. Decisions are joint ones (made with the family).

4. **Counselor versus client responsibility:** The counselor values the client helping himself. David may value the counselor giving him advice and telling him what to do.

5. **Confrontation of elders:** The counselor values expressing one's anger to one's parents via the open chair technique. David's Chinese culture does not value talking back to or criticizing elders; it is a sign of disrespect.

6. **David versus his parents:** David's parents value engineering. David is coming to value it less and less.

Critical Incident Number 5

Issues

1. **Individual blame versus system blame:** The counselor tended to attribute Felix's academic difficulties to personal deficiencies. What other external variables (sociocultural forces) may be contributing to Felixes feelings of loneliness, isolation, depression, and meaninglessness? Concentrate on the characteristics of white middle-class learning/teaching styles versus Hispanic ones. Can alienation come from the materials taught and the texts used? As a culturally different student, how might you feel in an environment that used material from a totally different perspective?

2. **Family obligations as a deficit:** The counselor may be distorting a cultural value into a deficit. For example, what does it mean to be the oldest in a traditional Hispanic family. Certainly, it is a position of importance and responsibility. Yet the counselor may be communicating to Felix that his values are outdated and pathological. What evidence do we have of this and what effect might it have on Felix?

3. **Felix's living situation:** What is there about Felix's living situation that may clash with Hispanic values, traditions, and modes of behavior? Speculate freely.

4. **Feelings of alienation, guilt, and shame:** What are the possible cultural and sociopolitical ramifications of these feelings? How does the strong family influences affect these feelings.

5. **What would you do and why?**

Conflicts

1. **Individual-centered approach of counselor versus sociocultural view by Felix:** The counselor views individual responsibility (IC-IR world view) as solely applicable to Felix. The reasons the counselor entertains about why Felix is doing poorly may clash with the client's perceptions.

2. **Institutional rules and regulations may clash with concepts of "personalismo":** Felix's dormitory situation may seem impersonal and devoid of the affective human qualities. In many Hispanic groups, human relationships take precedence over institutional policies.

3. **Individual competition versus group cooperation:** The alienation Felix experiences may be the direct result of the individual competitive elements in our educational system. Individual recognition and achievement are highly valued. Among Hispanic groups, cooperation to achieve mutually shared goals for the benefit of the group as opposed to the individual is highly valued.

Critical Incident Number 6

Issues

1. **Prejob knowledge:** How much of an idea of departmental politics, emphasis, and hierarchy should a job applicant have before the interview and before accepting the job offer?

2. **Generic versus cultural characteristics of counseling:** Is the "traditional counselor-client model" effective in counseling minorities (nontraditional clients)?

3. **Fellow counselor cooperation:** How much cooperation can you expect from the counselors, most of whom favor dealing with personal/emotional problems versus vocational educational problems?

4. **Minority participation with personal problems:** Will minorities be inclined to see counselors for personal reasons, no matter what the enticement?

5. **Why few minorities come to the counseling center?** Is the staff of the counseling center aware of the reasons why minorities have not come in before?

6. **Actual influence of a newly hired counselor:** As a newly hired counselor, how much influence do you have in changing institutional policies if you see a policy change as a means of increasing minority utilization of counseling center services?

7. **Priority of institution:** Does the institution's reputation of being a clinical training center take precedence over minority needs and recruitment?

8. **Self-defeating:** How does the institution discourage minorities by virtue of its traditional counselor-client model?

Conflicts

1. **Generic versus cultural characteristics of counseling:** The majority of counselors value traditional counselor-client models of counseling. Minorities do not value the same generic counseling characteristics.

2. **Revealing personal problems to counselors:** In all, 85% of counselors value dealing with clinical (personal/emotional) problems. Many minorities do not value revealing their personal problems to strangers (counselors). They would more likely come with vocational/educational concerns.

3. **Clinical versus vocational/educational counseling:** While 85% of the counselors value clinical problems, 5% of the counselors value vocational/educational problems.

4. **New counselor and the institution:** A newly hired counselor values minority utilization of the counseling center. The majority of counselors value clients with socioemotional problems. Will they value minorities with vocational/educational concerns?

Critical Incident Number 7

Issues

1. **Initial rapport:** Does the Black client initially feel he can be helped by and work with the white counselor?

2. **Inflexibility of counselor:** How is the counselor inflexible in his approach? The counselor immediately becomes uncomfortable and resentful when the student asks for advice and information. He cannot get away from being a nondirective counselor. This negatively affects his counseling session.

3. **Clarify goals and expectations:** Is there a need to clarify what the client expects of the counselor and what the counselor expects of the client?

4. **Referral?** When should a counselor refer his/her client? When does a counselor feel he/she cannot work effectively with a client so that a referral would be proper? If you realized you were biased, would you refer?

5. **Client taking off—leaving physically:** Should the counselor follow and catch up to the client after he has gotten angry and left the

counselor's office? Is it the responsibility of the counselor to see that the client gets help even if from another counselor?

Conflicts

1. **Approach:** The counselor values a nondirective counseling approach. The client values more a directive and structured approach.
2. **Needs of the client:** The client values getting advice and information from the counselor. The counselor values client finding information out for himself, taking responsibility for himself.
3. **Expression of feeling:** The counselor values focusing in on personal feelings. The client values focusing on academic issues and not on revealing intimate feelings to the counselor.

Critical Incident Number 8

Issues

1. **Significance of verbal and nonverbal messages in each culture:** Were there inaccurate interpretations in the sending and receiving of both verbal and nonverbal messages between the foreign and U.S. student (proxemics, eye contact, conversation, conventions)?
2. **Sending double messages:** How may the U.S. student consciously (or unconsciously) send double messages to the foreign student?
   (a) Let's be merely friends.
   (b) Sexual come-ons. Why did she single him out?
3. **Universal behaviors:** Did both students assume their own behaviors were understood universally rather than culturally?
4. **Experiences and attitudes:** What were the different experiences and attitudes regarding male/female relationships of the foreign student and of the U.S. student? He had not been alone with any other females outside his family. She had felt her actions were just part of being friendly to the foreign student.
5. **Distress:** Why did the foreign student sound distressed to the U.S. student when he came to her door late one night?
6. **Conservative culture:** What does "extremely conservative culture" mean? Is sex after knowing a woman for one week considered

conservative in the foreign student's culture? Was he not acting out of character?

Conflicts

1. **Sexual versus hospitable:** The foreign student valued the U.S. student's friendliness and their male/female relationship in a sexual way. The U.S. student valued the friendliness she offered the foreign student and their male/female relationship in a hospitable way.

2. **Who's the victim?** What is the difference in opinion between the U.S. and foreign student about who was the victim of the incident? The foreign student felt that he was the victim. The U.S. student felt that she was the victim.

3. **Verbal and nonverbal behavior:** The foreign student and U.S. student do not interpret and value all verbal and nonverbal language in the same way.

Critical Incidents Number 9

Issues

1. **Definition of "abusive language and aggressive behavior":** What is Mrs. Sakamoto's definition of these two terms? Are we dealing with Black language, street language in comparison to "good" standard English? Are we dealing with cultural dictates of behavior?

2. **Folder review:** Does a counselor decide to see a client's folder before or after the initial counseling session?

3. **How much of the folder to believe:** If a counselor chooses to review a client's folder, how much of the material in the folder should the counselor believe?

4. **"Paranoia":** Does Jimmy's paranoia stem from his contact with the white society? It could have been a reaction to being a minority in a predominantly white-ruled society and institution (high school). As a victim of oppression and racism, does distrusting whites and white institutions indicate pathology? How may it be a sign of health?

5 **Antagonism:** Does Jimmy feel picked on by the other students in the white high school? If the white students are antagonistic

toward him, Jimmy's language and behavior might be a reaction to this antagonism.

6. **Psychological tests:** Does the counselor feel that psychological tests are culturally biased, thus accounting for the negative or inaccurate interpretation in Jimmy's case?

Conflicts

1. **Language and behavior:** Jimmy or his culture may not regard his language as abusive and his behavior aggressive. Mrs. Sakamoto regards Jimmy's language as abusive and his actions aggressive.

2. **Race and culture of Mrs. Sakamoto:** If Mrs. Sakamoto is Asian, how may this influence your analysis?

3. **Contents of the folder:** The counselor may not value the contents of the folder and may even challenge the validity of some of its contents. The institution values the contents of the folder and sees them as being accurate and valid evaluations of Jimmy. He may be stereotyped for the rest of his school years because of the institutional belief in the contents of the folder (or lack of a better way to keep track of students).

4. **Contents of the folder:** The counselor may value the contents of the folder. Jimmy may not value the folder's contents; he may see the folder's contents as a bunch of institutional lies.

Critical Incidents Number 10

Issues

1. **Awareness of cultural differences (counselor):** Is the counselor aware of the cultural differences between Anglo and minority groups and between minority groups themselves?

2. **Training workshop emphasis:** Does the counselor's training reflect (i.e., did it teach her) what would work best with the minority society but not necessarily with minority group members?

3. **Goals/techniques:** Are the goals and techniques used by the counselor appropriate to all minority students? How are they inappropriate?

4. **Cultural oppression:** Is the counselor culturally oppressing the Asian American students by trying to force participation of the students (the "I know what's best for you" syndrome)?

5. **Lack of Asian Americans in the last group (personal problems):** Does the counselor know or understand the reasons for there being few Asian American students in the personal problem group?

Conflicts

1. **Verbal/expressive:** The traditional counselor values clients to be verbal, confrontive, and freely expressive of feelings. The Asian American students do not value or put as much value on these characteristics as does the counselor.
2. **Goals:** The counselor values assertiveness and being uninhibited as some of the goals of the workshops. The Asian American students do not value these things in the same way as does the counselor. Assertiveness and being uninhibited among peers is not the primary goal these Asian American students wish to achieve. These students may be able to benefit from the contents of the workshops without being verbal during the course of the workshop.
3. **Exposure of personal feelings:** The counselor values expressing personal feelings and discussing personal problems with group members. The Asian American students do not value discussion of and sharing their personal feelings and problems with "nonfamily" members.

Critical Incident Number 11

Issues

1. **Student's language barrier:** Did the foreign student understand the lectures and what was being asked of him in the assignments?
2. **Professors' language barrier:** Is the student really a bright individual but the professors misinterpret what the student says and what he does on assignments?
3. **Counselor's promises of optimism:** To lessen the student's state of depression, how much optimism or reference to "making everything OK" should the counselor present to the student? Would he be able to "deliver" what he had said he would?
4. **Acceptance of reality:** Is the student able to physically and mentally cope with and accept the decision the faculty makes? In the event of an unfavorable decision, would the disgrace be too much for him to handle?

5. **Alternatives:** Is there any other alternatives besides sending the student home with no degree or a partial degree? Is there some way the student could be able to finish his doctorate? Perhaps with a Chinese interpreter the student's knowledge of his subject could be tested in his own language.

6. **Other factors:** What other factors may have interfered with the student's barely adequate performance? Why had the student been at the university for more than four years before he was put on probation?

7. **Faculty diagnosis:** Was the diagnosis of the faculty (no chance for a PhD) an accurate one?

8. **Attitude to counselor:** Did the student see a counselor when he was on probation? What is the student's attitude toward counselors, since he chose to see one as a last resort? Does he really believe counselors can help him?

Conflicts

1. **Value placed on education:** The Chinese student's family valued an education for their son as a measure of his success and self-worth. The faculty members did not value education as much as did the Chinese family. The faculty members did not see failure in school to be as much a disgrace as did the Chinese family.

2. **Chinese values and issues on assignments:** In his papers and courses the student may have emphasized Chinese values and issues for which he received poor grades because his professors did not value the same items and issues.

3. **Counseling process:** The student did not value counseling as the first means of solving problems, only as a last resort. The counselor and counseling institution value the counseling process as a very good way of solving problems but probably not as a last resort way.

4. **Faculty split:** Part of the faculty values the Chinese emphasis placed on "losing face" and sympathize with the student and want to give him some type of degree. The other part of the faculty does not value the Chinese emphasis placed on getting an education and the disgrace that follows if one does not accomplish such. The latter faculty members only want to go by the rules and give the student nothing to show for his five years at the university.

5   Grades: The counselor may value looking at people as individuals
     and not merely as grades on a report sheet. The institution may
     value only grades and not the particular situation of the individu-
     al.

6.   **Family versus individual:** The Chinese student values highly what
     his family thinks of him, and his place in the family system is
     important. The counselor may take more of an individual
     approach with the student and not place as high a value on the
     student's being part of a family system. The counselor may say
     what is important is that the student can accept what will happen
     and not so much that the student's family will accept what will
     happen.

Critical Incident Number 12

Issues

1.   **Ignore racism or not?** Should Mark have ignored the biases of the
     other counselors? What are some ways he might have handled
     it?

2.   **Change in attitude:** Can a counselor, who is racially biased, be
     changed to be less so via awareness?

3.   **Should counselors criticize each other's work?** Should counselors
     criticize each others work even when their intentions are solely
     constructive? If so, what tactful tactics could be used by Mark?

4.   **Integrity, what price?** How much is an individual willing to risk
     for something he/she believes in, and how much is he/she willing
     to overlook? Mark felt he should speak up and as a result put
     himself in an uncomfortable position.

5.   **Is it worth the job, head counselor supervision?** Does Mark really
     want to remain and work in this type of atmosphere, one of racial
     bias toward minority clients and of hostility toward him?

6.   **Effectiveness after incident:** Can Mark continue to work effective-
     ly when teachers, fellow counselors and the principal do not appear
     to be giving him support or respect?

7.   **Who should Mark have seen first?** Should Mark have gone to his
     superior (principal) before confronting the counselor? What is the
     institution's policy on this matter? Could Mark have abided by
     this policy?

8.   **Politics and tact:** Could Mark have voiced his feelings and gotten

what he wanted without creating the hostile atmosphere that he did? Mark had several things against him:

(a) He is new to the staff, and his voice may not carry as much clout as that of a counselor who has been there for many years.

(b) He is newly graduated, which could affect his credibility.

(c) By threatening to resign, he is asking the principal to take sides with him. If the principal took sides with Mark this may create uneasy feelings among the rest of the counselors and the principal. Also, is threatening to resign like throwing a temper tantrum?

Conflicts

1. **Higher education:** Mark values counseling minorities to their full potential? The white counselor may not value higher education for minorities and may blanketly recommend vocation training programs for them.

2. **Institution backs white counselor:** The principal and the institution value the white counselor and his actions (counseling recommendation, seniority) more than they value those of Mark (confronting counselor, principal, school board, and threatening to resign).

3. **Mark's confrontation of the white counselor:** The white counselor does not value Mark, a new minority counselor, telling him/her how to counsel. Mark values telling the other counselor what he thinks in the interest of the minority student.

4. **Mark's approach:** The principal may not have valued the way Mark approached the problem. It put the principal in a situation where he had to choose between the other counselors and Mark.

Critical Incident Number 13

Issues

1. **Counselor interpretation of Martha's behavior:** Is the counselor making correct interpretations of Martha's behavior?
    (a) Lack of eye contact as passivity versus respect.
    (b) Restraint of feelings as repression versus a sign of wisdom and maturity.
    (c) Counselor doing all the talking as dependency versus respect for an authority figure.

2. **Career counseling:** Is Martha only seeking help in vocational counseling, or are other hidden requests present?

3. **Incorrect diagnosis:** Did the counselor know enough about Martha before coming to the conclusions or diagnosis that he did?

4. **Inappropriate technique, inappropriate goal:** Taking a personality test to help Martha see what she is repressing is probably not what Martha came in to see a counselor about. This error could have led to her termination of counseling with this counselor.

5. **Counselor competence:** Is the counselor competent and open minded, considering that he assumed he was correct just because Martha failed to show up for her tests? He did not question his own diagnosis.

Conflicts

1. **Generic versus cultural characteristics of counseling:** The counselor values generic counseling characteristics: eye contact, openness, and expressiveness. Chinese American culture values lack of eye contact as showing respect. Restraint of feelings is valued, for you don't tell strangers your personal business. It is also respectable to be silent and let the authority or elder do most of the talking.

2. **Conflict of goals:** The client's goal is to make a vocational choice. The counselor's goal is to see if Martha is repressed via a personality test.

3. **Diagnosis:** The counselor values his diagnosis. Martha does not value the repression diagnosis, which she shows by terminating counseling.

Critical Incident Number 14

Issues

1. **Lack of understanding the counselor may have of father's role in a traditional Hispanic family:** The family structure of traditional Hispanic families ascribe respect for the authority of a dominant father who rules the household. The hesitations on the part of the mother toward committing an appointment time may be a result of her having to consult with her husband for his decision. The counselor made arrangements with the mother and even suggested seeing her alone without the father. She ascribed the mother's

indecisiveness as avoidance. What cultural factors concerning male-female roles between Mr. and Mrs. Martinez may be operating?

2. **The counselor gave little consideration to Mr. Martinez's need to not miss a day's work:** This may be more of a class than Hispanic distinction. Nevertheless, many Hispanics are on the bottom of the economic scale in the United States, and that may make it very relevant. Missing a day's work may have significant financial impact on the entire family. Since counselors are usually middle class to upper-middle class, they frequently forget this point. The father's not wanting to miss a day's work may indicate strong love for the family rather than a lack of caring for a family member. The counselor saw the father's hesitations as something "negative."

3. **Anglo distortion of cultural values:** Can you point out instances where the counselor may have distorted traditional Chicano values? What effects may such distortions have in terms of the counselor's working with Elaina and her family?

Conflicts

1. **A task-oriented approach versus "personalismo":** Among many Hispanics, there is a strong preference for personal contact and individualized attention in dealing with power structures (social institutions). Anglos tend to be more task or business oriented. Following a chain of command and adhering to rules and regulations are important. In what way was this clash evident in Mrs. Johnson's contact with Elaina's parents? How else might she have handled it?

2. **The counselor misunderstood the extended family structure of many Hispanic families:** The "compadrazgo" (godfather) system is strong and influential. The tendency for counselors to view a godfather as an outsider or someone not directly involved in the immediate family is a mistake. The godfather is as much involved with the child as parents. Western tendencies to be individual centered as opposed to the Chicano family orientation can cause immense conflicts and misunderstandings.

Name Index

Subject Index